ROCKWELL

THE HERITAGE OF NORTH AMERICAN

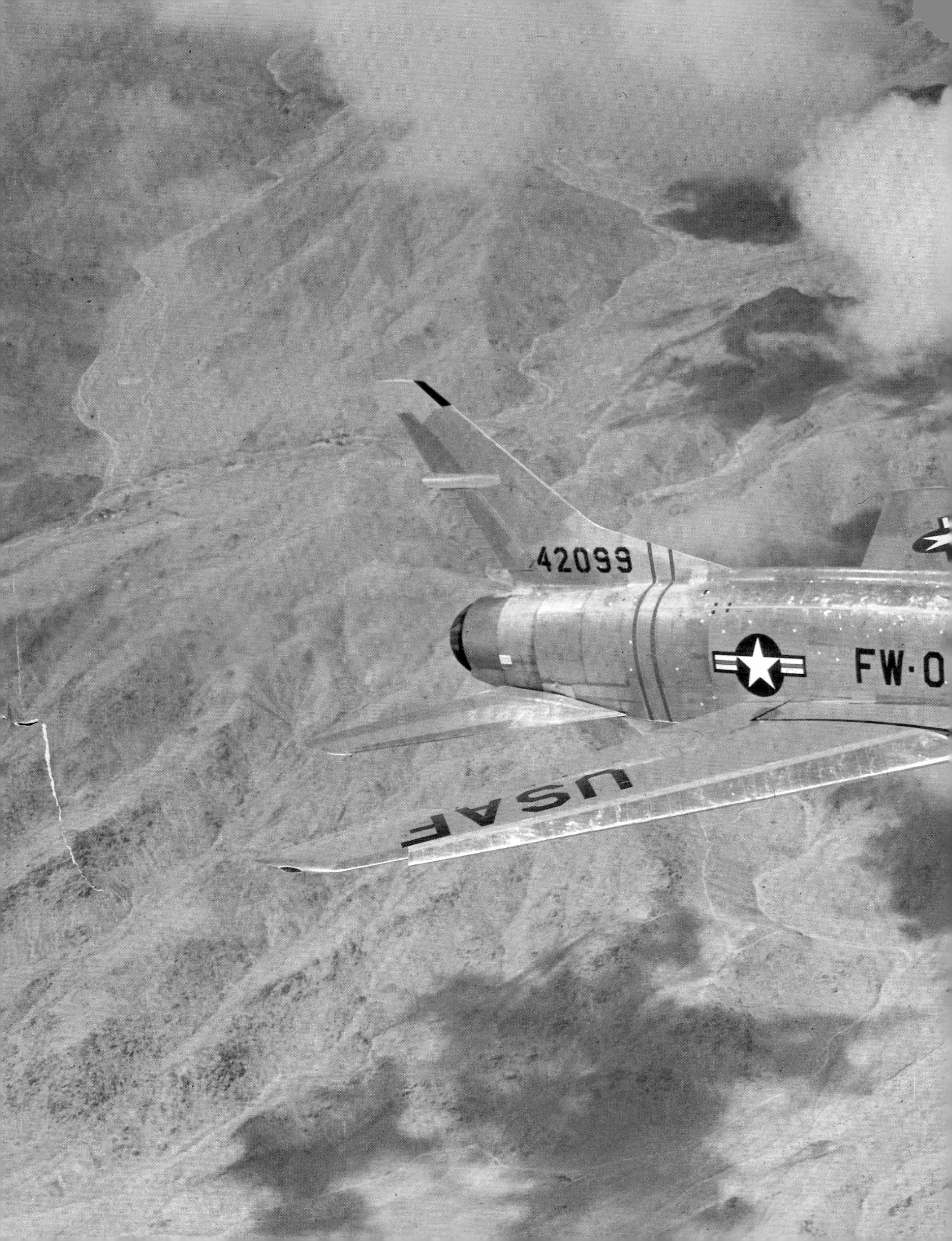
42099
FW-O
USAF

ROCKWELL
THE HERITAGE OF NORTH AMERICAN

BILL YENNE

Crescent Books
A Division of Crown Publishers, Inc.

The 1989 edition published by
Crescent Books, distributed by
Crown Publishers, Inc
225 Park Avenue South
New York, NY 10003

Produced by
Brompton Books Corp
15 Sherwood Place
Greenwich, CT 06830
USA

Printed in Hong Kong

ISBN 0-517-67252-9
h g f e d c b a

Preceding pages: North American's great F-100 Super Sabre was the first of the great Century Series fighters. Capable of speeds up to Mach 2, it was the Air Force's first fighter that operated routinely at supersonic speeds.

Below: A family portrait on the ramp at the North American Aviation plant at Inglewood, California in 1947. The first prototype XB-45 Tornado (NA-130) takes center stage with a P-82B Twin Mustang (NA-123) behind it.

In the foreground, and behind the P-82B are scores of NA-143 Navions, North American's one and only attempt at cracking the postwar general aviation market.

A pair of Douglas C-47s and a Beech 18 are on the runway in the distance.

ACKNOWLEDGEMENTS

The author wishes to thank Dick Barton, Sue Cometa and Bill Green of Rockwell International's Space Transportation & Systems Group; Joe Davies of Rockwell's North American Aviation Operations Palmdale/Edwards AFB office; Mike Mathews of Rockwell International's North American Aircraft Operations El Segundo office; Sam Petok, Senior Vice President and advisor to the office of the chief executive at Rockwell International's corporate office; Gail Rolka, who typed the manuscript; and Erik Simonsen of Rockwell International's North American Aircraft Operations El Segundo office. A special tip of the hat to Earl Blount, regional director of communications at Rockwell International's corporate office, for his undying support in the development of this project.

CONTENTS

INTRODUCTION:

Rockwell International is a multi-billion dollar, multi-industry corporation employing over 100,000 people at more than 100 facilities in two dozen countries worldwide. In the top two dozen American corporations in the *Fortune* 500, it is one of the world's industrial giants.

Based in El Segundo, California, Rockwell International today carries on the legacy of North American Aviation (NAA), a company which, between 1934 and 1967, built more military aircraft than any other planemaker in United States history—including 41,000 during World War II alone. Carrying on the NAA tradition has meant that Rockwell built the manned spacecraft which have carried all but five of the more than one hundred Americans to fly in space!

Rockwell's defense and aerospace electronics systems are found in most of the world's airliners and in defense systems, as well as in commercial computer and communication systems. Rockwell is also one of the world's largest independent suppliers of components for trucks, buses and automobiles. Through its Goss component, Rockwell is the world leader in the manufacturing of newspaper production systems, with two out of three American daily newspapers rolling off Rockwell's Goss presses.

The largest component within Rockwell's repertoire and the area of principal concern in this book, however, is aerospace. In 1988, for example, 52 percent of its earnings were derived from aerospace, versus 28 percent from electronics, 12 percent from automotive activities and eight percent from other, general industries.

In concise terms, Rockwell International is an amalgam of two companies—Rockwell-Standard (of Pittsburgh, Pennsylvania) and North American Aviation (of El Segundo, California)—which began with a 22 September 1967 merger. The company was known at first as North American Rockwell, but the name was changed to Rockwell International in 1973. However, the name 'North American Rockwell' probably best characterizes the heritage of the company.

For North American Aviation, the largest producer of military aircraft in United States history, it was the case a billion dollar aerospace giant with practically no non-government business, merging with the world's largest supplier ($600 million annual sales) of automotive mechanical parts. The California and Pennsylvania components of this new entity retained their separate identities as North American Rockwell and Rockwell Manufacturing respectively, until they were combined as Rockwell International in 1973.

Since 1967 Rockwell has acquired no fewer than 23 separate businesses as diverse as textile machinery and yachts. It was an era during which all of American industry saw diversification as the key to corporate survival in the uncertain times of an increasingly fickle marketplace. Rather than put all of one's eggs in a single basket (such as military aircraft, for instance), corporations sought to cushion them-

selves with a wide spectrum of interests. Among the Rockwell acquisitions were the well-known Admiral Appliance Company (founded in 1934) and Collins Radio (founded in 1933). The former would eventually be sold off, but Collins would go on to form an important core component in the Rockwell of today.

Indeed, the years from 1975 to 1980 found Rockwell's corporate philosophy change from one geared toward diversification to one geared toward getting back to the basic core of high technology aerospace, electronics and heavy industry. More than 20 previous acquisitions from appliances to yachts were sold off, and only a handful of new ones were acquired. This philosophy of focusing on the current group of *core* industries accomplishes the goal of insulating the corpo-

Above: The first Goss modular press control system which features a menu-driven display operates four, 70,000-copy-per-hour Goss Headliner Offset presses at the *Fort Worth Star-Telegram*. The presses, manufactured by Rockwell's Graphic Systems Division, went 'on edition' in 1986.
Right: The latest in a long tradition of military aircraft. Forward fuselages of B-1B long-range strategic aircraft for the US Air Force take shape at the company's Palmdale, California plant. The 100th aircraft was delivered in 1988, with spares and support work continuing for more than 20 years.

8

ration from the ups and downs of any particular industry cycle, while at the same time preventing Rockwell from spreading itself too thin.

Aside from aerospace, Rockwell's most important endeavor is in the area of high technology and electronics. This has been true since the establishment of North American's Autonetics Division in 1955, and it is likely to become even more so as Rockwell looks ahead to the twenty-first century. Today, a great deal of Rockwell's leading edge high tech activities take place within the Collins Division, which originated in 1933 as the Collins Radio Company and became part of Rockwell in 1973.

The Collins Radio Company was founded in the basement of a white, wood frame house in Cedar Rapids, Iowa by 24-year-old ham radio enthusiast Arthur A Collins. The company's first big break came in 1934, when Admiral Richard Byrd selected Collins equipment for the first radio broadcast from the South Pole. Collins went on to design and build radio equipment for commercial airliners, and for the Army and Navy during World War II. Indeed, General Douglas MacArthur made his immortal 'I shall return' speech using a Collins transmitter.

After World War II, Collins became the US Air Force's largest supplier of aircraft radios and radio navigation systems, including a total of 40,000 AN/ARC-27 radio units alone. Collins commercial radio transmitters were also very successful. They were used by radio stations in nearly every state in the United States and formed the backbone of the Voice of America effort in Europe during the 1950s.

WE OUTFOX THE BEAR.

Above and opposite: Examples of Collins products and advertising from the late 1980s, as the division became an increasingly important part of the Rockwell family.

ROCKWELL BEFORE NORTH AMERICAN

While this book is primarily about North American Aviation and the aircraft that it produced both before and after the 1967 merger, the story is clearly incomplete without some mention of the other half of the company.

American industrial development in the late nineteenth and early twentieth century is populated by a colorful breed of entrepreneurs who founded great empires on the basis of instinct and cunning. They built successful companies without the benefit of business textbooks and sponsored the innovation that paved the way for the greatness of the American industrial plant in its heyday. Such a man was Colonel Willard F Rockwell.

The story begins in 1919, the year after the first World War, when the Colonel took over the bankrupt Wisconsin Parts Company, an Oshkosh maker of motor vehicle axles. Over the next ten years, Rockwell's company developed the revolutionary double reduction axle, and in 1929 he was bought out by the larger Timken-Detroit Axle Company (founded in 1909).

Colonel Rockwell retained an interest in Timken, while in 1933 he moved to acquire the 19-year-old Standard Steel Spring Company of Coraopolis, Pennsylvania. Three years later Standard bought the Gary Structural Steel Company, and then acquired the Muehlhausen Spring Corporation in 1940. Between these interests, Colonel Rockwell had a hand in building the axles of 90 percent of the American tactical vehicles manufactured during World War II.

In 1953, Timken-Detroit merged with Standard Steel Spring to become the Rockwell Spring & Axle Company. In 1958 the name was changed to Rockwell-Standard.

Meanwhile, Colonel Rockwell held an interest in the Pittsburgh Equitable Meter Company, which had been formed in 1927 by a merger between Pittsburgh Meter and Equitable Meter. Pittsburgh Equitable became the Rockwell Manufacturing Company in November 1945, but remained separate from Rockwell-Standard until the Colonel merged his interests with North American Aviation in 1967.

Among the achievements of Colonel Rockwell's companies were the first double-reaction axles for heavy duty vehicles (1922), the first tandem driving axles (1925), the first two-speed, double-reduction axles for heavy duty vehicles (1933), the invention of the portable electric belt-sander (1935), the first die-cast aluminum meters (1945), the first axle-shaft that could be guaranteed for 100,000 miles (1949), the first portable electric band saw (1953), and the first nonmetal automobile body parts, which were made for the Chevrolet Corvette in 1953.

After the merger with North American on 22 September 1967, Colonel Rockwell became chairman of the new company, but he soon retired and was replaced by his son, Willard F 'Al' Rockwell, Jr who served as chairman for more than a decade.

Above: At this Oshkosh, Wisconsin plant in the early 1920s, Rockwell developed the first double-reduction axle, one of many technological advances introduced by the company for heavy-duty trucks.

THE COLLINS DF-206A. IT CAN SAVE YOU A BUNDLE.

If you're looking for an ADF that can save from 25% to 80% in space, power and weight over older military systems, look at the new Collins DF-206A Low Frequency Automatic Direction Finder.

The DF-206A can not only upgrade older aircraft at minimal cost, but it also meets the stringent requirements for new military applications.

It's designed to adapt to existing ADF mounts and to use existing aircraft wiring. There's no need to buy special factory wiring bundles with critical impedance matching. Separate loop and sense antennas have been replaced by a single lightweight, low-drag antenna.

We have also eliminated synchros and switching devices in the DF-206A's design, thus reducing installation components and improving reliability over the older electromechanical units. All components exceed MIL-E-5400 Class 1 environmental requirements, and the DF-206A is available with MIL-STD-1553B digital interfacing.

The DF-206A provides coverage in the 100-2200 kHz range plus 500 kHz and 2182 kHz preset emergency frequencies.

For all the time-saving, weight-saving, money-saving details and complete specifications, write Collins Government Avionics Division, Rockwell International, Cedar Rapids, IA 52498; or phone (319) 395-2208.

COLLINS AVIONICS

Rockwell International
...where science gets down to business

Unmatched in reliability, the Collins ARN-147 lasts 6 times longer and uses 40% less power than other military VOR/ILS receivers.

It's designed for 6000 hours MTBF, with 3 times the reliability required by government specifications. The ARN-147 is the U.S. Air Force standard VOR/ILS receiver.

The ARN-147 meets MIL E-5400 Class 2 military environmental specifications. This ruggedized receiver requires no shock mounts and can withstand severe gunfire vibration in helicopters and fighter aircraft.

COLLINS ARN-147. ONE TOUGH RADIO.

The solid-state ARN-147 runs cool, for longer component life. And it features all-modular construction with hinged modules and swing-out cards for easy maintenance.

The cost-effective ARN-147 can improve mission availability and flight safety through exceptional reliability. It is possibly the last VOR/ILS receiver military aircraft will ever need.

For more information contact: Collins Government Avionics Division, Rockwell International, Cedar Rapids, Iowa 52498. (319) 395-2208. Telex 464-421. COLLENGR CDR.

Rockwell International
...where science gets down to business

Aerospace / Electronics / Automotive
General Industries / A-B Industrial Automation

The Collins CP-1516/ASQ Automatic Target Handoff System (ATHS) helps ensure clear, quick, C³I communications. It facilitates air/air and air/ground interoperability, and provides target steering cues on HUDs or CRT displays.

Instead of vulnerable voice communications, Collins ATHS uses digital data bursts to minimize jamming and to reduce enemy detection while speeding the transfer of accurate battle information.

The system uses any MIL-STD-1553B or ARINC 429 transceiver to resolve target location and exchange target information between force elements. It's totally transparent to the system architecture.

NEVER SAY 'SAY AGAIN' AGAIN. COLLINS ATHS.

Now flying on U.S. Army OH-58D and AH-64s, the 10 lb. Collins ATHS can be easily integrated into aircraft and ground vehicles. And it's interoperable with TACFIRE and the Battery Computer System.

For more information contact: Collins Government Avionics Division, Rockwell International, Cedar Rapids, Iowa 52498. (319) 395-2208. Telex 464-421 COLLENGR CDR.

COLLINS AVIONICS

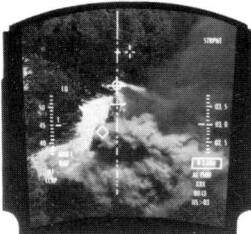

ATHS provides data for such HUD symbols as target, LL range and steerpoint.

Rockwell International
where science gets down to business

Aerospace / Electronics / Automotive
General Industries / A-B Industrial Automation

Circle 154 on Reader Card

TALK YOUR WAY ACROSS THE OCEAN WITHOUT LOSING YOUR VOICE.

COLLINS SATCOM LEADS THE WAY.

Collins Satellite Communications (SATCOM) is designed to give airlines reliable transoceanic communications that are not limited by range or atmospheric conditions.

Collins SATCOM will offer worldwide data link and voice services, and it's compatible with the ACARS and AIRCOM networks. It can help expand ATC flight-following, improve aircraft maintenance and provide in-flight passenger telephone service. Collins SATCOM will offer initial capability in data transmission with growth capacity to include two-way voice communications.

For more information, contact:

Collins Air Transport Division, Rockwell International, Cedar Rapids, Iowa 52498. (319) 395-1821. Telex 464-421 COLLENGR CDR.

Rockwell International
...where science gets down to business
Aerospace / Electronics / Automotive
General Industries / A-B Industrial Automation

COLLINS AVIONICS

This device has not been approved by the Federal Communications Commission. This device is not, and may not be, offered for sale or lease, or sold or leased, until the approval of the F.C.C. has been obtained.

Annual sales grew from $13 million in 1950, to $118 million in 1959, and to $440 million a decade later.

Collins radio equipment had been part of North American Aviation aircraft from the earliest days, but in 1958 the two companies began a particularly close collaboration when Collins developed specialized radio equipment for the X-15 and Apollo programs. Indeed, Collins radio equipment played a very significant part in America's early manned space flight effort. When the crew of Apollo 11 became the first human beings to set foot on the moon, Collins equipment transmitted the first words and pictures of the event.

However, the late 1960s were difficult times for the entire aerospace and high tech industry in the United States, and serious financial problems compelled Collins to seek a merger. In 1971 North American Rockwell began to invest in the ailing Collins, and in 1973 it acquired a controlling interest. Arthur Collins himself, however, resigned in 1972.

In the late 1970s, as the aerospace industry began to rebound, Collins once again became a world leader in electronic aviation systems. Collins developed the electronics for Rockwell's NAVSTAR navigation satellite and was a pioneer in the use of full-color CRT (cathode ray tube) display screens in aircraft cockpits.

While electronics in general, and avionics in particular, will play an increasingly prominent role in Rockwell's future, aircraft and spacecraft will also continue to be an important part. As programs such as the B-1 and Space Shuttle, that constituted a major part of Rockwell's operations in the 1970s and 1980s, are completed, new programs will come on line to take their place in the 1990s. These will include the X-30 National AeroSpace Plane (NASP) and the X-31 Enhanced Fighter Maneuverability (EFM) demonstrator. The X-30 will be a hydrogen-fueled, hypersonic transport aircraft capable of taking off and landing at conventional airports, yet also able to fly at Mach 25 in low Earth orbit. The X-31 project is being undertaken jointly by Rockwell and Messerschmitt-Boelkow-Blohm of West Germany. The outcome of this joint venture will be a pair of aircraft that can be used to study and evaluate a broad spectrum of techniques and technology that later may be utilized to maneuver fighter aircraft at extremely high speeds.

Above: An Eric Simonsen photo of the Rockwell X-30 high over the North Pacific. *Below:* A Rockwell engineer ponders the X-30's configuration. Rockwell's Rockdyne Division also has the contract for the X-30's engines.

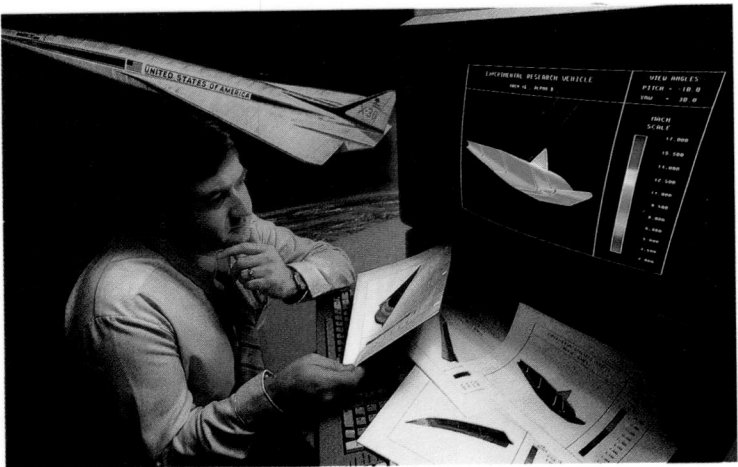

There are also two programs on the spacecraft side of the 'house of Rockwell' being developed under contract to the Defense Department. One ongoing project is Teal Ruby, an 11-foot-long, barrel-shaped telescope system that employs a staring, mosaic focal-plane array sensor system, which is housed in an Air Force Project 888 spacecraft. Designed as a space platform, its infrared sensor system uses mosaic focal-plane arrays to detect aircraft in flight over the Earth's surface.

The second program, Rockwell's NAVSTAR (Navigation System Using Time and Ranging) satellites, form the spacecraft element of the US Air Force/US Navy Global Positioning System (GPS). NAVSTAR spacecraft are three-axis stabilized and placed in several overlapping planes that circle the globe every 12 hours. They provide accurate, three-dimensional position fixes within 52 feet, with velocity to within four inches per second, as well pinpoint navigational accuracy to land, sea and air forces in the field, and are designed to function with a galaxy of 18 NAVSTAR spacecraft, which were launched between 1978 and 1985. The first of 28 Block 2 NAVSTARS was delivered in 1987 under a $1.3 million contract.

Above: A wind tunnel mock-up of the X-31, which is seen in a 3-view at right. *Below:* Technicians put finishing touches on a new NAVSTAR satellite at Rockwell's Seal Beach, California facility.

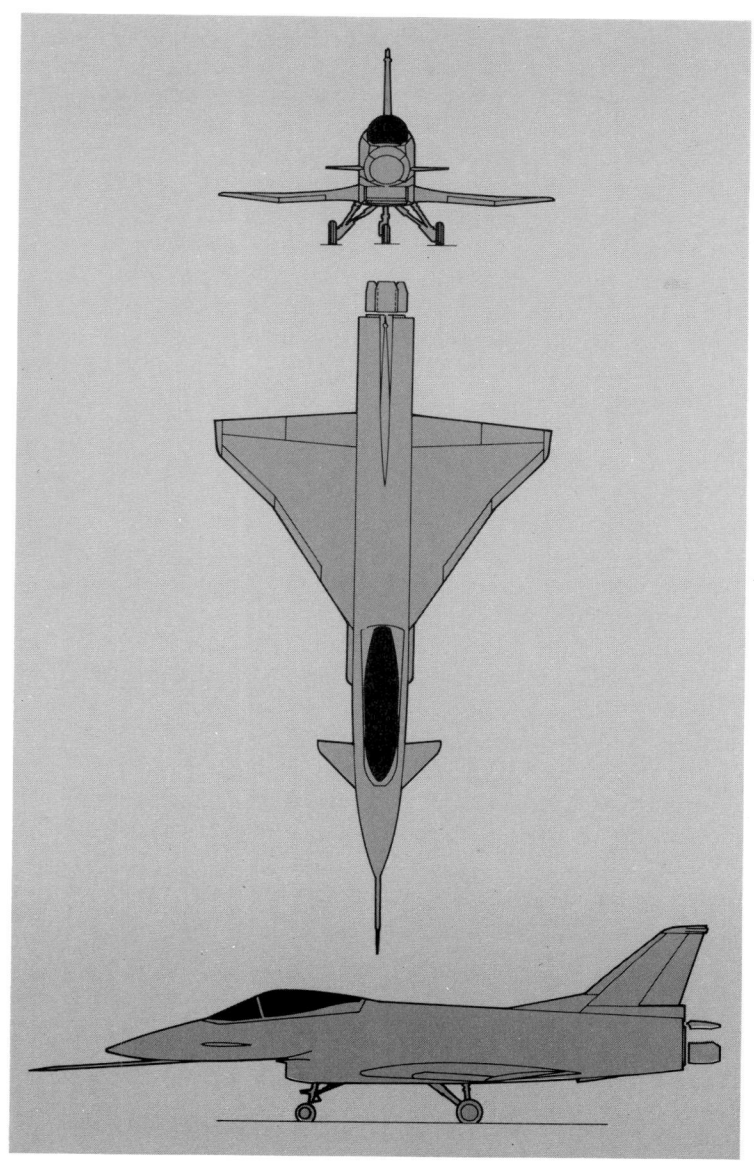

The ground portions of the GPS include a master control station at US Air Force Space Command (SPACECOM) Headquarters in Colorado and monitoring stations in the Indian Ocean (Diego Garcia), the Atlantic Ocean (Ascension Island) and the Pacific (Hawaii, Guam and the Philippines). Small user packs are also distributed to small units of all branches of the American armed services, including more than 7000 US Air Force aircraft, and as many as 4700 US Navy ships. Spacecraft, such as Landsat, also carry GPS receivers, and commercial users will also have access to GPS.

NAVSTAR carries an atomic clock to provide timing data that is accurate to within one millionth of a second. An L-band transmitter provides positioning data and has a pseudorandom noise code incorporated into the L-band transmissions, that requires a match by the receiving station in order to prevent an unauthorized user from accessing the system.

With such programs on the drawing board and in production, Rockwell is assured a continued place among the world leaders in aerospace development as we enter the twenty-first century.

THE BIRTH OF NORTH AMERICAN

The first chapter of the history of nearly every American aircraft manufacturer starts with a man and his passion to build airplanes. This is true of Beech, Boeing, Cessna, Curtiss, Douglas, Grumman, Lear, Martin, Northrop, Piper and Rutan. With Lockheed and Wright it was two men (albeit with the same name), but it's the same idea. This is not, however, exactly true of North American. There *was* a man, but his passion was directed more toward empire building than airplane building. By the time North American came to hang its appellation on a *new* aircraft, he had moved on, but in the meantime, the cast of players literally read like a Who's Who of the first 30 years of American aviation.

THE EMPIRE BUILDER

Clement Melville Keys was an investment banker who came into the world of aviation in 1916 as the man who would help Glenn Curtiss turn America's first successful airplane company (the Wrights' company had stagnated after the first few years) from a sole proprietorship into a public corporation. The deal that Keys struck brought John North Willys (of the Willys Car Company) into the deal as president, with Glenn Curtiss himself as chairman (and president of the engineering division), and Keys himself as vice president.

Less than a year later, the United States entered World War I and, thanks to Keys, the Curtiss Aeroplane & Motor Corporation was structured in such a way as to quickly develop the production capacity to take maximum advantage of the military's sudden, voracious appetite for aircraft and engines.

During World War I, Curtiss built over 5000 JN-series 'Jenny' biplanes, which came to be the most widely produced American airplane design for many years. After the war, as the market for new airplanes lagged dramatically, Willys sold his shares to Keys, who then became the largest shareholder in the Curtiss Aeroplane & Motor Company. For the wily Keys it was only the beginning.

In 1928 Clement Melville Keys laid out the plans for an elaborate and complex holding company, which would form a framework for his intended future plans. This holding company—North American Aviation, Incorporated—was to be owned 70 percent by Keys' own Curtiss Aeroplane & Motor Company, with 12 percent shares to each of two airlines: Transcontinental Air Transport (TAT) and the Curtiss Flying Service. Donald Douglas, the upstart plane builder in Santa Monica, California, bought into North American Aviation for the remaining six percent.

The following year Keys brought the Pitcairn Aviation Company (founded in 1927) and the Sperry Gyroscope Company (founded in 1910) under the North American Aviation umbrella. Pitcairn (started by Pittsburgh Plate Glass Pitcairns) also owned a fledgling airline, which now had become Eastern Air Transport (and which would ultimately become Eastern Air Lines). In August 1929—two months before the October stock market crash—Keys engineered a spectacular merger between his own Curtiss Aeroplane & Motor Company and Wright Aeronautical, a move which brought together under one roof America's two pioneering aircraft builders. Both Orville Wright and Glenn Curtiss—the old rivals —had lived to see the creation of the Curtiss-Wright Corporation by the deft hand of the empire builder.

The following year both the Ford Instrument Company (formed in 1916) and Berliner-Joyce Aircraft (formed in 1926) became part of the North American Aviation 'family' of companies.

By 1934 the holding company owned 27.6 percent of TAT (its former parent), and 52 percent of Western Air Express (WAE). These companies would ultimately become Trans World Airlines (TWA) and Western Airlines.

ENTER GENERAL MOTORS

In the meantime, other empire builders were taking the field. Henry Ford, twentieth century America's greatest entrepreneur, had developed an excellent trimotored airliner and was making noises about an airline company when General Motors, the world's largest corporation and Ford's bitterest rival, came into the game. General Motors' opening move was the May 1929 acquisition of 40 percent of Fokker

Aircraft, the firm started by Anthony Herman Gerald 'Tony' Fokker. Known in the industry as the 'Flying Dutchman,' the Java-born Fokker had designed the best Axis warplanes during World War I, and had built the best air transports in the world in the early twenties.

Renamed General Aviation Manufacturing Corporation in 1930, Fokker Aircraft was a true plum and formed the cornerstone of General Aviation Corporation (GAC), the holding company that General Motors formed as a parent company for aircraft interests. In 1933—through GAC—General Motors acquired a 30 percent share of North American Aviation and installed Ernest R Breech as Chairman of the Board. The world's largest corporation now owned the remnants of three important early aircraft builders—Berliner-Joyce, Fokker, and Pitcairn—as well as the seedling airlines that ultimately evolved into Western Airlines, Eastern Air Lines and TWA!

In 1934 the entire face of the commercial aviation industry in the United States changed when the newly elected Roosevelt administration pushed through the Air Mail Act, which decreed (in part) that an airline could not own an airplane manufacturer or vice versa. General Motors theorized that this controversial piece of legislation did not cover a *third* company owning one of *both*, but nevertheless, the industrial giant disposed of all of its holdings, except Eastern Airlines and North American Aviation, which were reconfigured as autonomous operating companies. Ultimately, General Motors sold its interest in Eastern Airlines in 1938 and in North American Aviation in 1948.

DUTCH KINDELBERGER

Technically, North American Aviation was founded in 1928, but it was really not 'born' until 1934, when Chairman Ernest Breech installed James H 'Dutch' Kindelberger as its president, and moved the company from Dundalk, Maryland to Inglewood, California the following year.

Born on 8 May 1895 in Wheeling, West Virginia, Dutch Kindelberger may not have been the father of North American Aviation

The Berliner-Joyce Aircraft Company became part of the NAA 'family' in 1930. Their output included 40 OJ-series observation floatplanes *(above)*, and a series of unsuccessful fighters such as the XFJ-1 *(below)*, the XF2J-1 *(bottom)* and the XF3J-1. Only one of each was built, but the XFJ-1 was rebuilt by NAA after a crash as NA-34.

(NAA) but he was the strict and familiar 'father figure' that would guide the company during its critical first three decades.

Kindelberger had worked as a draftsman for the US Army Corps of Engineers from 1913 to 1916 and had just enrolled at the Carnegie Institute of Technology when the United States entered World War I in 1917. He joined the Army and completed his tour of service as a second lieutenant in the Signal Corps' Aviation Section. Smitten by the aircraft bug, young Dutch went to Baltimore to work as a draftsman for Glenn Martin's aircraft company in 1918, where he came to know another young man by the name of Donald Wills Douglas, who also had pushed a drafting pencil for Martin in those days. Douglas quit Martin in 1920 to go west to start his own airplane company in Santa Monica, California. In 1925, Dutch Kindelberger was Glenn Martin's chief draftsman when he accepted a job offer from Don Douglas. Eventually, Kindelberger was promoted to chief engineer and vice president of the Douglas Aircraft Company.

In 1934, after nearly a decade in California, Dutch Kindelberger was hired by General Motors to return to Maryland as president of its General Aviation Manufacturing Corporation (GAMC) holding company. Later that year, when General Motors bought North American Aviation and decided to spin it off as an autonomous operating group, Kindelberger was named as its president and general manager. For his chief engineer, he chose John Leland 'Lee' Atwood, a man whose own contributions to North American Aviation over the years ahead would be surpassed by no one, with the sole possible exception of Dutch Kindelberger himself.

Lee Atwood was born in Walton, Kentucky on 26 October 1904 and earned his BS in civil engineering from the University of Texas in 1928. He worked as an engineer for the Army Air Corps at Wright Field, Ohio for two years before going west in 1930 to work for Douglas, where he became acquainted with Dutch Kindelberger.

NORTH AMERICAN AVIATION

Kindelberger and Atwood may well have had the moral support of General Motors at their backs in 1934 but, nevertheless, they were faced with literally starting from scratch. As a holding company, North American Aviation had never built a single airplane and existed as little more than a warehouse full of bits and pieces left over from the companies that it had held. There was a little modification work on some Berliner-Joyce P-16 (later PB-1) biplanes for the Army Air Corps, but the plane was now obsolescent and out of production. There was also one General Aviation GA-34 Pilgrim on the floor at Dundalk. A low-wing monoplane, the Pilgrim was unmarketable as a commercial transport because of its *single* engine. Coming from Douglas, where the DC-3 program was brewing, Kindelberger and Atwood certainly knew that the future belonged to multi-engined commercial transports.

Right: A suave Dutch Kindelberger in Santa Monica in 1929. 'You're a native Californian as soon as you've parked your trailer' he would say, and four years later, he quit his job at Douglas Aircraft to pull NAA's trailer west from Dundalk, Maryland to establish it as one of California's—and the world's—premier plane-makers. Modification work on Berliner-Joyce P-16 fighters *(above)* was almost the only thing on the floor when Kindelberger arrived in Dundalk in 1934.

One thing that NAA *had* inherited from the amalgam of companies that had been funneled into it was the excellent craftsmen that Tony Fokker had brought over from Europe. These men formed the nucleus of Kindelberger's plan to propel the former holding company into the real world.

Though starting from scratch, Kindelberger knew that NAA would be up and running *faster* if it set its sights on building small single-engined planes rather than trying to compete with Boeing, Douglas and Lockheed in the world of large, multi-engined aircraft. Kindelberger also reasoned that the government market held greater stability in the depths of the Depression than the gamble of a headlong plunge into commercial aircraft. Around the end of 1934 Kindelberger heard of the Army Air Corps' desire to commission the development of a new basic trainer, and he talked board chairman Ernest R Breech into investing $35,000 in a project he hoped would launch NAA as a viable airplane builder.

The drawing boards at NAA's Dundalk, Maryland facility sizzled with various configurations before one was chosen and designated number NA-16. This plane, a fixed-gear, two-place, low-wing monoplane, would be the first North American Aviation model numbered aircraft to be flown. The NA-16 made its first flight on 1 April 1935, with the noted test pilot Eddie Allen at the controls. The NA-16's first flight was a success, as was its debut before the Air Corps Materiel

Command at Wright Field. On the basis of that presentation, the Army ordered 42 trainers under the designation BT-9 and with the name Yale. It was at this point that Kindelberger moved NAA's operations from Dundalk to Inglewood, California, a few miles from Santa Monica, where he'd worked for Douglas just a year earlier.

THE YALE FAMILY

The production version of the NA-16 would be built in California after the 1935 move as model NA-19. This airplane was first flown on 15 April 1936 at Inglewood, with Paul Balfour at the controls. The Air Corps went on to order a total of 267 BT-9 Yales with 400 hp R-975 engines, including one that was re-engined with a 600 hp R-1340 engine in 1938, and redesignated BT-10. This aircraft put North American Aviation on the map as a plane builder, and went on to evolve into several other groups of similar trainer aircraft.

The initial follow-on to the BT-9 series was the BC-1 series of 'basic combat trainers.' The 'BC' desgination came about because there was money in the budget for combat planes but not trainers, and the Air Corps needed trainers! The first of these made its maiden flight on 11 February 1938, again with pilot Paul Balfour. A total of 300 BC-1s were built, including 30 BC-1I instrument trainers. An additional three aircraft were built in 1938 with 600 hp R-1340 engines (and three-

Below and opposite: Two views of the NA-16, North American's first airplane, soon after it was rolled out onto the grassy field at Dundalk, Maryland on a blustery March day in 1935. It first flew on 1 April and launched an incredibly successful family of training aircraft.

bladed props)—like the BT-10—and these were designated as BC-2. In 1937, a single BC-1-type aircraft was completed under the NAA model number NA-33. Finding its way to Australia, it went on to evolve into the Commonwealth Wirraway trainer, which had a parallel development to the North American AT-6 Texan.

The last major permutation of the Yale family was the BT-14 series, which Paul Balfour premiered on 10 February 1939, almost one year after the BC-1. There were 251 BT-14s built with 450 hp R-985-2 engines, and in 1941 27 of these were re-engined with less powerful 400 hp R-985-11 engines and redesignated as BT-14A.

In the meantime, the US Navy ordered 40 model NA-28 trainers under its training designation NJ-1. These were essentially BT-9s with 500 hp R-1310-6 engines, although one was modified by the Navy with an experimental XV-770 water-cooled engine and redesignated NJ-2.

From overseas came an order from the French government for 460 model NA-57 trainers, which were essentially the same as the BT-9 and were also powered by R-975 engines, along with 300 NA-64 models. Deliveries of unassembled NA-57s began in August 1939 to the French base at Nantes, but by the time France fell to the Nazis in June 1940, only 100 NA-57s and 56 NA-64s had reached the French air force, with 30 NA-57s having gone to the French Navy. Fifty of these aircraft were ultimately integrated into service with the German Luftwaffe in November 1942.

Like many American aircraft ordered by France but not delivered before June 1940, the remaining 230 NA-57s and 244 NA-64s were diverted to the Royal Canadian Air Force (RCAF) in 1940 under the designation Yale I. The US Navy, meanwhile, ordered 77 NA-52s (BC-1s with metal-covered rear fuselages), under the Scout trainer designations SNJ-1 and SNJ-2.

The program that had begun modestly in Dutch Kindelberger's nearly abandoned hangar in Dundalk resulted in 1577 aircraft being produced. It was not a bad start, particularly in light of the fact that it would lead to the development of the AT-6 Texan, the greatest American trainer of the age of propeller-driven airplanes and one of a half dozen airplanes for which North American will always be remembered.

THE O-47 PROGRAM

Inherited from the General Aviation days but first flown in November 1935 after the NA-16's initial flight, she was the only bird in the North American family tree to have gotten her start under a General Aviation model number. Designated GA-15 while still on the drawing boards in 1934, the plane was a large, low-wing observation monoplane whose tail surfaces were reminiscent of the NA-16 series.

Like the NA-16, the GA-15 was developed to meet a US Army Air

Corps requirement, and like the NA-16, the prototype plane was built at NAA's original Dundalk, Maryland plant, but the production aircraft would all be built at the new Inglewood, California plant. Equipped with an 850 hp R-1820-41 engine, the one and only GA-15 prototype made its first flight in November 1935 under the Air Corps designation XO-47.

With the great test pilot Eddie Allen at the controls, the XO-47 successfully secured the production contract and 164 production O-47As were ordered for delivery in 1936-37. Built with the NAA model number NA-25, they were powered by 975 hp R-1820-49 engines, and each was armed with two .30 caliber wing-mounted machine guns. The O-47 carried a three-man crew, which included an observer, who rode in a specially designed compartment on the *bottom* of the fuselage.

Though the 0-47A program wasn't as successful in terms of production numbers as the BT-9/Yale program had been, it was well received by the Air Corps, and it did lead to orders for 74 O-47Bs that were similar to the O-47As, except for its increased fuel capacity and a 1060 hp R-1820-57 engine. The O-47Bs were built under the model number NA-51 and were delivered during the 1939 fiscal year.

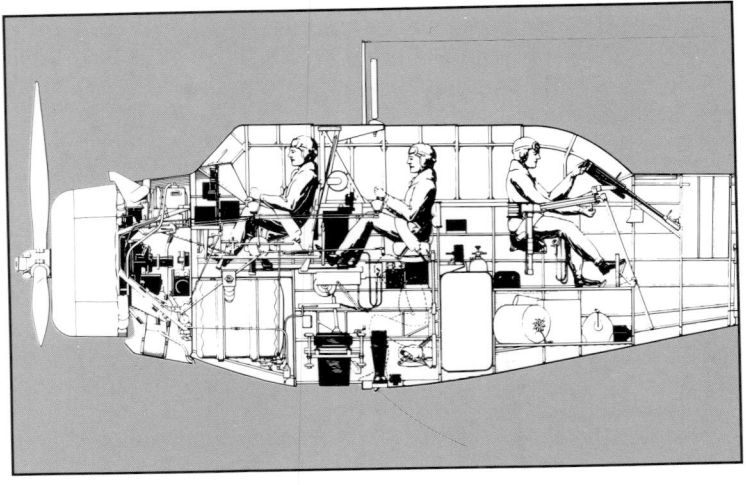

Above: The interior layout of the O-47—with its downward firing gun and below-deck observer's station. *Below*: The NA-35 was designed by NAA but produced by Lockheed's Vega Division when NAA capacity became saturated by Yales and Texans. *Facing page*: The Yale family, as represented by (from top) the BT-9 (NA-19), the BT-19 (NA-22) and the BT-9C (NA-29).

Below: Sporting Army Air Corps colors, a shiny New BT-9 Yale awaits delivery on the tarmac at Inglewood, California. The Yale made NAA's fortune in the late 1930s, but it was only a harbinger of the great things to come. This sprawling rural setting is today the site of Los Angeles International Airport. The oil wells (right distance) are still present, but everything else has changed.

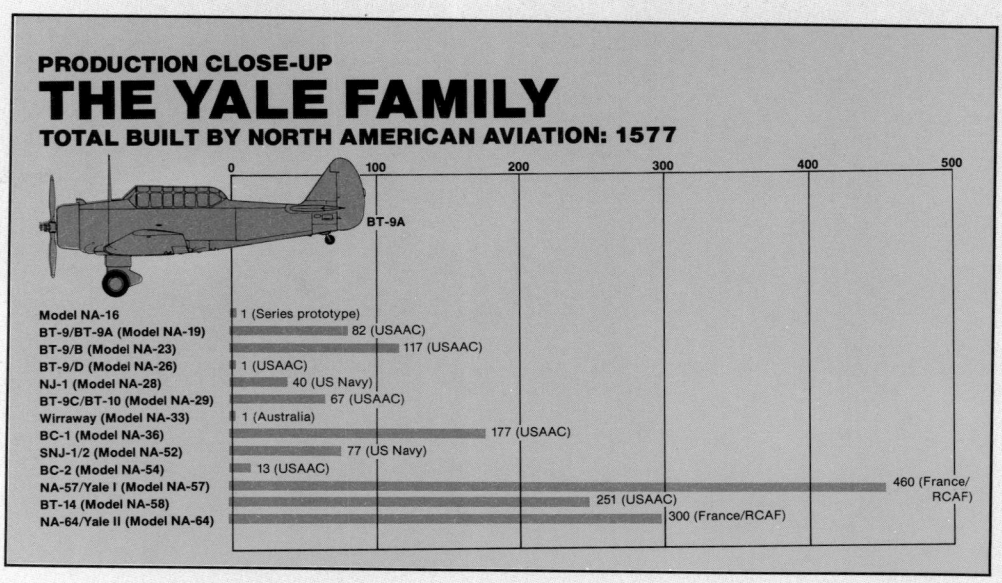

PRODUCTION CLOSE-UP
THE YALE FAMILY
TOTAL BUILT BY NORTH AMERICAN AVIATION: 1577

BT-9A

Model	Production
Model NA-16	1 (Series prototype)
BT-9/BT-9A (Model NA-19)	82 (USAAC)
BT-9/B (Model NA-23)	117 (USAAC)
BT-9/D (Model NA-26)	1 (USAAC)
NJ-1 (Model NA-28)	40 (US Navy)
BT-9C/BT-10 (Model NA-29)	67 (USAAC)
Wirraway (Model NA-33)	1 (Australia)
BC-1 (Model NA-36)	177 (USAAC)
SNJ-1/2 (Model NA-52)	77 (US Navy)
BC-2 (Model NA-54)	13 (USAAC)
NA-57/Yale I (Model NA-57)	460 (France/RCAF)
BT-14 (Model NA-58)	251 (USAAC)
NA-64/Yale II (Model NA-64)	300 (France/RCAF)

THE TEXAN DYNASTY

S he has been called the 'most universally used plane in history' and, while that *may* be an exaggeration, she is certainly the most universally used trainer ever built. With the possible exception of the Soviet Polikarpov Po-2, the AT-6 Texan and its kin added up to the biggest production totals—15,495 by company records—of any trainer in history. Today, it still stands as one of North American's half dozen most important programs.

HER ORIGINS

T he AT-6 (Air Corps advanced trainer, sixth) was a *direct* outgrowth of the BC-1 (basic combat) program, which had evolved from the BT-9 (basic trainer) program. Indeed, nine of the first 94 AT-6s built for the US Army Air Corps were slightly modified NA-55s (BC-1As)! At the same time, another BC-1 equivalent—North American model NA-49—was being developed for the Royal Air Force as Harvard I, and still another—NA-50—was being developed for Peru as a fighter! The NA-49 first flew on 28 September 1938, just seven months after the original BC-1 (NA-26), and the first NA-50 flew on 1 August 1938. However, further development of the definitive American trainer version lagged for more than a year, until the remaining 85 AT-6s, built as NA-59, began to be delivered on 10 February 1940.

The Royal Siam (Thailand) Air Force ordered six enclosed cockpit fighter versions, which were virtually identical to the NA-50, but which were completed as NA-68. The first NA-68 flew on 1 September 1940, but the planes were diverted to the US Army Air Corps before they could be delivered to Siam. Despite their P-64 pursuit designation, the NA-68s were used as trainers rather than fighters. Meanwhile, the Royal Siam Air Force also had ordered an attack version, which was built as NA-69. Also commandeered by the USAAC, these twelve planes were designated A-17. Other combat versions were also considered but largely rejected.

The RAF even toyed with a fighter version, which was ordered as NA-73. In Australia, meanwhile, Commonwealth Aircraft was developing its homegrown Wirraway fighter, which also was based on the NAA BC-1.

THE WORLD IN TUMULT

B y the time that the US Army Air Corps became the US Army Air Forces (USAAF) on 20 June 1941, it was clear that the ever expanding Second World War would soon engulf the United States, and

The BC-series begat the idea of armed Yales with retractable gear, which in turn begat the Texan dynasty. In the meantime there was the NA-50 *(below)* for Peru and the NA-64 *(above)* for Siam (now Thailand) which were conceived as fighters. These aircraft were heavily armed and had underwing attach points for bombs.

Only a handful of these planes were made, and indeed the NA-64 wasn't even delivered to Bangkok. All six were drafted by the USAAC for use as trainers! All of this in turn helped to lead to the idea of arming Texans with forward-firing Brownings.

that American readiness to fight the war would be the key to winning. France had fallen to the Germans just a year before; Britain was hanging on by its fingernails; and the USSR was invaded on 22 June 1941.

The USAAF was born into a tumultuous world with a mandate of rapid expansion in terms of both men and airplanes. This meant that thousands—and ultimately hundreds of thousands—of new pilots would have to be trained practically overnight. They would have to be trained to fly fighters and bombers at the front as well as to fly the airplanes *to* the front. The key to this great fifteen-fold expansion was neither a fighter nor a bomber, it was the trainer that would make it possible for the would-be pilots to learn to fly the fighters and bombers. The AT-6 was the airplane of the hour, the keystone of what would become the biggest air force the world would ever see.

Whereas the US Army Air Corps had ordered 94 AT-6s, the USAAF ordered 1847 AT-6As (NA-84) with the same 600 hp R-1340-49 engines of the AT-6, and 400 AT-6Bs, with 600 hp R-1340-AN-1 engines (also NA-84). Like the AT-6 and the BC-1 before it, the new NA-84 Texans were armed with .30 caliber forward-firing machine guns, and the AT-6B also carried such a gun in a dorsal mount.

Midway through the AT-6A program, production demands on the NAA Inglewood plant became so great that a sprawling new factory complex was built in Dallas, Texas. Eventually, 1330 of the AT-6As and all of the AT-6Bs, as well as a large number of other NAA aircraft, were built in this Dallas plant.

The US Navy, which had ordered 77 SNJ-1/2 scout trainers (NA-52) based on the BC-1, was now placing an order for 270 NA-77s to be delivered as SNJ-3. The Royal Air Force (which was training many of its pilots in Canada) and the Royal Canadian Air Force, (which was training *all* of its pilots in Canada), jointly received 526 NA-76s (NA-75 for the RCAF) and 1056 NA-81s under the Lend Lease program as Harvard II and Harvard IIA, respectively.

THE NA-88 TEXAN

Simply put, nearly two-thirds of all Texans built were of the NA-88 variety. These included 2970 AT-6Cs and 3588 AT-6Ds for the USAAF, 2400 SNJ-4s for the US Navy and 229 Harvard IIs for the RAF. Most were delivered in the hellish year 1942, when the Allies were desperately battling to hold back the Axis tide and the need for trained pilots was truly urgent. Because they were used almost entirely within North America, the NA-88s would remain as the backbone of the Allied pilot training effort throughout the war.

The NA-88 began as a true offspring of the war effort. The earlier models in the series, such as the AT-6A and Harvard II were, like most other aircraft of that and later times, built of aluminum, a light, strong metal that was ideal for airframe construction. In the uncertain world of 1942, however, aluminum and many other strategic materials became a vital necessity at precisely the same time that advancing Axis

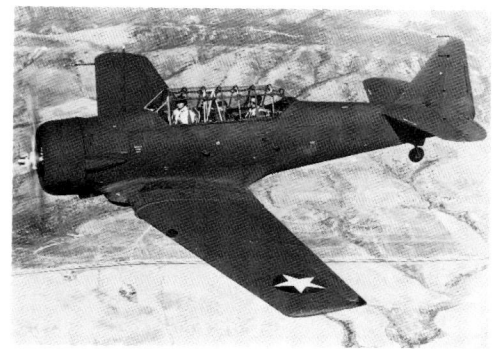

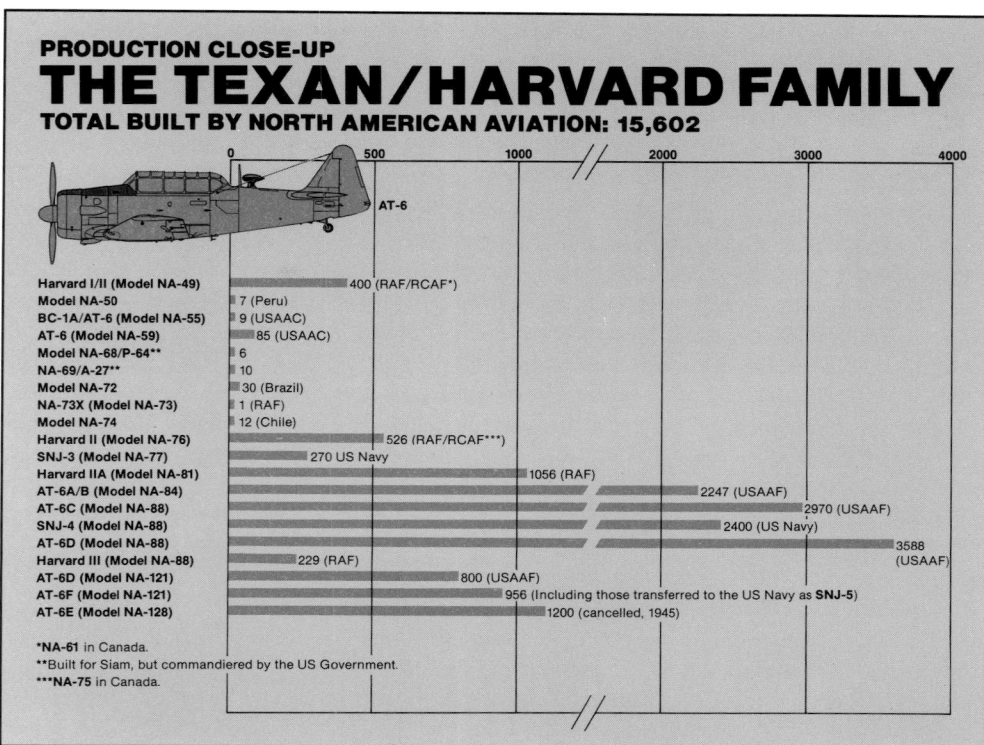

PRODUCTION CLOSE-UP
THE TEXAN/HARVARD FAMILY
TOTAL BUILT BY NORTH AMERICAN AVIATION: 15,602

AT-6

Harvard I/II (Model NA-49)	400 (RAF/RCAF*)
Model NA-50	7 (Peru)
BC-1A/AT-6 (Model NA-55)	9 (USAAC)
AT-6 (Model NA-59)	85 (USAAC)
Model NA-68/P-64**	6
NA-69/A-27**	10
Model NA-72	30 (Brazil)
NA-73X (Model NA-73)	1 (RAF)
Model NA-74	12 (Chile)
Harvard II (Model NA-76)	526 (RAF/RCAF***)
SNJ-3 (Model NA-77)	270 US Navy
Harvard IIA (Model NA-81)	1056 (RAF)
AT-6A/B (Model NA-84)	2247 (USAAF)
AT-6C (Model NA-88)	2970 (USAAF)
SNJ-4 (Model NA-88)	2400 (US Navy)
AT-6D (Model NA-88)	3588 (USAAF)
Harvard III (Model NA-88)	229 (RAF)
AT-6D (Model NA-121)	800 (USAAF)
AT-6F (Model NA-121)	956 (Including those transferred to the US Navy as **SNJ-5**)
AT-6E (Model NA-128)	1200 (cancelled, 1945)

*NA-61 in Canada.
**Built for Siam, but commandiered by the US Government.
***NA-75 in Canada.

Below: The NA-49 launched the entire Texan/Harvard Dynasty. This aircraft is the first of 400 that were ordered for the Royal Air Force and the Royal Canadian Air Force as Harvard I and Harvard II. It bears the US civil registry N7000 while already wearing the RAF roundels. Also note the single wing-mounted cannon.

The NA-88 *(above)* became the definitive member of the family with over 9000 units being produced—most of them during 1942! Most of the NA-88s, including the one above, served the USAAF as AT-6C and AT-6D, but many also served the US Navy and the RAF.

armies began to threaten the source of ores and raw materials, as well as the shipping lanes that brought them to the United States. Even if the bauxite *did* arrive safely, existing aluminum plants were strained beyond capacity to produce the amount of finished aluminum that would be required by the war effort.

A decision was reached, therefore, to preserve critical aluminum for use only in *combat* aircraft, so North American devised a way to build Texans almost entirely without aluminum. The first result of this was 2970 plywood AT-6Cs that started rolling out of the new NAA Dallas plant.

The AT-6D series followed immediately after the AT-6Cs and was identical to its predecessor, except for the conversion to a 24-volt electrical system. Both types were equipped with the standard 600 hp R-1340 engine, except for 1573 AT-6Ds that were transferred to the US Navy under the SNJ-5 designation and were powered by 550 hp R-1340s. The SNJ-5s were also armed with an AT-6-type .30 caliber machine gun in a dorsal mount, as well as with two wing-mounted .30 caliber machine guns.

Though most Texans were armed only for training purposes, a handful actually were designated as combat aircraft during World War II. Siam had ordered the NA-68 and NA-69 variants as six fighters and ten attack bombers respectively, but these eventually wore American markings as the P-64 and A-27, respectively. The NA-72, NA-73 and NA-74 types were built as warplanes, but none saw service. The NA-73X designation was used to disguise the Mustang 1 project, while the 30 NA-72s and ten NA-74s were built for Brazil and Chile, respectively. They were (like the A-27) powered by 785 hp R-1820 engines and equipped to be armed with 400 pounds of bombs, as well as their guns.

When the Japanese were moving down through Malaya in 1941, the Australian-built version of the plane, the Wirraway, rose to give battle over New Britain Island with its single .30 caliber machine gun—and promptly knocked down a Japanese Zero. In July 1942 one of a group of USAAF Texans sent to Mexico at the outbreak of war scored two direct hits on a German submarine off the coast of Tampico. The sub was believed to have been sunk.

THE LATER TEXANS

In 1943, as the production line was winding down on the first 3588 AT-6Ds, an additional batch of 800 were ordered, which were built as NA-121. The same model number was used as an additional 956 AT-6Fs were ordered, also in 1943. The AT-6F was identical to the AT-6D, except for a strengthened fuselage and some minor detail differences, and so the retention of the NA-121 model number was justified. During production of the AT-6F, a total of 411 were diverted directly to the US Navy under the designation SNJ-5.

The AT-6E (actually XAT-6E) designation went to a single AT-6D, which was experimentally re-engined with a 550 hp V-770 in-line engine. It was the only Texan ever officially tested with a water-cooled, rather than air-cooled, power plant. The XAT-6E tests might have led to an AT-6E production run, but, as the saying goes, why tamper with a good thing?

The AT-6 series is often confused with the AT-16 series. The latter were, in fact, nearly identical to the AT-6, but the designation was applied to 1800 aircraft built in Canada by Noordyn for Lend Lease to the RAF. Paid for by the US Government, they were given a USAAF designation and USAAF serial numbers, even though they never saw the United States and never wore American markings.

Dependable durability was one of the plane's chief assets. Late in 1942 cadets at Craig Field, Alabama set a record by completing 23 million miles of flying Texans without a single accident attributable to mechanical failure. In October 1944 an AT-6 set a record for continuous service when it completed its 5000th hour of flying time per day, or about 111.5 hours a month; flew about 750,000 miles, or about 30 times around the world; and used up seven engines. An example of the kind of wear to which the Texan was subjected is shown by the history of an AT-6 at Craig Field which flew 2000 hours, was involved in 11 crackups, had seven new wings, five new landing-gear struts, and six

Below: Compare this view of the US Navy's first SNJ-1 (NA-52) to the NA-49 on the previous page. Note the all-aluminum fuselage, the Yale-type radio-mast and the absence of a forward-firing machine gun.

propellers. During one period, this particular plane was in the air 22 hours a day.

Easy to maintain and repair, it could do anything a fighter could do—and more. Although not as fast, it had more maneuverability and was easier to handle. A pilot's airplane, it could roll Immelmann, loop, spin, snap and vertical roll. It was designed to give the best possible training in all types of tactics, from ground strafing to bombardment and aerial dogfighting, and contained such versatile equipment as bomb racks, blind flying instrumentation, gun and standard cameras, fixed and flexible guns, and just about every other device that military pilots had to operate. Lt EC Dickinson, the most decorated Navy flier of World War II, called the SNJ 'the best scout trainer in the world.'

Other uses included training pilots in dive-bombing, training aerial gunners, and as a tow for target sleeves. Some Texans were equipped with skis for service in the Arctic and helped to rescue crews of planes downed in the snows of Greenland and Iceland.

When the war ended there were still thousands of Texans in the USAAF and US Navy, as well as hundreds of Harvards in Canada and the United Kingdom. Though production had wound down by 1945 at NAA's Dallas factory, Canadian Car & Foundry (CCF) went on to build a number of them under NAA license in 1946 as Harvard IV. Many of the surviving NAA-built Texans were scrapped, but a great many remained in service to train the postwar pilots of the original services. Others were sold to countries such as Brazil, France, Greece, Portugal, Spain and Sweden.

In 1947, when the USAAF became the US Air Force, the remaining Texans were redesignated simply T-6, a designation that they had already carried unofficially for some time. Between 1949 and 1953, 2068 of the surviving Texans were rebuilt with an improved cockpit layout, updated radio equipment, greater fuel capacity, a steerable tail wheel and a square-tipped prop with an enclosed spinner. These aircraft were redesignated T-6G and given new serial numbers. In the early 1950s, several hundred CCF Harvard IVs were acquired by the US Government for transfer (under the military assistance program) to Italy as T-6H, and to Belgium, France and West Germany as T-6J.

In the early days of the Korean War T-6 Texans were employed as spotter planes for fighter-bombers. Flown by volunteer pilots armed only with .45-caliber pistols, the sturdy little planes often carried Army observers in the rear seat to help seek out ground targets at low levels.

'When the planes with bombs and rockets showed up,' reported Lieutenant General Lauris Norstad after a visit to the front, 'the T-6s more often than not *led* them to the attack to make sure they'd hit the right things. They would go right down and blow the leaves off the targets so the pilots behind them could see what they were supposed to blast.'

	AT-6 Texan	SNJ Texan
First Flight:	1940	1940
Wingspan:	42 ft	42 ft
Length:	29 ft	29.5 ft
Height:	11 ft, 9 in	10.8 ft
Engine:	Pratt & Whitney R-1340-49 Wasp	Pratt & Whitney R-1340-AN-1 Wasp
Engine hp:	600	550
Gross Weight (lb):	5300	5617
Armament:	two .30 cal machine guns	two .30 cal machine guns
Crew:	2*	2*
Operating Altitude (ft):	24,200	24,750
Top Speed (mph):	208	212
Range (miles):	750	870

* Instructor plus one student.

Below: One of the ubiquitous NA-88s—a Navy SNJ-4—just after its delivery in 1942. *Facing page:* A sight familiar to thousands of USAAF pilots—and would be pilots—the instrument panel of the AT-6 Texan!

Below: This T-6G was among the first 371 of an eventual total of 2068 earlier model Texans that were 'remanufactured' by North American between 1949 and 1954. They were rebuilt at NAA's Fresno, California plant with modifications, including an improved cockpit layout, increased fuel capacity and a steerable tail wheel. The most notable feature was, of course, the enclosed prop spinner.

Some T-6Gs were armed, redesignated LT-6G and assigned to the 6147th Tactical Air Control Squadron during the Korean War for use as target spotter aircraft. After Korea, 10 LT-6Gs were transferred to Austria. The T-6Gs continued to serve until the 1970s.

SNJ-3

LANDING LIGHTS
(BOTH SIDES)

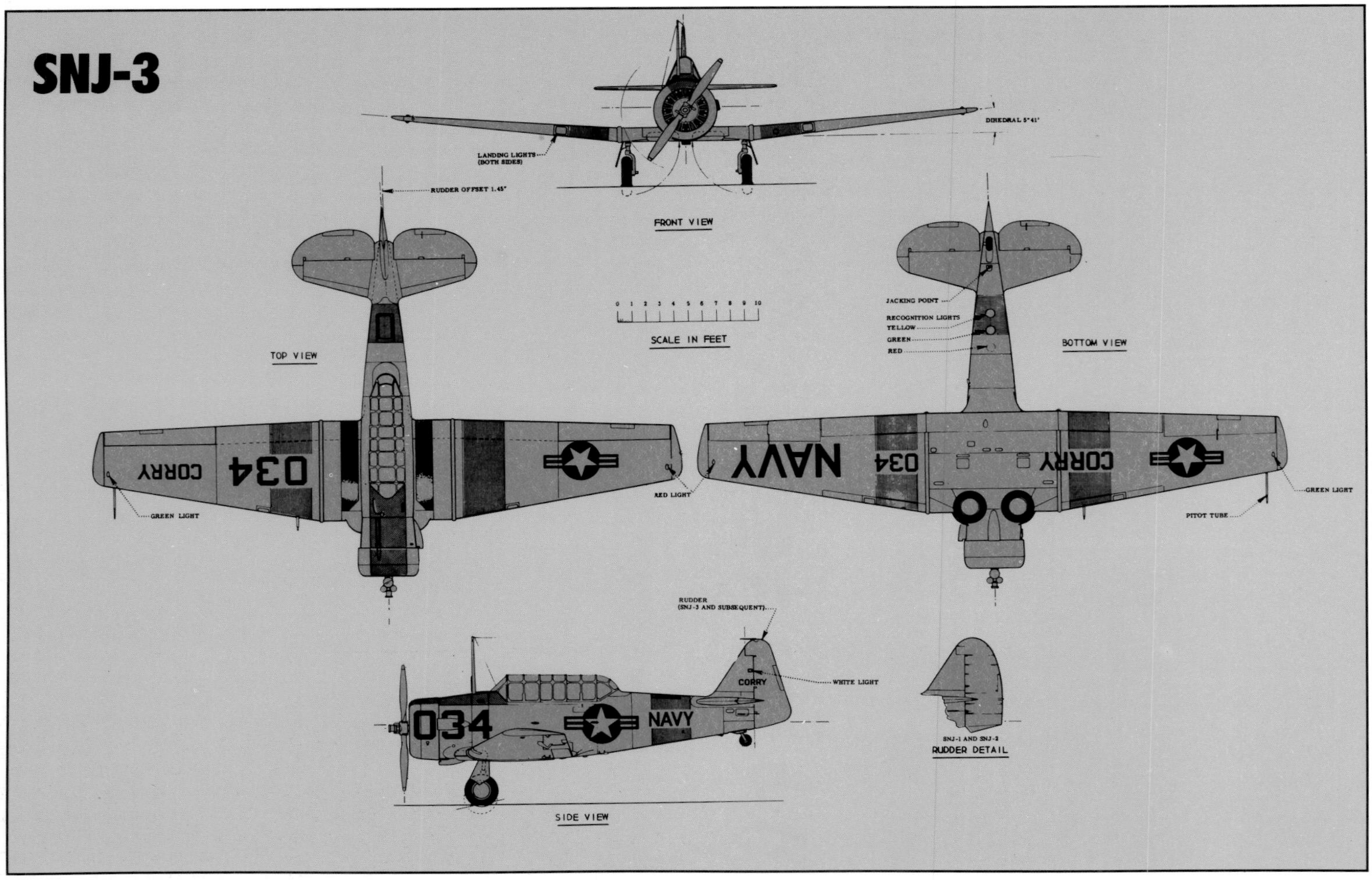

DIHEDRAL 5°41'

FRONT VIEW

RUDDER OFFSET 1.45°

TOP VIEW

0 1 2 3 4 5 6 7 8 9 10

SCALE IN FEET

JACKING POINT

RECOGNITION LIGHTS
YELLOW
GREEN
RED

BOTTOM VIEW

CORRY

034

RED LIGHT

GREEN LIGHT

NAVY

034

CORRY

GREEN LIGHT

PITOT TUBE

RUDDER
(SNJ-3 AND SUBSEQUENT)

CORRY

WHITE LIGHT

034

NAVY

SIDE VIEW

SNJ-1 AND SNJ-3
RUDDER DETAIL

T-6G

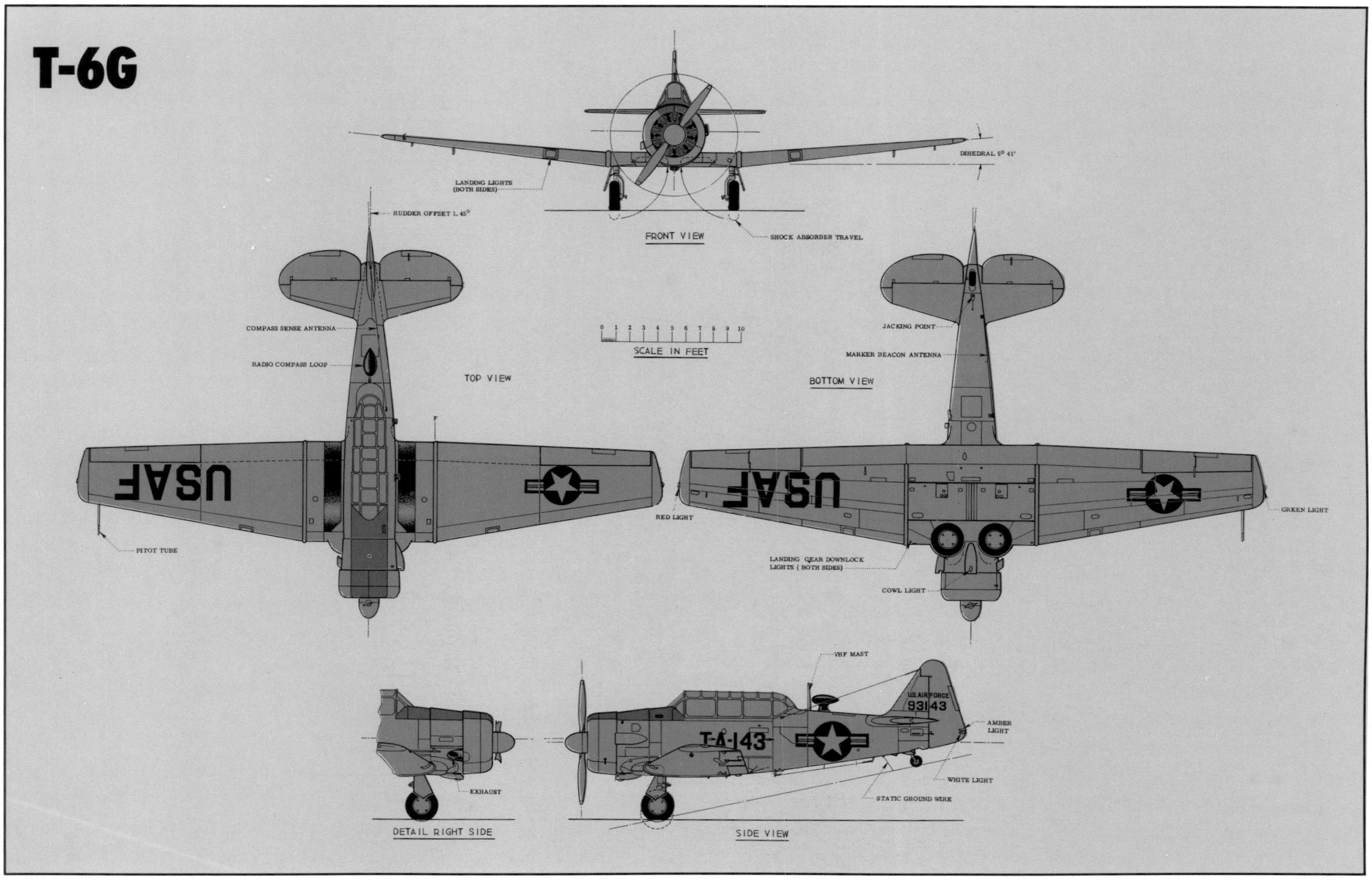

DRAGONS AND MITCHELLS

The early, astounding success of North American Aviation in the first half dozen years of its existence as an autonomous aircraft builder was due almost entirely to a series of small, single-engine aircraft, beginning with the NA-16 and leading up through all the permutations of the Texan family. This vast series of durable little workhorse airplanes turned NAA into one of the giants of the American aircraft industry. These aircraft, however, were only one—albeit vital—part of the company's activities during the 1935-1941 period.

Dutch Kindelberger had moved NAA from Dundalk, Maryland to Inglewood, California in 1935 in order to expand, and to build trainers. He built a huge factory adjacent to Mines Field (today's Los Angeles International Airport) and hired hundreds of new workers to help cope with the orders that began to mount up. He was, however, not content to rest on the laurels of current orders. He had the future on his mind. Kindelberger was fond of the phrase 'You're a native Californian as soon as you've parked your trailer,' and it was very soon after Kindelberger had parked *his* trailer that he began thinking about bigger airplanes.

The US Army Air Corps had toyed briefly with the idea of very large, long-range aircraft at the end of World War I, but had shelved the idea in deference to the Navy, which perceived *itself* as the country's first line of defense. USAAC also deferred to the traditionalists within its own ranks, who saw airpower only as a tool to support ground forces—little more than an adjunct to artillery.

Alone among Air Corps general officers was General William Lendrum Mitchell. As field commander for US Army airpower in France during World War I, Billy Mitchell, like everyone, was horrified by the senseless carnage of trench warfare. Unlike his contemporaries, however, he conceived a strategy for theoretically shortening a conflict and reducing loss of life by simply circumventing the battlefield with airplanes that could fly *over* the front and destroy the enemy's *ability to wage* the war. This would, of course, necessitate large airplanes. Billy Mitchell favored larger airplanes, but the Army and Navy considered them a waste of both time and money in the overall defense of the United States. 'Why, an airplane could never sink a battleship,' they said.

Mitchell accepted the challenge, and a demonstration was arranged in 1921, whereby a group of captured German warships would be anchored in Chesapeake Bay and Mitchell's airplanes, based at nearby Langley Field, Virginia, would try to sink them. When the bombers sent the mighty battleship *Ostfriesland* to the bottom, the Navy was red-faced. Public opinion, as well as that of all the junior officers in the

Army's air service, was clearly on Mitchell's side, but the Army and Navy hierarchy wouldn't budge. Billy Mitchell became the nation's leading exponent of long-range, or 'strategic,' airpower. He became more and more outspoken until he insulted the Navy one too many times. Court-martialed for insubordination, he was drummed out of the service in 1925. The prophet had become a martyr, but he left behind a huge coterie of young Air Corps officers who were converts to his doctrine of strategic airpower.

It took nearly a decade for these young men to percolate to higher levels of decision-making within the Air Corps, but by 1934 the stage was set for consideration of long-range strategic bombers. The first to be contracted for was the experimental Boeing XB-15, a vast, four-motored monster that was more than double the size of the bombers that Mitchell had used to sink the *Ostfriesland*. Boeing received the contract for the XB-15 in June 1934, but just two months later the Air Corps solicited proposals from various manufacturers for another 'multi-engine' bomber. Whereas the XB-15 was seen as being an experimental 'one-of' aircraft, the latter was to be an aircraft of somewhat smaller size that the Air Corps was interested in buying *in quantity*.

Less than a year later, three manufacturers showed up at the Air Corps Logistics and Research facility at Wright Field, Ohio with new prototype airplanes. Boeing presented its Model 299 Flying Fortress, Douglas its Model DB-1, and Martin its Model 146. The latter was eliminated from competition for the contract, and the competition was narrowed down to the Boeing and Douglas models, which were provisionally designated XB-17 and XB-18, respectively. Boeing's entry had four engines and a longer range, while the Douglas DB-1 had two engines and lower cost. The Boeing bomber was offered at a $196,730 unit price, compared to $58,000 for the Douglas entry. The Air Corps ordered 133 Douglas bombers under the designation B-18, but only 13 Boeings under the designation B-17. Ultimately, the Boeing B-17 would distinguish itself as one of the greatest airplanes of World War II, but in 1935 the handwriting on the wall clearly favored twin-engine bombers.

THE XB-21 PROGRAM

Dutch Kindelberger was watching the Boeing-Douglas playoffs with keen attention. Located in Santa Monica, Douglas was only a few miles up the Pacific Coast Highway from the North American plant in Inglewood, so Kindelberger was acutely aware of the

Heavy bombers circa 1935: *(from top)* The Boeing B-17 Flying Fortress, the Douglas B-18 Dragon and the North American B-21, which was also named Dragon. The B-17 went on to become the most famous heavy bomber of all time. The B-18, which was favored by the Air Corps 'number-crunchers' over the B-17, was ordered in modest quantities and lived an undistinguished life chasing U-Boats in the Caribbean throughout World War II. The B-21 never went into production, but it led to the B-25, one of the greatest *medium* bombers of World War II.

remarkable success that Douglas was having with its twin-engined DC-2 and DC-3 commercial airliners, as well as that of the huge order that they'd just received for their B-18 'Bolo.' The performance of the B-18 was, however, not as high as had been hoped, and Air Corps flyers found themselves favoring their handful of B-17s. Thus, there was a sudden window of opportunity opened within the American aircraft industry for a twin-engined bomber that could beat the performance of the B-18 and the cost of the B-17. It was into this window that Dutch Kindelberger climbed.

North American's twin-engined bomber, its Model NA-21, was proposed. In turn, the NAA proposal was ordered by the Air Corps under the conveniently coincidental designation XB-21. Nicknamed Dragon, it first flew on 22 December 1936, with Alex Burton and 'D' Tomlinson at the controls. The XB-21 had a wingspan of 95 feet, compared to 89.5 feet for the B-18 and 110 for the B-17. It offered a maximum range of 3100 miles, which was about ten percent less than the early B-17s but nearly one-third greater than the B-18. Powered by two Pratt & Whitney R-2180-1 twin Hornets, the XB-21 offered 2400 total horsepower, compared to 1620 hp for the B-18 and 3280 hp for the four-engined B-17.

Facing page: Dutch Kindelberger (center) presided over a wartime meeting from the head of the table. Lee Atwood is in the lower right and chief engineer Ray Rice (in glasses) is at Atwood's right.

Standing second from right is Harold Rainer, who headed the B-25 program. JS Smithson (with mustache), VP of production, and PR man Lee Taylor are seated (right). The subject of their discussion would have included the B-25 program. *Below:* The NA-40 prototype nears completion in 1936. A Texan can be seen in the background.

On the cost side, however, North American lost out to its neighbor from Santa Monica. Douglas met the XB-21 challenge with a much improved B-18A Bolo for $63,977 to counter NAA's bid of $122,600 for production model B-21s. North American was paid for the prototype—Lee Atwood recalls 'Dutch coming in waving the check'—but a series of five YB-21 service test aircraft were canceled.

THE BIRTH OF THE B-25

Kindelberger did not, however, lose faith in the idea that North American should build a twin-engine bomber. The next step was a twin-engined, twin-tailed, medium-size bomber, which NAA developed as Model NA-40. Produced during 1938, the NA-40 prototype made its first flight on 10 February 1939 with test pilot Paul Balfour in the cockpit. Smaller and trimmer than the pudgy XB-21, the new bird attracted a good deal of interest within the Air Corps.

A total of 8500 drawings and, ultimately, 195,000 engineering man hours, produced a three-place bomber in the medium bomber class. The NA-40 was initially powered by two 1100 hp Pratt & Whitney R-1830 Wasps, and later re-engined with a pair of 1350 hp GR-2600 engines and redesignated NA-40B (aka NA-40-2). This plane fared much better in its evaluation trials, and the Air Corps, requesting only minor detail changes, placed an order on 20 September 1939 for 184 aircraft at $63,970 each, three weeks after Germany invaded Poland, and World War II began. Designated B-25 by the Air Corps, the revised NA-40s were given the model number NA-62 and were first flown on 19 August 1940, two months after France fell to the Germans.

The B-25 differed in design from the NA-40 by its lowered wing,

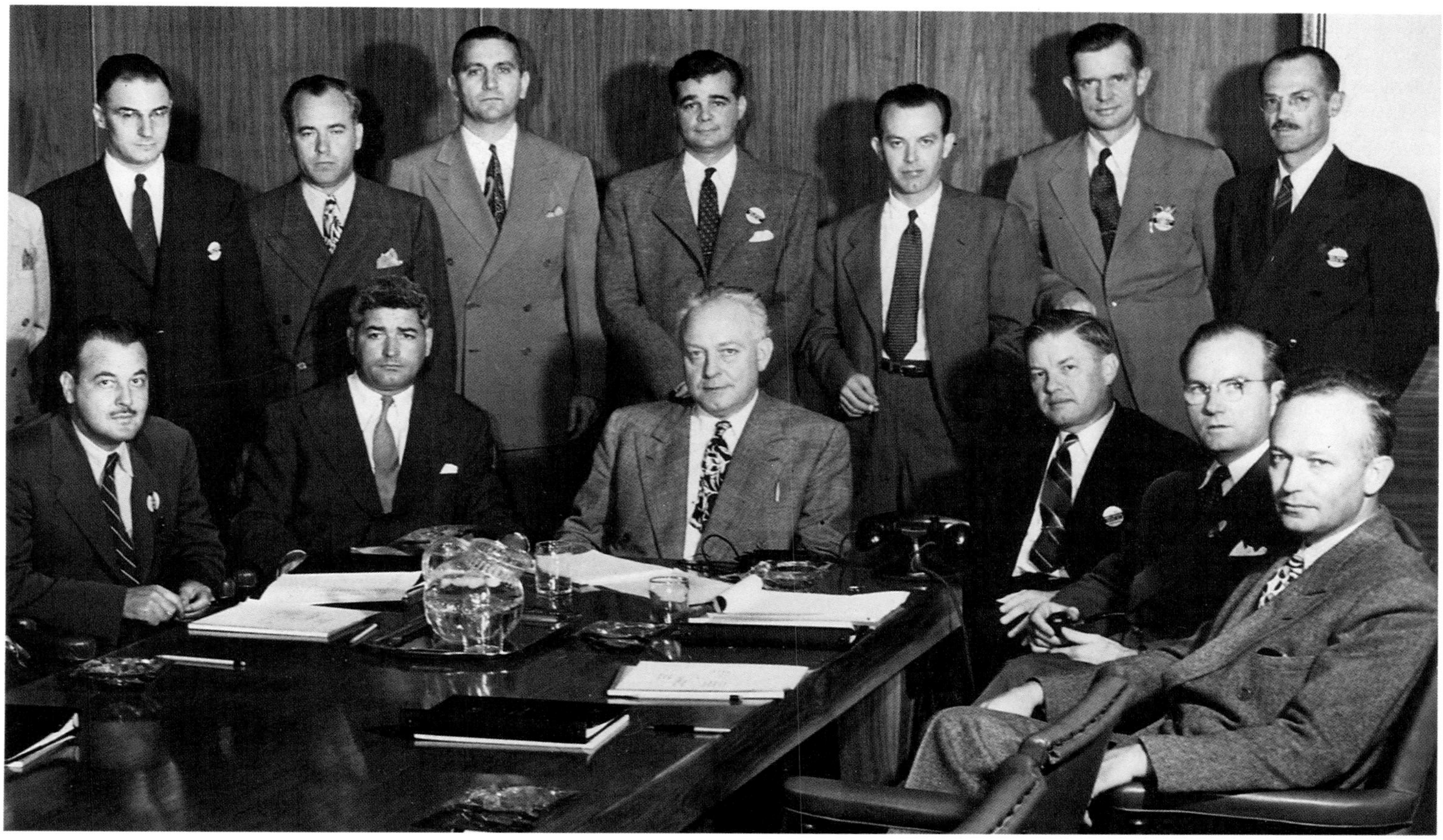

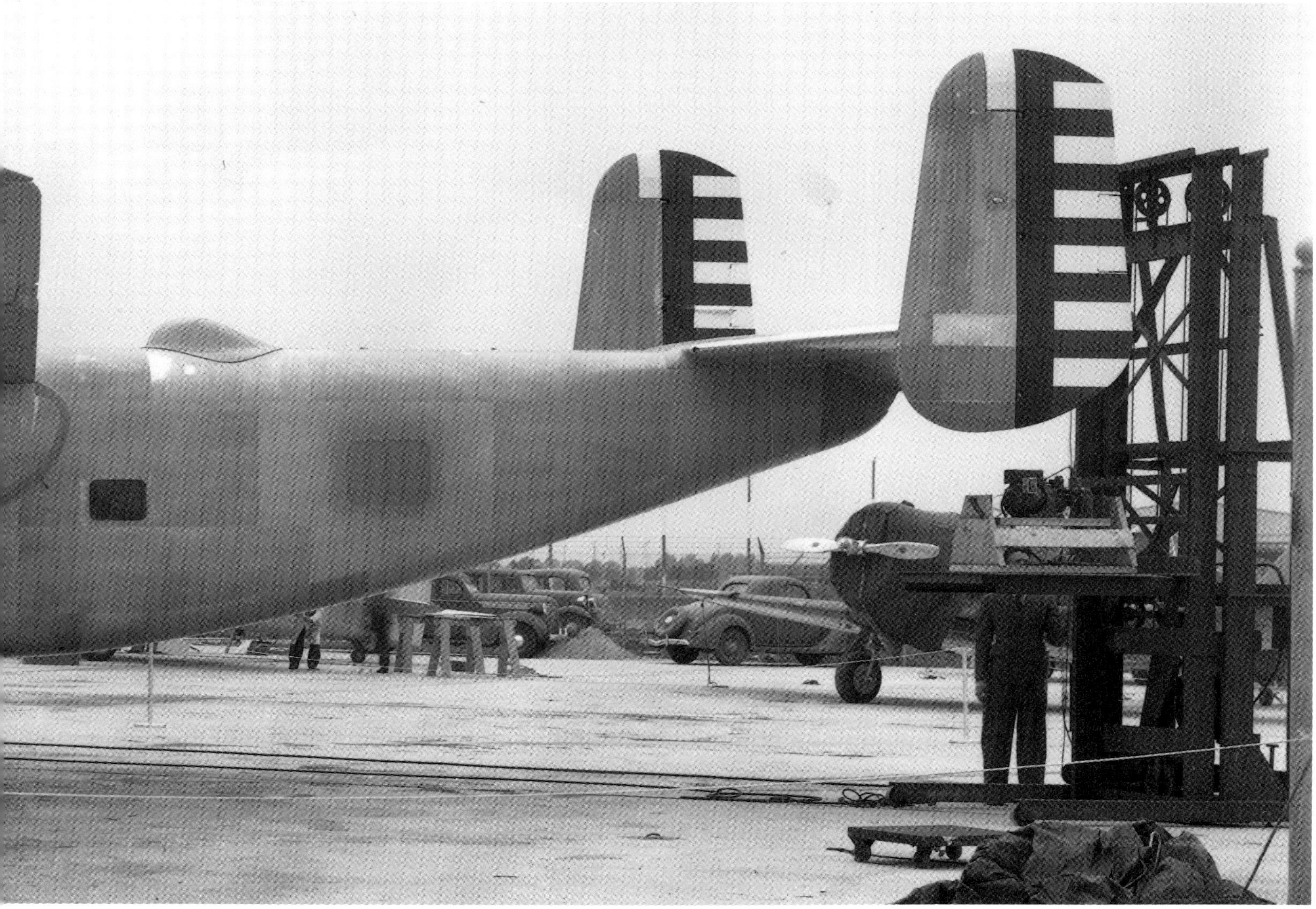

redesigned fuselage, three .30 caliber machine guns (two in the waist, one on the nose), and two 1700 hp R-2600-9 engines. The first 24 B-25s were delivered by September 1940, at which time the Air Corps ordered the remainder to be built with increased armor and the newly developed self-sealing fuel tanks under the designation B-25A. There were 40 of these aircraft built as NA-62A and delivered as B-25A between May and August 1941. At that time, the specifications again were changed, this time to a B-25B standard, which involved replacing fixed 30mm machine guns with power turrets that had .50 caliber guns.

During this time period, the war was going badly for Britain, the sole surviving Allied power, and it was believed that only a matter of months remained before the United States would be drawn into the conflict. On 20 June 1941 the Air Corps became the semi-autonomous US Army Air Forces (USAAF), a service with the mandate to build the largest air force on Earth. The B-25 medium bomber series—which

was now ironically named 'Mitchell' after General Billy Mitchell—would be destined to play a key role in the rapid expansion of the USAAF.

A modest number of B-25Bs was followed by a major order for 1625 B-25Cs, which began to roll out of North American's Inglewood plant in January 1942, just a month after the United States entered World War II. In the meantime, the USAAF's projected need for this durable, medium bomber had outstripped NAA's California production ability, so a new factory was built in Kansas City, Missouri. The planes constructed at this plant, beginning in February 1942, were designated B-25D, although they were identical to the Inglewood built B-25Cs except for modified exhaust outlets.

THE DOOLITTLE RAID

Even as North American's factories were gearing up for massive production of B-25s, the USAAF had earmarked the Mitchell for what was to be one of the most important missions of the war. The strategic situation in the Pacific during the early months of 1942 was desperate. The Japanese had destroyed a major portion of the US fleet at Pearl Harbor, they had overrun Southeast Asia and the Philippines and had captured Singapore. They had also occupied parts of Alaska

Below: A B-25B Mitchell in olive drab over the rugged California coastline.
Opposite: Jimmy Doolittle, in a B-25 cockpit after the raid. In this photo he sports his shiny new brigadier general's stars, reflecting the promotion he received as a result of the Toyko mission. More promotions were in store for Jimmy as he moved to England later in 1942 to head the Eighth Air Force.

and now threatened Australia and the American West Coast. Japan appeared invincible. The Imperial Navy ruled the Pacific like it was a Japanese lake, and there was no place that the Americans could overpower them.

In Washington DC, however, the Joint Chiefs of Staff had dreamed up an incredible, almost absurd, plan. They wanted to bomb Tokyo immediately! How could this be done when no airplane in the world had half the necessary range? Aircraft carriers, like the Japanese had used to destroy Pearl Harbor, were unfeasible because the Japanese knew the range of carrier planes and had mounted patrols to prevent aircraft carriers from getting too close to their territory. Furthermore, it would be suicidal to cross thousands of miles of the Pacific, only to come within range of every warplane in Japan.

A large long-range bomber couldn't be used because it needed a longer runway than was afforded by a carrier's flight deck. It was at this point that the idea arose to try *medium* bombers. They *might*—at full throttle—be able to take off from a carrier, *and* their range would permit them to be launched farther away from Tokyo than the Japanese might expect, and hence be outside the patrol radius of shore-based Japanese bombers.

Colonel Jimmy Doolittle, a well respected pilot who was known for his willingness to take chances, was assigned to the task of mounting the raid. The plane he chose for this mission was the B-25B. After weeks of practiced take-offs from distances equal to a carrier flight deck, Doolittle, 16 USAAF crews and 16 B-25Bs sailed west aboard the USS *Hornet*. On 18 April 1942, a day before the raid was to have been launched, the *Hornet* and her escort ships encountered Japanese patrol ships. Fearing that the element of surprise would be lost if they waited for the *Hornet* to get closer to Japan, Doolittle decided to launch the raid immediately.

Despite heavy seas and Army, rather than Navy, crews, the 16 B-25Bs managed to get into the air, and all 16 completed the trip to Japan. Each plane carried 1141 gallons of fuel and 2000 pounds of bombs. Those 16 tons did little physical damage, but the psychological effect of American bombers raiding Tokyo only four months after Pearl Harbor was immense. The positive morale factor in the United States was inversely proportional to the negative morale factor in Japan.

Because of having to take off short of the intended launch point, none of Doolittle's B-25Bs made it to the Chinese airfields where they were supposed to land, but nearly every crewman survived forced landings elsewhere. A few weeks later, Jimmy Doolittle, promoted to general, received the Medal of Honor from President Roosevelt in ceremonies at the White House. The B-25 had succeeded in its baptism of fire. The bombers named for Billy Mitchell had bombed Tokyo!

THE MITCHELL AT WAR

The Doolittle mission was, however, just one of many for the B-25. Even as the *Hornet* was setting sail for its rendezvous with destiny, other Mitchells were being pressed into service from the jungle airstrips of the southwest Pacific, from steel mats laid across sand dunes in North Africa and the Middle East, and from the tundras of Alaska and the Aleutians. Throughout 1942, together with its sister medium bomber, the twin-engined Martin B-26 Marauder, the B-25 was striking enemy targets from Sicily to New Guinea.

Many also served with the Royal Air Force, the Nationalist Chinese Air Force and the air force of the exiled Netherlands government. Lend-leased to Russia, Mitchells were soon striking German targets on the eastern as well as the western fronts.

While the B-25 and B-26 medium bombers carried a modest bomb load when compared to that of the B-17 and B-24 heavy bombers, their speed, maneuverability and ability to fly at a very low level made them a very potent weapon when used to strafe enemy targets with their .50 caliber machine guns. In January 1943 North American Aviation converted five B-25Cs to carry a nose-mounted 75mm howitzer, the largest gun that had ever been carried by a United States warplane. The experiment was successful, and 400 B-25Gs were built with the howitzer as standard equipment. Pity the tank or enemy warship that came into the sights of a B-25G gunner!

In August 1943 the USAAF ordered 1000 even more potent Mitchells. The B-25H, like its predecessor, carried the 75mm gun, but this weapon was, in turn, augmented by four nose-mounted and four side-mounted, forward-firing .50 caliber machine guns, as well as a top turret, two waist guns and a tail turret. This gave the B-25H the capability of bringing to bear ten machine guns coming and six going! This was in addition to the 75mm cannon, a brace of eight five-inch wing-mounted rockets and 3000 pounds of bombs! The US Navy even ordered 248 of these deadly weapons to be delivered to the Marine Corps as PBJ-1H.

The final model in the Mitchell family was NAA's Model NA-108, which the USAAF designated B-25J. With a glazed bombardier's compartment in the nose, the B-25J was the successor to the B-25D. The B-25J had a normal bomb capacity of 5000 pounds but could carry up to 6746 pounds. More B-25Js were built than any other sub-variant. There were 4318 delivered to the USAAF, 255 delivered to the US Navy as PBJ-1J, and 316 to the RAF as Mitchell Mk III. While the B-25H assembly line at Inglewood wound down in July 1944, the B-25J remained in production until the end of the war.

The Mitchell at war, *counter clockwise from below*: A B-25C releases a string of 500 pound bombs on the Germans in the Apennines in 1945. A B-25J crew in China reached a personal milestone in 1944 in the war against the Japanese. The armament of the B-25G, including a 75mm howitzer (left chin), was truly formidable, and the scourge of the enemy.

Left: From executives in suits and ties to riveters without shirts, from women in saddle shoes to janitors with bow ties, they were—black and white, male and female—the people of North American who made the B-25 possible and the end of the war nearer. They are gathered here on the occasion of the rollout of the first B-25J in 1943. As can be seen in the background, more would follow—soon. *Above:* Her smile was not for the recipient of this 75mm shell that would help make the B-25G and B-25H such awesome ground attack aircraft.

	B-25H Mitchell	**B-25J Mitchell**
First Flight:	1943	1943
Wingspan:	67 ft, 7 in	67 ft, 7 in
Length:	51 ft	53 ft, 6 in
Height:	15 ft, 9 in	16 ft, 4 in
Engines:	two Wright R-2600-13 Cyclones	two Wright R-2600-29 Cyclones
Engine hp:	1700	1700
Gross Weight (lb):	33,500	27,560
Empty Weight (lb):	19,975	19,940
Max Payload (lb):	3200	3200
Armament:	fourteen .50 cal machine guns one 75mm T13E-1 cannon	eighteen .50 cal machine guns
Crew:	5	6
Operating Altitude (ft):	23,800	24,500
Cruising Speed (mph):	230	242
Top Speed (mph):	275	293
Max Range (miles):	2700	3240

POSTSCRIPT TO A GREAT CAREER

When World War II ended, the North American B-25 Mitchell had earned a justifiably important place in the history of American combat aircraft. It had served with distinction on every front and with a better overall operational record than Martin's B-26 Marauder, the only other American medium bomber of note. Nearly *ten thousand* had been built, yet only 380 were lost in combat!

After VJ Day on 3 September 1945, 1767 Mitchells remained in the USAAF, compared with 719 Marauders. On 26 September 1947, when the USAAF became the independent US Air Force, the new service inherited more than 600 B-25s, mostly B-25Js. Most of these were converted to TB-25J crew trainers, but 157 were converted to TB-25Ks and TB-25Ms by Hughes Aircraft, to be used to test E1 and E5 radar fire control systems. A handful also had their guns removed and became CB-25J utility transports and VB-25J staff transports.

As North American was ready to point out, the postwar use of the fast and durable Mitchell for these various roles saved 'a good share of defense dollars by reducing [the] need for completely new trainer and transport aircraft.' By the time of the Korean War, however, only about a dozen Mitchells remained in active service, and the last of these was retired in 1953.

THE XB-28 PROGRAM

A little known stable mate of the immensely popular B-25 was the plane that North American Aviation knew as NA-63, that the USAAF designated as XB-28, but which could well be called the 'Super Mitchell.'

The original idea for the NA-63 dated back to the earliest days of the B-25 program. The Second World War had just begun. North American had the B-25 on the drawing board, as did Martin with their B-26. Foreseeing a need for pressurized aircraft with turbo-supercharged engines to operate at very high altitudes, the Air Corps asked both North American Aviation and Martin to extrapolate from their B-25 and B-26 designs a twin-engined, high altitude bomber. The Martin design was rejected, but on 13 February 1940, the Air Corps ordered NAA to go ahead with two examples of its NA-63 design under the designation XB-28.

Powered by two turbo-supercharged Pratt & Whitney R-2800-11 Wasps, the XB-28 made its first flight on 24 April 1942, less than a week after the Doolittle raid. It was only slightly larger than the B-25, and like the B-25, it had a tricycle landing gear. Unlike the Mitchell, however, the XB-28 had a single, rather than double, vertical tail surface.

Despite its excellent performance, the new plane was not ordered into production. Even as the XB-28 prototype was being test flown, the USAAF was re-evaluating its need for a high altitude *medium* bomber. In theory, it sounded like a good idea, but in practice the USAAF found that medium bomber missions were actually being flown at *low* altitudes. Rather than infringe on North American's B-25 production capacity for an untried newer type, the USAAF canceled the whole program.

The second XB-28 was reconfigured on the assembly line as an unarmed, high altitude reconnaissance aircraft under the NAA model number NA-67, and it was delivered as XB-28A.

Above: The XB-28 suffered only from bad timing. However, see page 69.

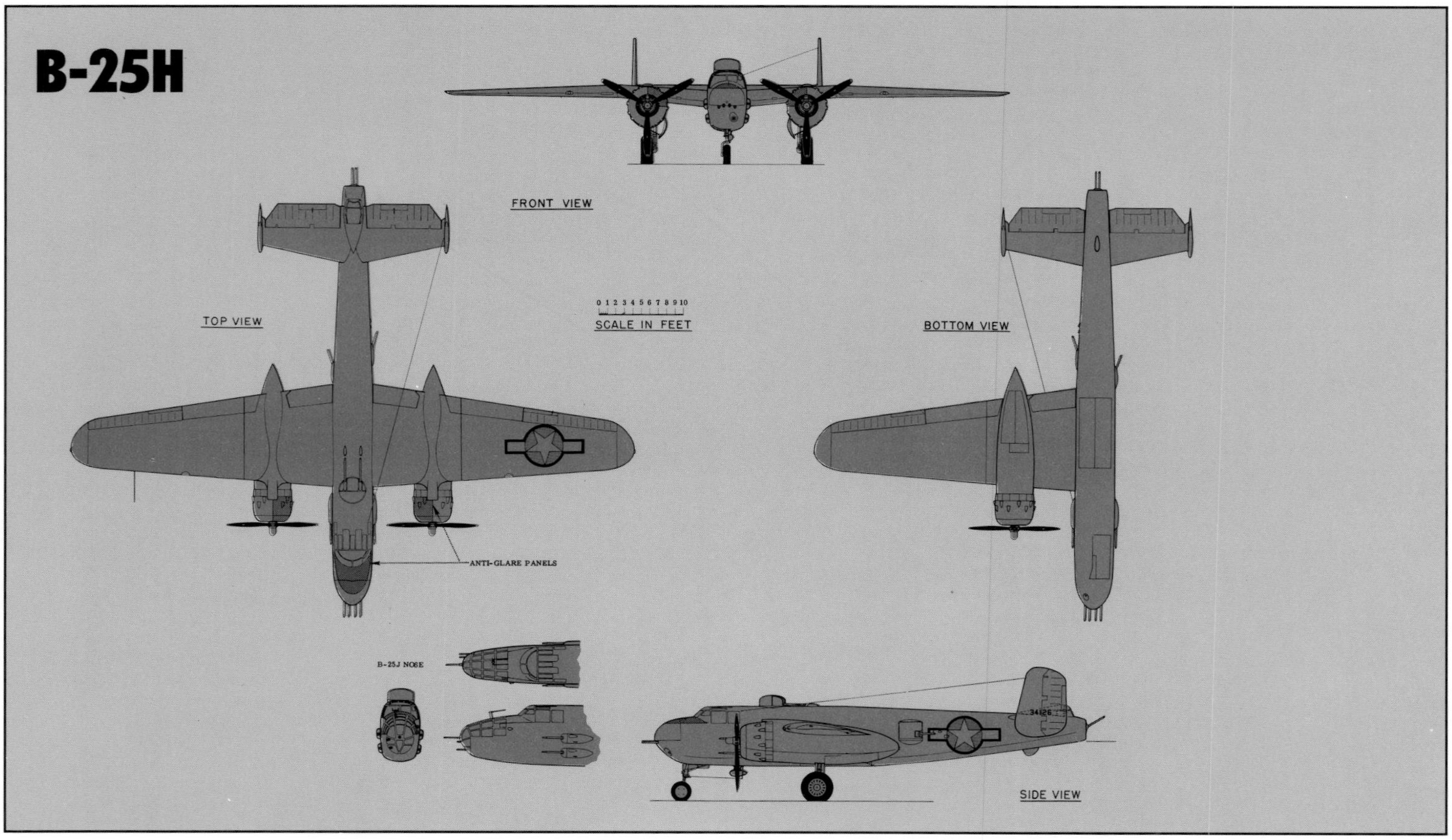

B-25H

FRONT VIEW

TOP VIEW

0 1 2 3 4 5 6 7 8 9 10
SCALE IN FEET

BOTTOM VIEW

ANTI-GLARE PANELS

B-25J NOSE

SIDE VIEW

PRODUCTION CLOSE-UP
B-25 MITCHELL
TOTAL BUILT BY NORTH AMERICAN AVIATION: 11,433

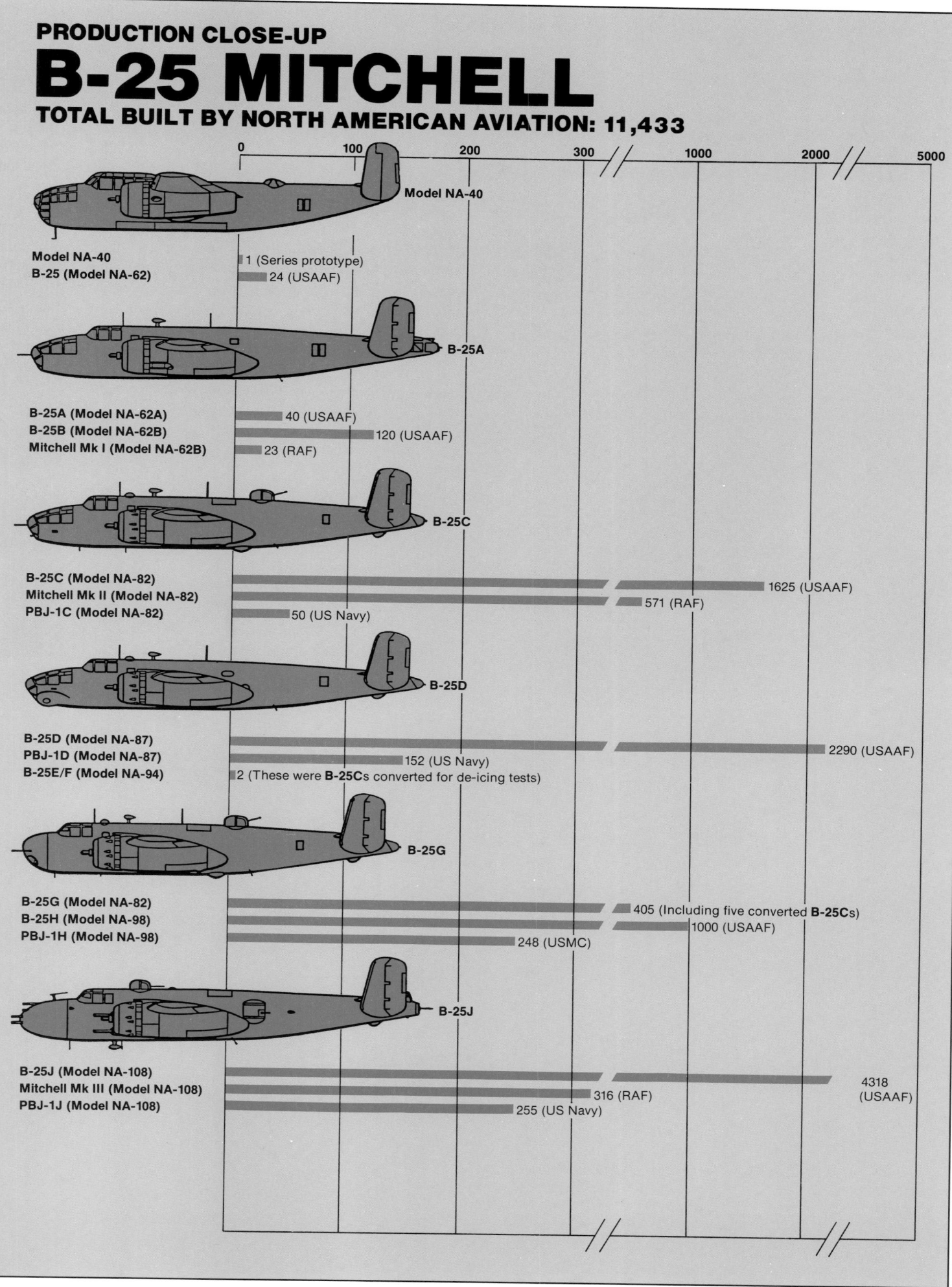

Model NA-40

Model NA-40
B-25 (Model NA-62)

1 (Series prototype)
24 (USAAF)

B-25A

B-25A (Model NA-62A)
B-25B (Model NA-62B)
Mitchell Mk I (Model NA-62B)

40 (USAAF)
120 (USAAF)
23 (RAF)

B-25C

B-25C (Model NA-82)
Mitchell Mk II (Model NA-82)
PBJ-1C (Model NA-82)

1625 (USAAF)
571 (RAF)
50 (US Navy)

B-25D

B-25D (Model NA-87)
PBJ-1D (Model NA-87)
B-25E/F (Model NA-94)

2290 (USAAF)
152 (US Navy)
2 (These were B-25Cs converted for de-icing tests)

B-25G

B-25G (Model NA-82)
B-25H (Model NA-98)
PBJ-1H (Model NA-98)

405 (Including five converted B-25Cs)
1000 (USAAF)
248 (USMC)

B-25J

B-25J (Model NA-108)
Mitchell Mk III (Model NA-108)
PBJ-1J (Model NA-108)

4318 (USAAF)
316 (RAF)
255 (US Navy)

112823

Above: Still marked with the chalk mark on her nose that she received at the factory, a B-25C heads out over California's rugged San Gabriel Mountains toasted brown by the summer of 1943. By nightfall she will be at a USAAF field and within a week she will be heading out from Newfoundland across the wild North Atlantic bound for her rendezvous with wartime Europe where the guns in her plexiglass turret will face the Messerschmitts and Focke Wulfs of Hitler's Luftwaffe.

THE P-51 MUSTANG

Of the great air superiority fighters of World War II, there is probably none other that has earned more votes for 'best' of its genre than the North American P-51 Mustang. Arriving relatively late in the war, it really began its illustrious career after the venerable Spitfires, P-47s, Bf-109s, P-38s and Zeros had established their reputations. The P-51 was the long-awaited long range fighter escort for the American strategic bombers penetrating the heart of the German Reich, the first Allied fighter to pose a serious threat to Nazi interceptors in the skies over the fatherland itself. In the Pacific the Mustangs swarmed into Iwo Jima after its capture and used the former Japanese stronghold as a base from which to seize air superiority over the Japanese home islands.

Of World War II's great piston-engine fighters, the P-51 was the only one to be conceived after the war began. Its origin is traceable to a British Air Ministry shopping trip to California in April 1940. The seven-month-old war had British aircraft factories working double-time and still not meeting the RAF's demand for aircraft, so the Air Ministry was looking to buy additional types of American design which could be produced in the United States. On the medium bomber side, Douglas was building Bostons for the British and Lockheed was building Hudsons. Curtiss, meanwhile, was building Tomahawk fighters (equivalent of the US Army Air Corps P-40 Warhawk) and North American was already building the Harvard trainer (equivalent of the US Army Air Corps AT-6 Texan) for sale to the British. By April 1940, however, the British were interested in a fighter to supersede the Tomahawk, and they went to North American because of their satisfaction with the Harvard.

The Mustang Is Born

At the outbreak of World War II in September 1939, North American Aviation was involved in the production of the Harvard trainer for the British and French governments and had established a very good record for quality aircraft and prompt delivery. It was at this time that Dutch Kindelberger promoted Lee Atwood from vice president and chief engineer to vice president and assistant general manager. At about the same time, J Stanley Smithson moved from chief project engineer to vice president of manufacturing and production, and Raymond H 'Ray' Rice moved from assistant chief engineer to chief engineer (see photo on page 37). This put in place the team that would be responsible for what well may be the greatest piston-engined fighter of all time.

Meanwhile, in the late fall of 1939, the British Purchasing Commission suggested to Kindelberger that North American consider establishing a second production line for the Curtiss P-40 to augment production for this fighter aircraft. The request was not made with any urgency and, according to Lee Atwood, 'This proposal was not seriously considered at that time.'

However, North American had been thinking about the possibility of designing a fighter and had, at various times, examined the Curtiss P-40. 'It seemed apparent to me,' Atwood wrote later, 'that a considerably better design could be developed, and I evolved a design concept which involved placing the coolant radiators back of the wing and designed a ducting system to recover some of the cooling energy in an efficient manner. This principle had been developed to some extent in literature, both in the United States (at the National Advisory Committee for Aeronautics, NACA) and in England, as the "Meredith effect." It involved discharging the heated air under as much pressure as was possible in a rear facing jet as in the yet-to-be-developed ram-jet engine. Thus, the cooling drag could be reduced to very little or even nothing at all in theory. The P-40 had the radiators, both engine heat rejection and oil coolers, suspended under the engine, giving a poor aerodynamic entry, and no effort was made to restore the momentum of the cooling air, the discharge merely leaking out through openings in the cowling at the firewall.

However, as far as Atwood remembered, no drawings of this new concept were made at that time, and he did not authorize any design work until later.

In January 1940, the British renewed their suggestion that North American build some P-40s, and this time, with the concurrence of Kindelberger, Atwood approached the British Purchasing Commission, which was then headed by Sir Henry Self, with the idea that North American could design and build a fighter plane *superior* to the P-40 in a reasonably short time. This suggestion was taken under consideration, and Atwood was called upon to confer with Colonel William Cave and Air Commodore Baker of Self's staff from time to time on North American's background, technical capabilities and further questions about the configuration that NAA had proposed.

Atwood made several trips to New York between January and April, meeting with the British at their offices at 15 Broad Street. Atwood was assisted in these discussions by the General Motors offices at 1775 Broadway and periodically by RL Burla of the NAA staff and LR Taylor, then based in Washington, DC, for the company. AT Burton, who had been stationed in England with North American's Harvard

program and had developed an understanding of RAF requirements, also assisted them.

Atwood began by making it clear to the British that NAA had no design, *but* if authorized to proceed, *could design* and build the aircraft in accordance with the specifications advanced by the British Purchasing Commission. These conversations went on until the last week in March, when apparently affirmative recommendations were made to Sir Henry Self, and he called Atwood in to discuss the project, asking him for a definite proposal for 320 aircraft. Atwood recalls that Self made the reservation, however, and took note of the fact that North American had never actually designed a fighter plane. He asked Atwood whether he thought NAA could get copies of the wind tunnel tests and flight tests of the Curtiss P-40. He told Atwood that if NAA could do this, it would increase Britain's confidence in NAA's ability to move forward in a timely way. Atwood recalls that, 'I told him we would try, and that night I took the train to Buffalo, where I called upon Mr Burdett Wright, who was general manager of the Curtiss Division at Buffalo. After negotiating with him for most of a day, I arranged to purchase copies of the wind tunnel test and the flight test report for the sum of $56,000, which would cover out-of-pocket expenses and some proportion of the cost of the test.'

Atwood then went back to New York and indicated to Sir Henry that he had been able to secure the data, and presented him with a draft of a letter contract which called for 'the production of 320 NA-73X aircraft equipped with an Allison engine and certain armaments to be furnished by the British, and an airframe to be designed and built by North American Aviation.' The letter added that the total cost to the British government (excluding engine and armaments), would not exceed $40,000 per airplane.

Although some technical work was by then being done in California, North American had not at that time presented the British Purchasing Commission with drawings or specifications of any kind, except for the free-hand sketches Atwood had used to demonstrate the concept during the informal conversations, and the letter contract was the *sole* document available. Sir Henry Self executed this document, after having it edited by his legal staff, on 10 April 1940. With this instrument, the project got underway, with the name 'Mustang' having

The North American P-51 was born as a result of a British request that NAA open a production line to produce Curtiss P-40 Warhawks *(above)* under license. Lee Atwood (see picture on page 37) decided that NAA could go one better with its own design, which originated as the NA-73X Mustang I, and in turn evolved into the NA-97 *(center above)* and the NA-102 *(top)* which were designated P-51A and P-51B respectively by the USAAF.

The Mustang was noticeably more angular than the Warhawk in order to facilitate faster production. The P-51A, as well as the nearly identical A-36 Invader attack plane, had an Allison engine and a 3-bladed prop, while the P-51B had the Packard engine and 4-bladed prop that would become standard for the rest of the Mustang series.

been selected for the new NA-73X aircraft by the British Purchasing Commission.

The original concept did not include the laminar flow wing, which was eventually incorporated in the Mustang. This wing design came from the aerodynamics department of the North American Aviation engineering group headed by LL Waite, from a concept originated by Edward Horkey, who was one of NAA's aerodynamic specialists. His work was based on what were then very recent developments at NACA (the National Advisory Committee for Aeronautics, which later became NASA, the National Aeronautics and Space Administration).

THE EVOLUTION OF THE MUSTANG

The North American Model 73 (NA-73X) was built in 117 days and first flew on 27 October 1940, with Vance Breese in the cockpit. The NA-73X bore a strong resemblance to the Curtiss Tomahawk/Warhawk in the fuselage, although the wing and tail surfaces were distinctively its own. Its straight lines and sharp corners were dictated by the need for production simplicity. The first NA-73X crashed in November 1940, and it was not until a year later that the first NA-73X 'Mustang I' arrived in England for service with the RAF. In the meantime, the US Army Air Corps (US Army Air Forces after June 1941) showed only a passing interest in the North American Mustang. Of the first ten that were built, the Air Corps did purchase two for its own flight tests, and these were delivered to its Wright Field, Ohio

flight test center under the designation XP-51—and the long forgotten name 'Apache.'

When initially tested in England, the Mustang proved faster than the Supermarine Spitfire V, but the RAF decided to retain the latter as its frontline interceptor because it would be easier to maintain a domestically-produced airplane for such a critical role. The RAF Mustangs were then first assigned to the Royal Army Cooperation Command to serve in support of ground troops. A Mustang had conducted a strafing attack on a Luftwaffe base in France on 10 May 1942, but they first saw action in large numbers and in this ground support role as part of the abortive British commando assault against Dieppe on the coast of Northern France three months later.

While the Mustang I was armed with two .50 caliber Browning machine guns below the nose and two .30 caliber Brownings in each wing, experience led North American to develop its Model 83, which was armed with a pair of 20mm cannons in each wing. North American produced 150 NA-83s under the USAAF designation P-51 (no suffix). Most of these were promptly delivered to the RAF under the Lend-Lease Act, whereupon they were redesignated as Mustang IA. Nearly all the P-51s retained by the USAAF were, meanwhile, modified as photo-reconnaissance aircraft under the designation F-6A.

However, the first serious USAAF production order for the airplane destined to become the best USAAF fighter of World War II cast it as a dive bomber! Produced as North American's NA-97, it was basically an NA-73X fitted with dive brakes. Designated as A-36A and called

Invader, 500 of the NA-97 dive bombers eventually were delivered to the USAAF, with which they were to see service in campaigns in Sicily and Italy in 1943.

The A-36As were followed by the P-51A series, which were intended for delivery to the USAAF and immediate transferral to the RAF as Mustang II. Most, however, were retained by the USAAF and assigned to the Fourteenth Air Force in the China-Burma-India theater, where they turned in a remarkably good performance against Japanese air and ground forces during 1943.

The Allison V-1710 engine that was standard equipment in the thousand RAF Mustangs and USAAF P-51s and 500 A-36As prior to the end of 1942 had made it a surprisingly reliable and capable airplane, but not a great airplane. In the spring of 1942, however, the RAF had experimented with the idea of retrofitting Mustangs with the Rolls Royce Merlin 61 engine. The resulting aircraft, called 'Mustang X,' turned out to be amazingly powerful, and the reviewers of Merlin-powered Mustang's performance were unanimous in their praise. Major Thomas Hitchcock, the American air attaché in London, immediately recommended that his boss, USAAF commanding General Henry 'Hap' Arnold, consider acquiring Merlin-powered Mustangs for the USAAF. Coincidentally, the Merlin was being produced under license by Packard as the V-1650 in the United States, so North American was able to seriously plan a series of factory-built Merlin-powered Mustangs. Originally designated XP-78, the aircraft became the P-51B, as well as being the first USAAF subseries to take the name

Above: General Hap Arnold, Chief of the USAAF poses shyly with a new P-51B at NAA's Los Angeles factory. *Below right:* A beautiful laminated hardwood wind tunnel model of the NA-73 prototype. *Below:* The A-36 Invader (NA-97) was identical to the early P-51s.

Mustang. The initial flight of the XP-51B (itself a modified P-51) took place on 30 November 1942, and a production order was placed on 28 December. The improvement was marked. The Packard V-1650 could deliver 1595 hp, as against 1470 hp for the Allison V-1710. North American went on to produce 1988 P-51Bs at the Inglewood, California factory and 1750 nearly-identical P-51Cs at Dallas, Texas.

The only major problem with the Mustang that still remained to be rectified was limited pilot visibility. A few Mustangs were retrofitted with the British Malcom canopy that was used on the Supermarine Spitfire, but this measure was rejected as not going far enough. North American solved the problem with a full 'bubble' canopy, which afforded the pilot a 360-degree field of vision. Developed as North American Model 106 (NA-106), the new Mustang went into full-scale production at Inglewood in February 1944 and at Dallas in July. Designated P-51D by the USAAF, it quickly became the definitive Mustang variant, with 6502 being built in California and 1454 in Texas. Among these were 136 photo-reconnaissance aircraft that served as F-6D and 281 that went to the RAF as Mustang IV. The

Dallas series was originally supposed to be designated as P-51E, but the P-51D designation was retained.

The P-51F and P-51G designations went respectively to three light-weight experimental Mustangs and a pair of experimental aircraft with five-bladed props, both of which carried the NA-105 model number. The P-51H (NA-126) was a lengthened NA-106 with a taller rudder, and the designation went to 555 built at Inglewood. The P-51L designation was to have gone to an additional 1700 of the type to be built at Dallas as NA-129, but the project never came to fruition. The P-51J series (also NA-105) consisted of 52 aircraft similar to the P-51F. The P-51K (NA-111) were a series of 1500 Dallas-built Mustangs that were distinguished from the P-51D only by having a smaller Aeroproducts prop and provisions for carrying five-inch rockets. P-51M, like the P-51L designation, was destined for a Dallas-built version of the P-51H, but only one was built. Meanwhile, 120 Mustangs were built under license by Commonwealth Aircraft in Australia during and immediately after World War II. Based on the P-51D, they received the Royal Australian Air Force designations Mustang Mk 20 through Mk 23.

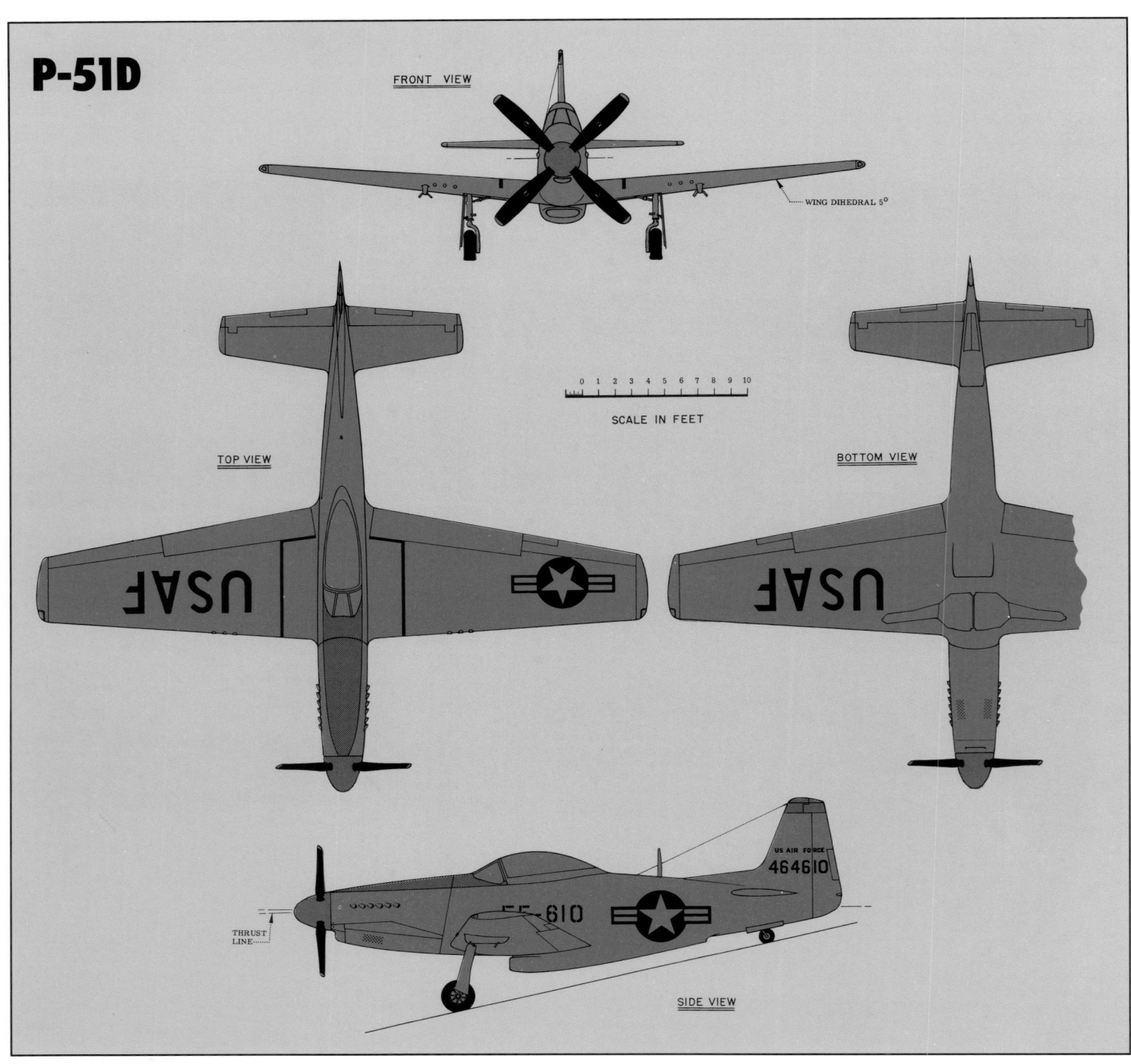

PRODUCTION CLOSE-UP
P-51 MUSTANG
TOTAL BUILT BY NORTH AMERICAN AVIATION: 16,241

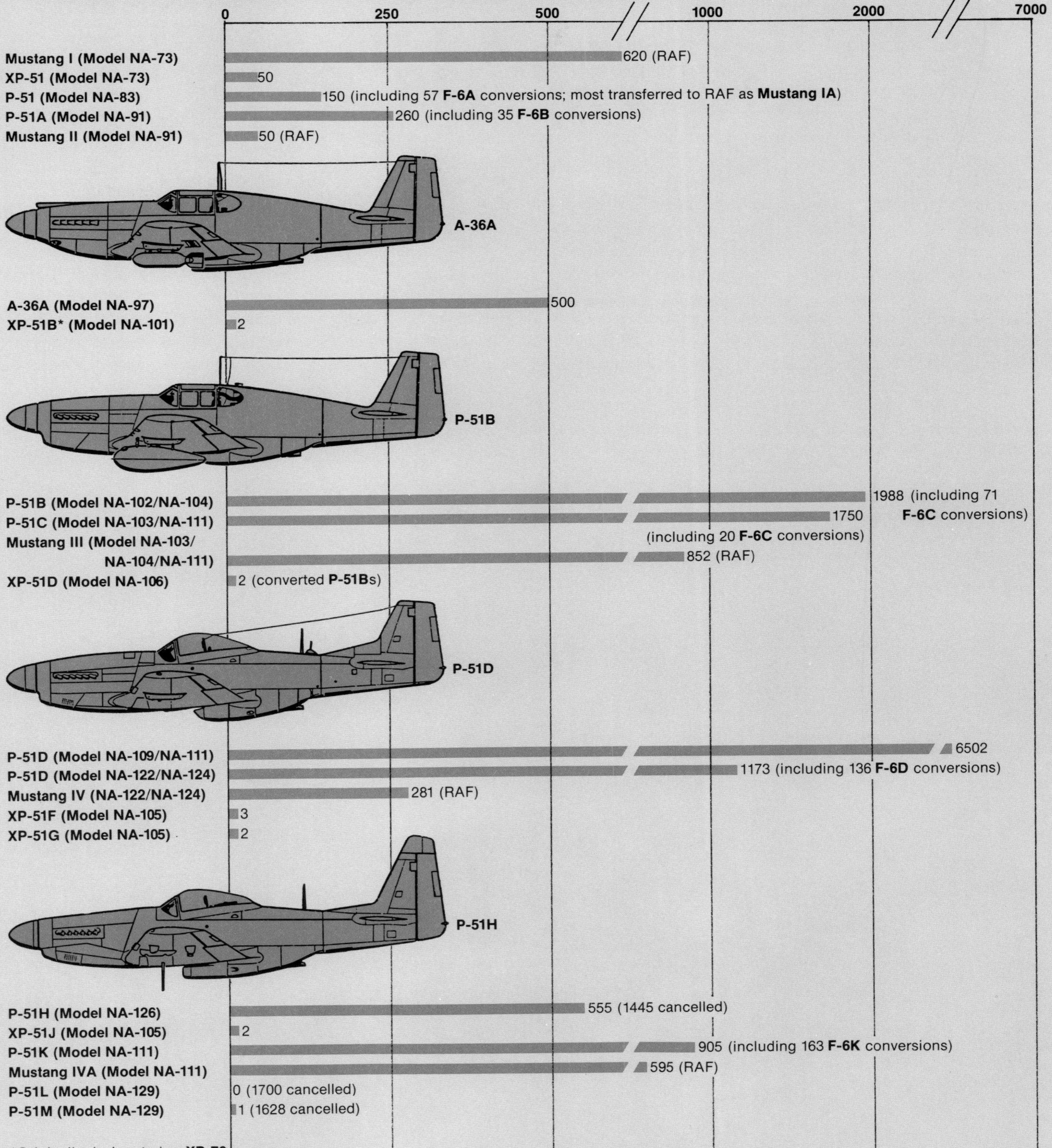

Scale:	0	250	500 //	1000	2000 //	7000

Mustang I (Model NA-73) — 620 (RAF)
XP-51 (Model NA-73) — 50
P-51 (Model NA-83) — 150 (including 57 **F-6A** conversions; most transferred to RAF as **Mustang IA**)
P-51A (Model NA-91) — 260 (including 35 **F-6B** conversions)
Mustang II (Model NA-91) — 50 (RAF)

A-36A

A-36A (Model NA-97) — 500
XP-51B* (Model NA-101) — 2

P-51B

P-51B (Model NA-102/NA-104) — 1988 (including 71 **F-6C** conversions)
P-51C (Model NA-103/NA-111) — 1750 (including 20 **F-6C** conversions)
Mustang III (Model NA-103/ NA-104/NA-111) — 852 (RAF)
XP-51D (Model NA-106) — 2 (converted **P-51B**s)

P-51D

P-51D (Model NA-109/NA-111) — 6502
P-51D (Model NA-122/NA-124) — 1173 (including 136 **F-6D** conversions)
Mustang IV (NA-122/NA-124) — 281 (RAF)
XP-51F (Model NA-105) — 3
XP-51G (Model NA-105) — 2

P-51H

P-51H (Model NA-126) — 555 (1445 cancelled)
XP-51J (Model NA-105) — 2
P-51K (Model NA-111) — 905 (including 163 **F-6K** conversions)
Mustang IVA (Model NA-111) — 595 (RAF)
P-51L (Model NA-129) — 0 (1700 cancelled)
P-51M (Model NA-129) — 1 (1628 cancelled)

*Originally designated as **XP-78**.

Note: The **F-6** was the photoreconnaissance version of the **Mustang**. Most conversions were made by adding cameras without deleting armament. In 1947, when the USAAF became the US Air Force, all 2800 remaining **P-51**s were redesignated **F-51** and all the **F-6**s were redesignated **RF-51**.

THE MUSTANG AT WAR

When it first arrived in the European theater in October 1943, the Packard-powered P-51B was still saddled with the stigma of its being an attack plane in the A-36A mold. It was intended that the 354th Fighter Group—the first USAAF P-51B group—should be assigned to the Ninth Air Force, an England-based organization dedicated to tactical fighter-bomber operations. As luck would have it, however, the 354th was still under the control of the Eighth Air Force, and the P-51Bs were pressed into service as long range fighter escorts for the B-17 and B-24 heavy bombers that the Eighth was sending against strategic targets deep inside Germany. On 13 December 1943 the P-51Bs accompanied 649 heavy bombers to the U-boat pens at Kiel, bringing the first of many surprises to the homeland of the Nazi interceptors.

Three days later a USAAF Mustang downed a German fighter for the first time, but only the first of many, for on 5 January 1944 Mustangs scored 18 victories. Just six days later Major James Howard shot down four Germans in a single engagement, earning himself the Congressional Medal of Honor.

The long-range escort capability of the Mustang was the key reason that it is regarded as one of World War II's most important fighters. It was a necessity discovered the hard way. Two 1943 bombing missions

(17 August and 14 October) over Schweinfurt, Germany had resulted in the loss of 120 B-17s (more than 25 percent of those engaged) and the death or capture of 1200 airmen. This prompted the USAAF to rush modification of the Mustang's fuselage to insert an extra tank that would extend its range to more than 800 miles. This modification resulted in P-51Ds being able to reach Berlin and to engage the Luftwaffe over all of the major cities of Germany's northern industrial heartland. Mustangs saved the Allied strategic bombing offensive and made themselves legendary in the process.

The great American test pilot Charles 'Chuck' Yeager flew the P-51D over Europe, calling it the 'the best American fighter in the war, equal to anything the Germans [could] put up against her.' He ought to know, because in 1944 he became an ace (five aerial victories) in one day flying a Mustang! Luftwaffe chief Reichsmarschall Hermann Goering also paid tribute to the Mustang when he admitted privately that he realized the war was lost when P-51Ds began appearing over Berlin.

Mustang production, particularly of the P-51D, moved at a rapid rate in 1944, and the fighter strength of the Eighth and Ninth Air Forces in England increased steadily. There were 14 P-51 fighter groups within the former and three within the latter. Of these, the 357th Fighter Group was the highest scoring group, with 609 aerial victories. Meanwhile, there were four P-51 groups with the Fifteenth Air Force in Italy,

Both hauling external tanks and sporting the bold black and white 'Invasion Stripes' adopted by the Allied air forces at the time of the 6 June 1944 Normandy incursion, a Malcolm-hooded P-51C *(top right)* and a bubble-canopied P-51D *(below)* head out from British bases to face the Luftwaffe. Judging by the victory markings beside their cockpits, the previous encounters with the enemy by these USAAF Eighth Air Force pilots were successful.

four with the Fourteenth Air Force in China, and three with the Fifth Air Force in the Pacific.

The VII Fighter Command of the Seventh Air Force, which was organized to escort B-29 bombers on raids over Japan, also had three P-51 groups—designated as Very Long Range Fighter Groups—assigned to it. Based at airfields on the hard-won island of Iwo Jima, the P-51Ds of the VII Fighter Command began Very Long Range Fighter operations on 16 April 1945. They quickly proved themselves by shooting down 34 Japanese interceptors in their first week over the Chrysanthemum Empire, and by shooting up nearly 30 more on the ground during strafing runs.

While the Mustang was prominent within the RAF arsenal and clearly the cream of the USAAF, it is a little known fact that the US Navy also briefly considered adapting the Mustang for use aboard its carrier fleet. Preliminary testing of a USAAF P-51D for shipboard service by the US Navy was begun in early 1944. Initial flight tests to establish feasibility were made at North American's Inglewood plant by engineering test pilot RC 'Bob' Chilton. Results of these tests being favorable, the program was carried through to carrier tests at sea. Proposals were also prepared for carrier adaptation of other P-51 variants, including the P-51H.

The airplane selected for the tests was a USAAF P-51D, serial Number 44-14017, which is reported to have been modified with an arresting hook installation by North American's plant at Dallas, Texas. After completion and testing of the work, the airplane was flown to the Norfolk, Virginia and Philadelphia, Pennsylvania Navy yards for ground catapult tests. These were so successful that planned catapult tests at sea were scratched from the schedule.

The aircraft carrier USS *Shangri La* was chosen for the actual carrier tests. It departed Norfolk Navy Yard in the evening on 13 November 1944 and proceeded to a point about 85 miles east of Chesapeake Bay. The following day the *Shangri La* headed into the wind, and after a 90 mph approach, the test pilot, Navy Lieutenant Robert Elder, executed an excellent landing to the cheers of hundreds of Navy personnel. The ship's captain permitted all personnel who desired to witness the tests, as it was a red letter day for the ship as well as the Mustang. Four more landings and takeoffs were made, and all were considered excellent.

Some of the Navy Bureau staff had reservations that the P-51 could make successful carrier takeoffs, but the North American engineering representatives aboard for the tests stated that if the carrier provided a 35 knot head wind, that no more than a 600 foot deck run would be required. The first trial was from the 700 foot line and, although Lieutenant Elder failed to trim properly due to excitement, the Mus-

tang got off promptly. The second trial began at the 600 foot line and Elder was quickly airborne after a 250 foot run. The maximum arresting cable runout on landing was 82 feet, with the airplane at a gross weight of 9600 pounds.

After the final landing, the airplane was placed on the elevator and lowered to the hangar deck for inspection and found to be in excellent condition. Here it remained for about an hour for the benefit of those crew members who wished to see it. Lieutenant Elder then flew it back to Norfolk.

The Mustang was subsequently scheduled to perform several off center landings at the Philadelphia Navy Yard, but no information on these tests is available, and Norman L Avery, who later researched the P-51D carrier tests for the NAA, found no evidence that the Navy proceeded any further toward adopting the USAAF's best as one of its own. Indeed, after the fall of Okinawa in April 1945, Japan—the war's final objective—was within easy range of the land-based USAAF P-51s, and there was little practical need for the Navy to adopt the Mustang.

The USAAF P-51D was not only a match for the renowned Messerschmitt Bf-109 and Focke Wulf Fw-190 fighters, but they held their own against the jet-propelled Messerschmitt Me-262 fighters that became operational in 1944. The German jet fighters were clearly faster than the Mustang, but the P-51 had an edge in terms of maneuverability. According to Chuck Yeager, who flew against them and shot one down in 1945, the Me-262 pilots 'tried to avoid dogfights, concentrating instead on hammering bombers… The Mustang, with its laminar-flow wing, could easily turn and dive with them, but in a level chase it was no contest; the Me-262 easily sped beyond gun range.' In Yeager's words, it was like 'a fat man running uphill to catch a trolley.'

The P-51 Mustang ended the war as USAAF's top fighter, if not the top fighter of the war. Nearly half of the enemy aircraft shot down in Europe were claimed by Mustangs, while in the Pacific the P-51s controlled the skies over the Japanese homeland. From an inventory of 57 Mustangs at the end of 1942, USAAF inventory increased to 1165 at the end of 1943, 3914 at the end of 1944, and 5595 at the end of June 1945. After the war, Mustangs were retained in greater numbers than any other fighter type, with 3303 still remaining in service at the end of 1946, though most were being transferred to units of the Air National Guard (ANG). In 1947, when the USAAF became the US Air Force, the P-51 was redesignated as F-51.

Below and opposite: The P-51D was the ultimate Mustang, and North American built nearly 8000 of them. They rolled out of NAA's plants at Inglewood, California (NA-109 and NA-122) and Dallas, Texas (NA-111 and NA-124) at a rate of nearly a dozen a day for two years.

58

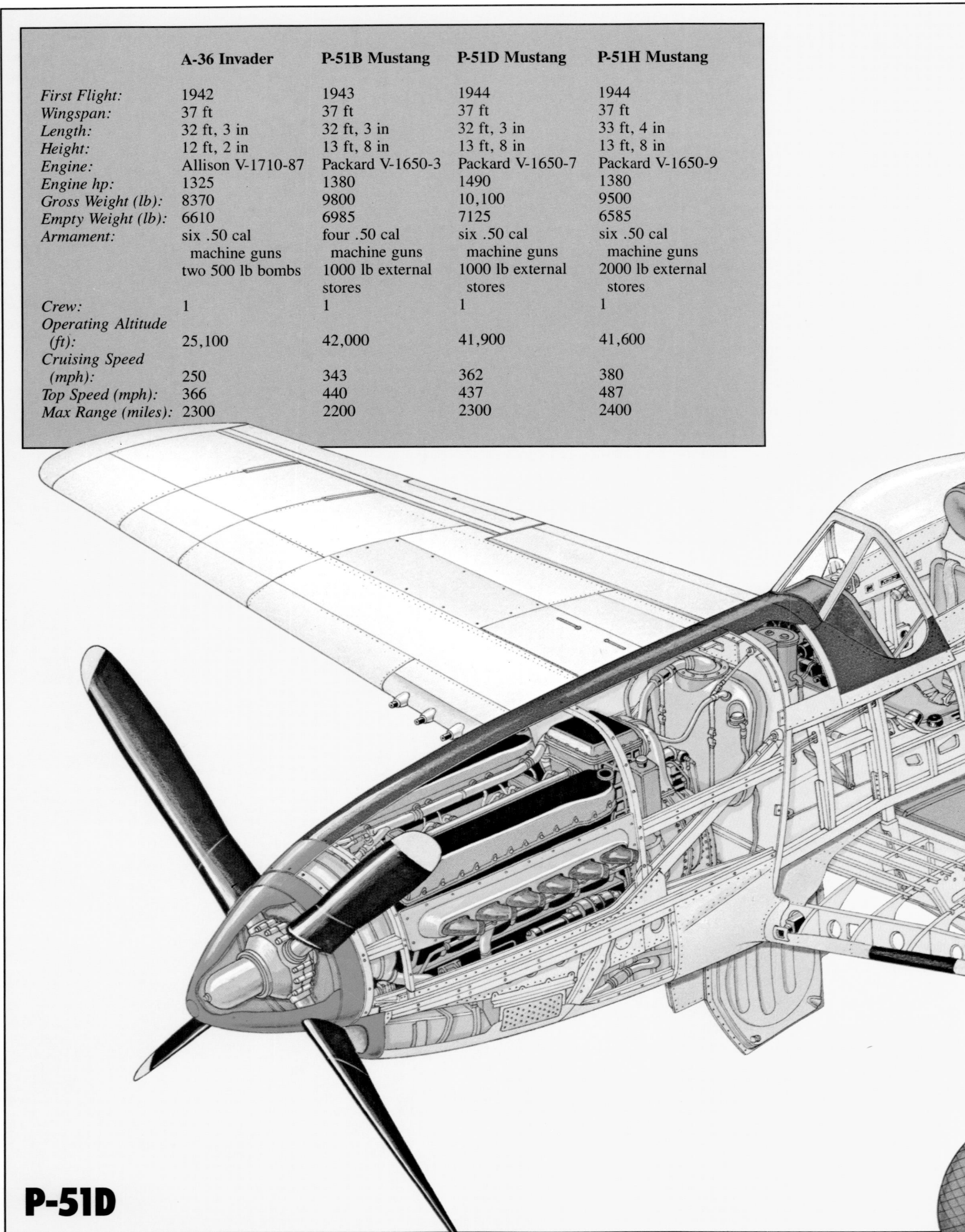

	A-36 Invader	P-51B Mustang	P-51D Mustang	P-51H Mustang
First Flight:	1942	1943	1944	1944
Wingspan:	37 ft	37 ft	37 ft	37 ft
Length:	32 ft, 3 in	32 ft, 3 in	32 ft, 3 in	33 ft, 4 in
Height:	12 ft, 2 in	13 ft, 8 in	13 ft, 8 in	13 ft, 8 in
Engine:	Allison V-1710-87	Packard V-1650-3	Packard V-1650-7	Packard V-1650-9
Engine hp:	1325	1380	1490	1380
Gross Weight (lb):	8370	9800	10,100	9500
Empty Weight (lb):	6610	6985	7125	6585
Armament:	six .50 cal machine guns two 500 lb bombs	four .50 cal machine guns 1000 lb external stores	six .50 cal machine guns 1000 lb external stores	six .50 cal machine guns 2000 lb external stores
Crew:	1	1	1	1
Operating Altitude (ft):	25,100	42,000	41,900	41,600
Cruising Speed (mph):	250	343	362	380
Top Speed (mph):	366	440	437	487
Max Range (miles):	2300	2200	2300	2400

P-51D

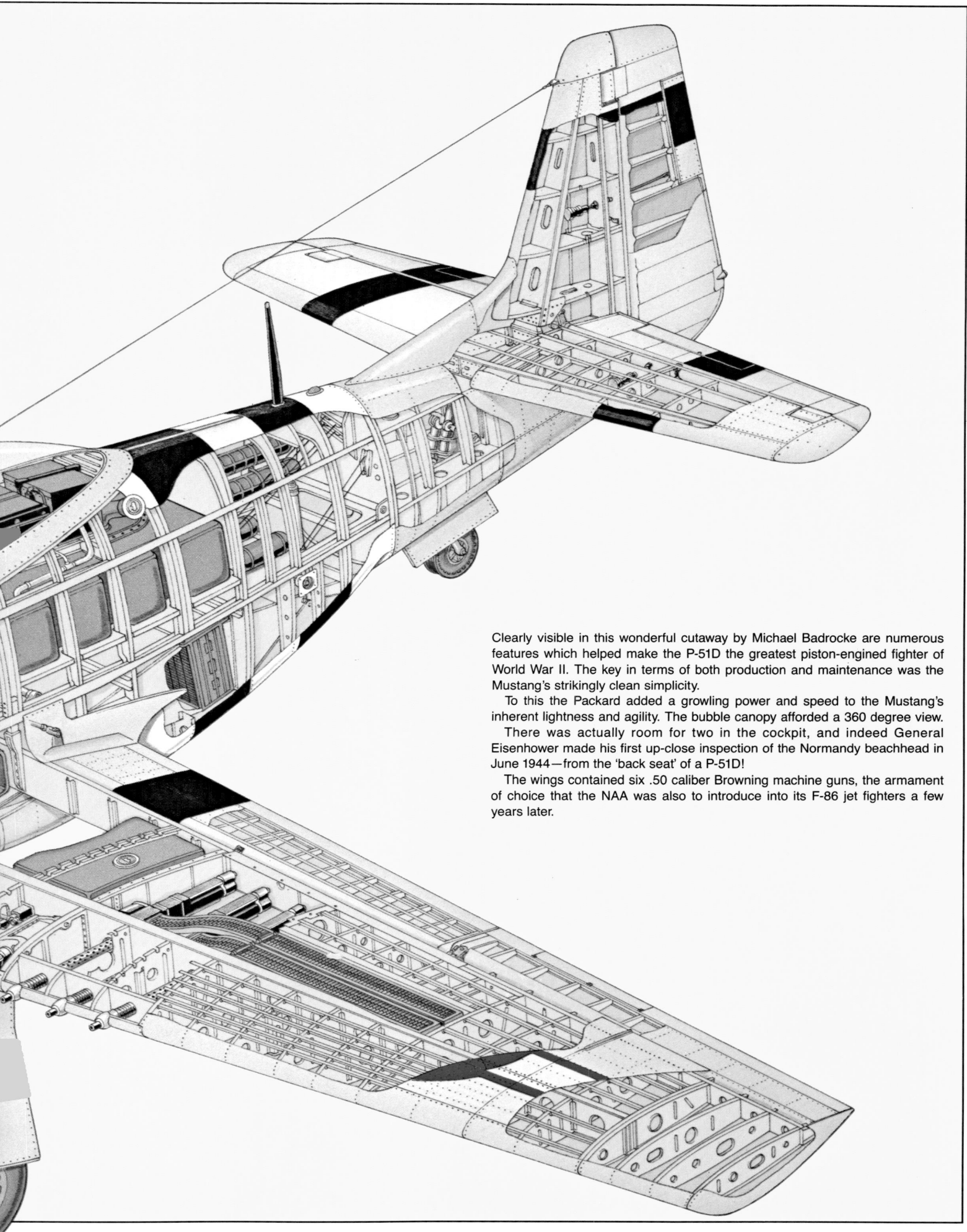

Clearly visible in this wonderful cutaway by Michael Badrocke are numerous features which helped make the P-51D the greatest piston-engined fighter of World War II. The key in terms of both production and maintenance was the Mustang's strikingly clean simplicity.

To this the Packard added a growling power and speed to the Mustang's inherent lightness and agility. The bubble canopy afforded a 360 degree view.

There was actually room for two in the cockpit, and indeed General Eisenhower made his first up-close inspection of the Normandy beachhead in June 1944—from the 'back seat' of a P-51D!

The wings contained six .50 caliber Browning machine guns, the armament of choice that the NAA was also to introduce into its F-86 jet fighters a few years later.

To make a longer range Mustang, North American simply bolted two together! It wasn't quite that simple, but it was close. As shown in this cutaway by NAA staff artist Reynold Brown, the interior structure of the P-82 (later F-82) Twin Mustang was very similar to that of the P-51 Mustang seen on the previous pages.

The six .50 caliber Browning machine guns were deleted from the wings, in favor of four of the same on the stub wing which connected these 'Siamese twins.' Also shown in this drawing are the wing-mounted braces of 'Mighty Mouse' High Velocity Aerial Rockets (HVAR), which were also carried as optional equipment by the P-51, but are not shown in the drawing on the previous page.

The big difference here was the Air Forces' insistence on Allison rather than Packard Merlin engines. This was primarily because the Packard Merlin factory was dismantled in 1945.

P-82B

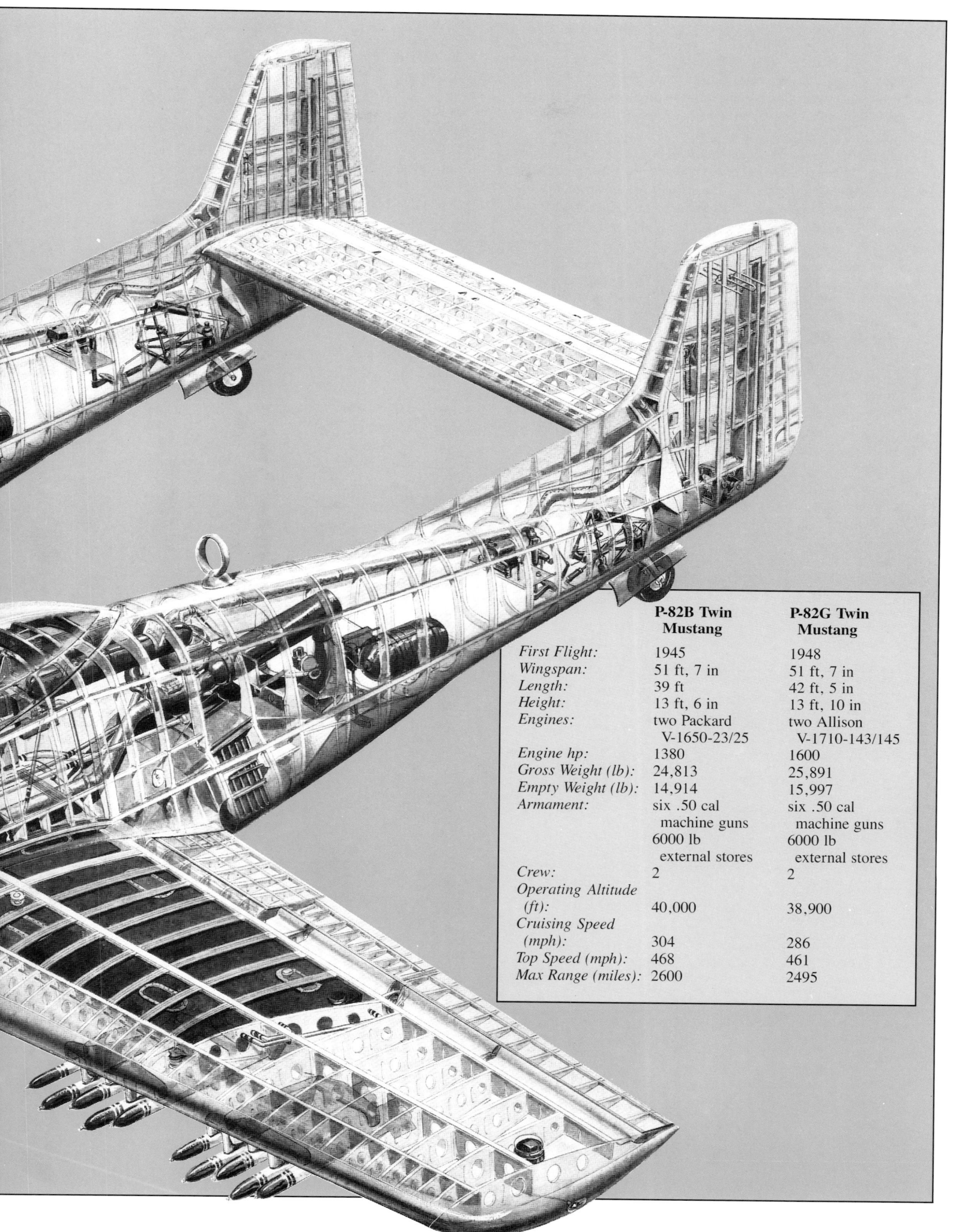

	P-82B Twin Mustang	P-82G Twin Mustang
First Flight:	1945	1948
Wingspan:	51 ft, 7 in	51 ft, 7 in
Length:	39 ft	42 ft, 5 in
Height:	13 ft, 6 in	13 ft, 10 in
Engines:	two Packard V-1650-23/25	two Allison V-1710-143/145
Engine hp:	1380	1600
Gross Weight (lb):	24,813	25,891
Empty Weight (lb):	14,914	15,997
Armament:	six .50 cal machine guns 6000 lb external stores	six .50 cal machine guns 6000 lb external stores
Crew:	2	2
Operating Altitude (ft):	40,000	38,900
Cruising Speed (mph):	304	286
Top Speed (mph):	468	461
Max Range (miles):	2600	2495

ANOTHER WAR

In June 1950, as the Korean War began, the Air Force had 1804 F-51s, still more than any other fighter type. Thirty were in storage in Japan, and they went into service quickly, while another 145 ANG F-51s were shipped from the United States aboard the carrier USS *Boxer* in July.

Though the air war over Korea was owned primarily by jets, the Air Force ultimately sent three wings of F-51s, which flew a total of 62,607 missions, primarily in the ground attack role. A number of victories over enemy fighters were claimed, with nine confirmed and 13 listed as 'probable.' A good many Mustangs were also transferred to the Republic of Korea Air Force (ROKAF) during the war. Others served with the South African Nr 2 'Cheetah' Squadron and Australian units in Korea, with many of the latter being among those that were built in Australia.

THE POSTWAR YEARS

By the 1950s Mustangs were in service with a great many air forces around the world, from Europe to Latin America, and on *both* sides during the 1946-1949 Chinese civil war. In service with Israel's air force, Mustangs served with distinction in both the 1948 and 1956 Middle East wars. At one point in the latter conflict an Israeli Mustang pilot literally cut communication lines between Suez City and the Egyptian front lines by using his propeller on telephone wires!

In the United States, the Air National Guard phased out its last P-51 in 1957, when the last Virginia ANG F-51D was delivered to the Air Force Museum on 27 January.

When World War II ended, the USAAF's hottest weapons began to trickle into the civilian market, where they became a valued commod-ity on the air race circuit. Though they were procured by the USAAF for $50,985 in 1945 (roughly $300,000 in current dollars), surplus Mustangs were disposed of for a fraction of their original cost. There were even stories of new P-51s still in their crates that went for as little as $5000.

Surplus Mustangs owned by Paul Mantz promptly won the 1946 and 1947 Bendix Trophy Races between California and Ohio with record speeds. Most notable of the Mustang racers was the P-51D delivered to the USAAF in 1944 under the serial number 44-84961, but which was never sent overseas. Having languished on the used aircraft market for two decades, 44-84961 entered the circuit in 1966 and soon became the most extensively-modified Mustang racing. By 1972, under the owner-ship of Gunther Balz and flying in the markings of the Roto-Finish Company, the aircraft began claiming speed records the way its stable mates once claimed Messerschmitts. Purchased in 1974 by Ed Brown-ing of Idaho Falls and renamed *Red Baron*, it was reconfigured with a contra-rotating propeller. In 1979, shortly after setting a record speed of 499 mph, the *Red Baron* was destroyed in a crash during the Reno National Championship Air Races. Another highly visible Mustang on the racing circuit until the mid-1980s, was the all-yellow P-51D with Rockwell International markings that was flown by former NAA test pilot Bob Hoover.

Today, Mustangs remain an important part of the air racing scene at Reno and other venues, where they will likely continue to set and hold speed records for piston engine aircraft well into the twenty-first century.

Below: It wasn't the ideal taxiway, but neither was it an obstacle for this Fifth Air Force F-51 fighter-bomber enroute to a North Korean target in September 1951. *Right:* Bob Hoover and the Rockwell Mustang. *Bottom right:* The flight line at the 1984 Reno Air Races.

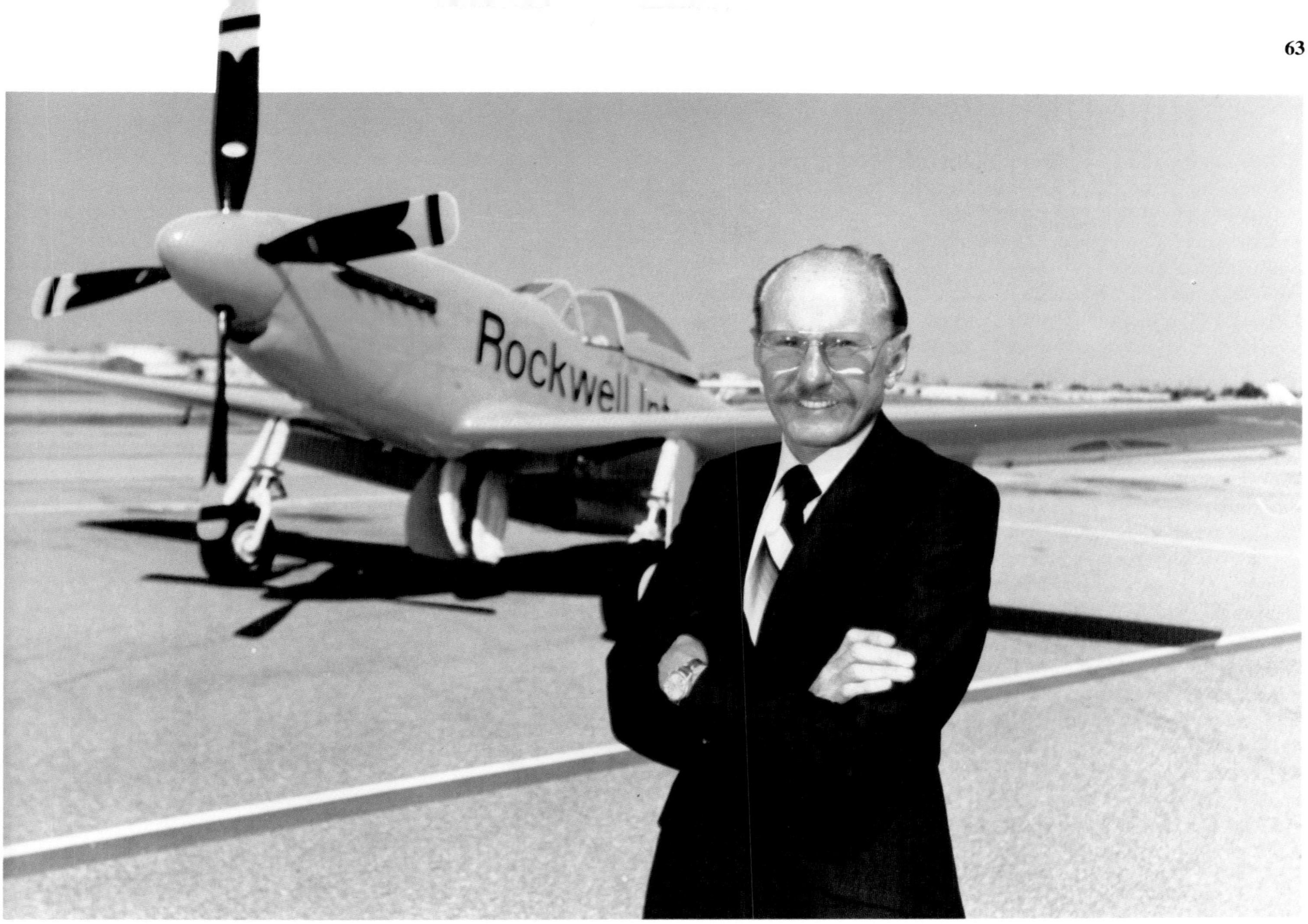
Rockwell

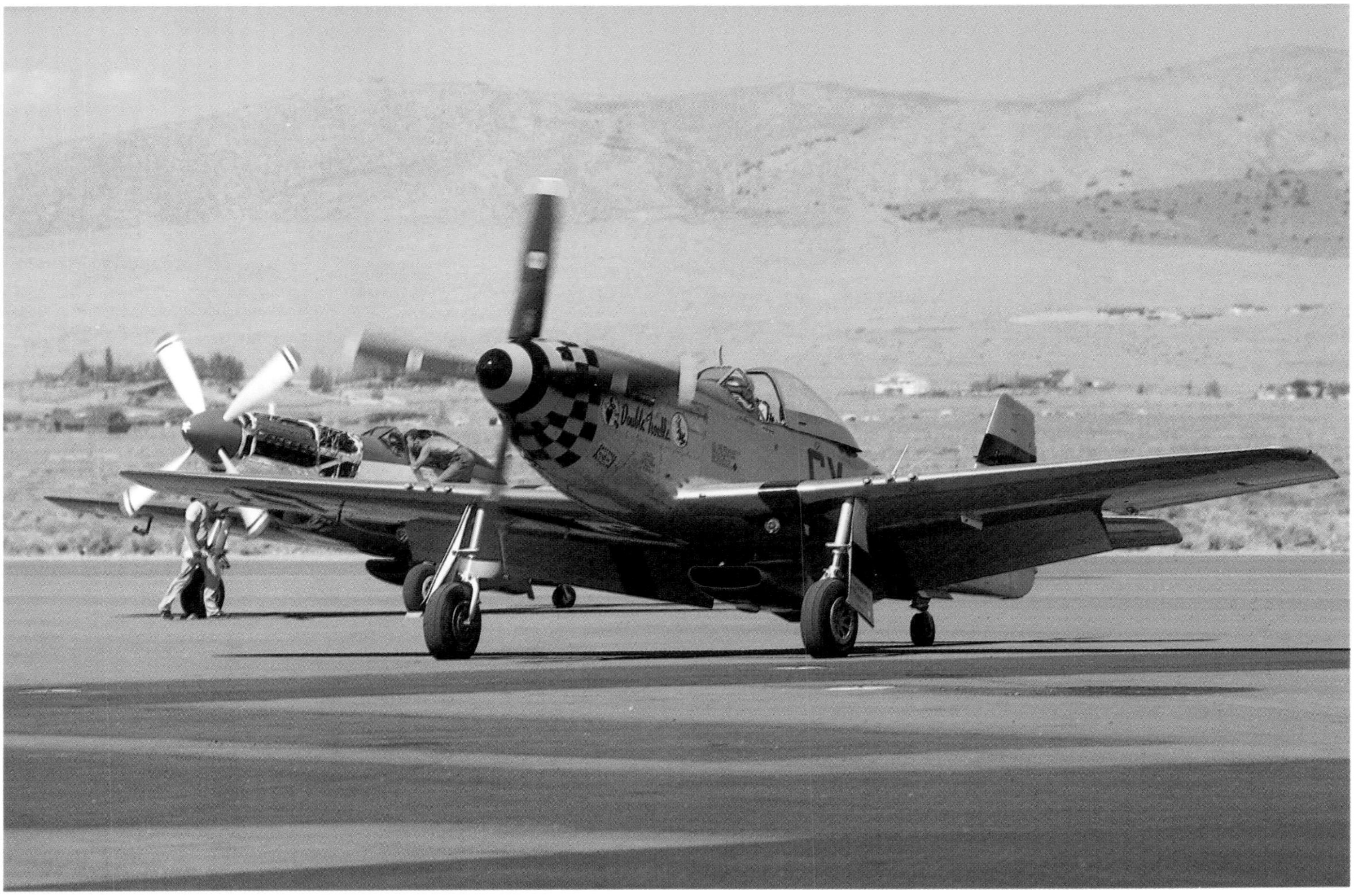

THE F-82 TWIN MUSTANG

It was an obvious solution to the problem of how to develop a long range fighter to escort long range bombers: they took the fighter that was the longest-ranging type then in service and *spliced two of them together*!

North American's idea of joining two standard, well-proven, P-51 fuselages (complete with engine) was not unique. It was reminiscent of the He-111Z transport and glider tug, a 'Siamese Twin' arrangement of two He-111 bombers, built by the Germans earlier in the war. In any case, NAA's plane proved to be the sole American example.

Ordered in January 1944 under the designation XP-82, the North American NA-120 combined two P-51D wings and a modified horizontal stabilizer. It was powered by a pair of Packard V-1650 Merlin engines (like those of the P-51D), driving P-51D propellers that turned in opposite directions to provide stability. The two cockpits featured identical controls so that pilot and copilot—or more properly, the two *co*pilots—could trade off control on long, tedious flights. Given that the range of the Twin Mustang would be nearly double that of the very long range Mustang, those flights would, in fact, be quite long.

In June 1944, as the Allies were storming ashore at Normandy, the USAAF ordered one XP-82A, to be powered by two Allison V-1710 engines, for evaluation purposes, along with 500 P-82Bs (NA-123) to be powered by the Packard V-1650 Merlins. The first XP-82 flew on 16 June 1945 with Edward Virgin and Joseph Barton at the dual controls. They flew the XP-82A in October, but by the time they took the first P-82B up for a try on Halloween 1945, the end of the war had resulted in P-82B production being slashed by 96 percent.

Early in 1946, two P-82Bs were tested with two different types of radar systems in an effort to evaluate the potential of the Twin Mustang as a night fighter. Redesignated P-82C, the first of these flew on 27 March with World War II-vintage SCR-720 radar, and two days later the second one flew under the P-82D designation with newer AN/APS-4 radar. In the meantime, the decision had been made to continue production of the basic fighter version, but to use the Allison V-1710 instead of the Merlin engines. This aircraft was built as NA-144 and first flown by George Welch on 17 April 1947, with the Air Force designation F-82E.

The government had always wanted to give its Twin Mustang a purely American and stronger engine than the foreign-born V-1650 (built at Packard plants, which were dismantled after the war). Therefore, in August 1945 the USAAF had negotiated with the Allison Division of the General Motors Corporation for a new version of the V-1710. Various models of this engine had equipped the P-38 and P-40, and Allison promptly agreed to buy surplus government V-1710 parts for the new project. Even so, the F-82 program's new V-1710 engines proved costly in the long run—reaching $18.5 million after many amendments. The airplane engine combination was never satisfactory. Meanwhile, on 28 February 1947 an F-82B set a nonstop distance record for fighters, flying the 4968 miles from Honolulu to New York in 14 hours, 31 minutes and 50 seconds, with an average speed of 341.9 miles per hour.

Versatility of the F-82 made it adaptable to a wide variety of roles. Ultimately, it was adapted to be used as a fighter, a long range escort, a long range reconnaissance plane, night fighter, attack bomber, rocket fighter and as an interceptor. Comparison with contemporary jet

Above and opposite: To boldly and graphically demonstrate the tremendous range of the P-82, the USAAF Air Material Command conceived the idea of flying one non-stop from Honolulu to New York in February 1947. The pilot for the mission was Lt Col Bob Thacker, and his co-pilot was Lt Johnny Ard. The airplane was named *Betty Joe* after Thacker's wife. To put the feat into perspective, the distance covered was equivalent to more than *four* roundtrip flights from England to Berlin!

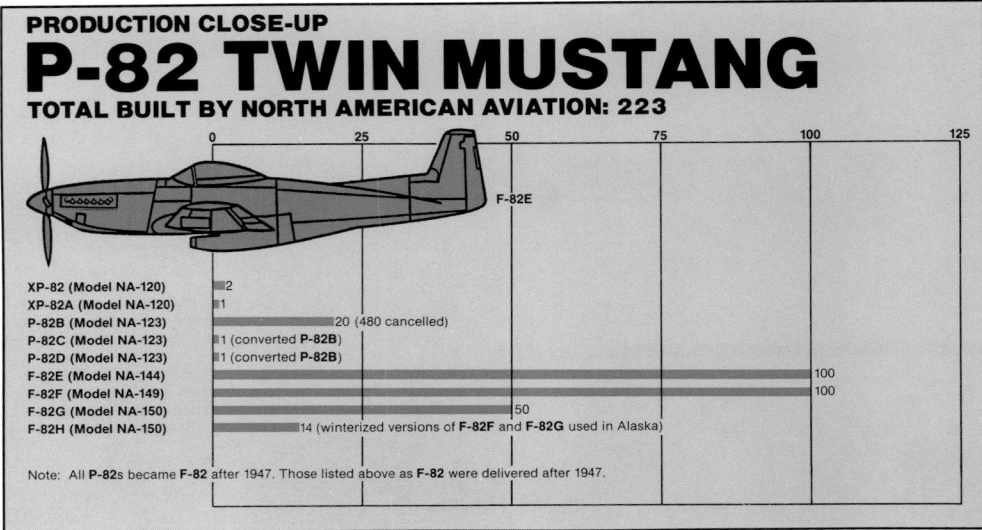

PRODUCTION CLOSE-UP
P-82 TWIN MUSTANG
TOTAL BUILT BY NORTH AMERICAN AVIATION: 223

	0	25	50	75	100	125

F-82E

XP-82 (Model NA-120) — 2
XP-82A (Model NA-120) — 1
P-82B (Model NA-123) — 20 (480 cancelled)
P-82C (Model NA-123) — 1 (converted P-82B)
P-82D (Model NA-123) — 1 (converted P-82B)
F-82E (Model NA-144) — 100
F-82F (Model NA-149) — 100
F-82G (Model NA-150) — 50
F-82H (Model NA-150) — 14 (winterized versions of F-82F and F-82G used in Alaska)

Note: All P-82s became F-82 after 1947. Those listed above as F-82 were delivered after 1947.

fighters shows the F-82 had more than twice the range and took off in a considerably shorter distance.

Having completed the radar testing on the P-82C and P-82D, the Air Force decided to go into production with two night fighter variants of the Twin Mustang. The F-82G (NA-150) was developed around the old SCR-720 radar and was first flown in December 1947, while the F-82F (NA-149) with the more advanced AN/APS-28 radar wasn't test flown until March 1948. Both of these night fighter types were heavier and longer—by two feet—than the F-82E, but all three were powered by Allison V-1710 engines. These Twin Mustangs, along with Northrop P-61s left over from World War II, provided the backbone of the US Air Force night fighter force until the advent of jet propelled all-weather interceptors in the early 1950s.

The final Twin Mustang variant, F-82H, was actually five F-82Gs and nine F-82Fs that were winterized prior to being delivered for all-weather interceptor duty with the US Air Force's Alaskan Air Command.

The Twin Mustang first entered service in 1948 with both the Strategic Air Command (SAC), where it would serve as a long range bomber escort, and with the Air Defense Command (ADC), where it would serve as an all-weather interceptor, supplementing the wartime vintage P-61s still in service. By the end of 1948 overseas assignments included service with the Caribbean Air Command (CAC) in Panama and with the Fifth Air Force of the Far East Air Forces (FEAF) in Japan.

The latter were among the only combat ready American aircraft that were available when the Korean war started on 25 June 1950. Three FEAF F-82s were dispatched immediately, and one of them scored the first aerial victory of the war against a North Korean Yak-11 on 27 June. Eventually, F-82s would be credited with 20 enemy aircraft destroyed, but only four of these were in air-to-air combat. The major reasons were the superiority of most enemy aircraft (jets were deployed by the end of the year) and the lack of spare parts for the Twin Mustangs.

When F-82 production ceased in 1948, no provision had been made for an adequate supply of spare parts, and further, the Air Force did not have many F-82s to begin with. It could ill afford to weaken the F-82 units committed to the Pacific Northwest's defense or to draw from the 14 F-82Hs in Alaska. Hence, although a few of the SAC-surplus F-82Es went to FEAF, all F-82s were withdrawn from combat in February 1952. If the Fifth Air Force had continued to use F-82s over Korea, only 60 days of extra supply support would have been supplied. The last remaining Twin Mustangs were withdrawn from service in June 1953.

Above (both): Two views of the second XP-82 (NA 120) Twin Mustang prototype in 1945. *Below:* The P-82C (NA-123) with its enormous, ungainly and soon to be obsolete SCR720 radar pod is seen here at the time of its rollout in 1946.

POSTWAR BOMBERS

North American Aviation entered the postwar field of first generation jet fighters and produced what was to become the most successful aircraft of that genre—the F-86 Sabre Jet. The company intended to do the same with jet propelled medium bombers. It would also go on to carve a niche for itself in the development of a new class of aircraft, the Navy's 'Heavy Attack,' carrier-based, strategic bombers.

THE B-45 TORNADO

As early as 1944, the USAAF realized that in order to maintain its qualitative superiority in aircraft technology, it would have to develop jet bombers *as well as* jet fighters. In the last year of the war the USAAF began to accept jet bomber designs from all the major airframe builders. These included the Douglas XB-43, the Consolidated XB-46, the Boeing XB-47, the Martin XB-48 and the North American XB-45 Tornado. All were initially designed as conventional, straight-winged aircraft, but only the Boeing proposal was eventually built with straight wings. They were all about the same size as the World War II heavy bombers, but much smaller than the huge Consolidated B-36 that was also in development. The six-engined B-36 was the largest and last propeller driven bomber that the USAAF would order, and it represented the end of an era. The quintet of new jet bombers were, on the other hand, the first of an all-new era.

By the end of 1947 all the new jets had made their first flights. The B-45 Tornado, which made its first flight on 17 March 1947, was the

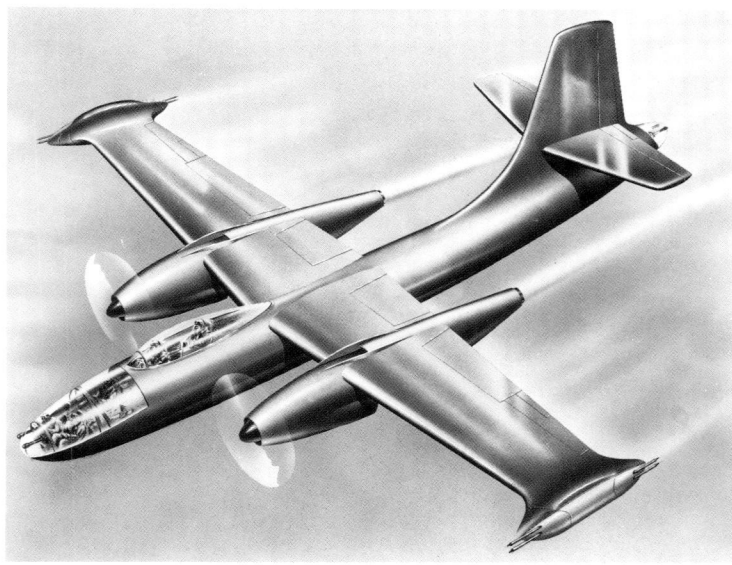

Above: Two early concepts for a twin-engined turbo-prop bomber that emerged at NAA in 1945. The basic layout eventually grew longer wings and tail surfaces, acquired turbojets in place of its turboprops and evolved into the B-45 Tornado.

Below: An early production model B-45A (NA-147) and *(far left)* the first B-45C (NA-153), which in turn evolved into the RB-45C reconnaissance version.

first to go into production. Among the others, only the Boeing B-47 would eventually see service.

The B-45 was a four-jet bomber, with the engines paired into one nacelle on each wing. The flight deck and canopy were configured in a fighter style, with the pilot *ahead* of, rather than *beside*, the copilot. Aside from these features, the B-45 was very similar in overall appearance to NAA's earlier B-28 project.

Three XB-45s (NA-130) were followed by the first of 97 B-45As (NA-147) in February 1948. The B-45B was to have been similar to the B-45A, but with a radar-controlled tail turret. However, the system for operating such a turret did not become available, so the B-45B designation was bypassed and the manned tail turret was used on the B-45A, as well as on the B-45C (NA-153).

Among the B-45A's milestones were the distinctions of being the first four-jet aircraft flown in the United States; the first jet bomber to go into production in the United States; and an unofficial speed record of 675 mph, set on 1 March 1949 by Captain LH Stoker in a B-45A based at Eilson AFB, Alaska. The B-45A's internal bomb bay could accommodate up to 22,000 pounds of conventional, as well as nuclear, bombs. First flown by Joseph Lynch on 3 May 1949, the B-45C was the last and longest ranging of the Tornado subtypes. Most of these aircraft were ordered in the photo reconnaissance configuration as RB-45C. Nicknamed 'flying cartographer' by the company, the RB-45C had wingtip fuel tanks to increase its range and a lengthened nose designed to accommodate five cameras. An additional seven-camera installation was also made in the area which was a bomb bay on conventional B-45s. It was in this reconnaissance role that the Tornado saw service during the Korean War.

In 1952, with the aid of two inflight refuelings, an RB-45C made the first nonstop trans-Pacific flight by a multiengined jet bomber. The ten-hour, 3640-mile flight from Alaska to Japan earned Tornado the 1952 MacKay Trophy for the year's 'most meritorious flight.'

Clockwise from right: A B-45A, undergoing the first RB-45C conversion from B-45C configuration, and the second RB-45C being refueled by a KB-29 over Edwards AFB in 1951 (see page 73). Equipped with five camera stations, the RB-45C saw action in Korea as a reconnaissance bomber.

	B-45A Tornado	B-45C Tornado
First Flight:	1947	1949
Wingspan:	89 ft	89 ft
Length:	75 ft, 4 in	75 ft, 4 in
Height:	25 ft, 2 in	25 ft, 2 in
Engines:	four General Electric J47-GE-7/9 turbojets	four General Electric J47-GE-13/15 turbojets
Engine Thrust (lb):	5200	5820
Gross Weight (lb):	81,418	110,050
Empty Weight (lb):	45,694	48,969
Max Payload (lb):	22,000	22,000
Armament:	two .50 cal machine guns	two .50 cal machine guns
Crew:	4	4
Operating Altitude (ft):	42,800	37,550
Cruising Speed (mph):	470	466
Top Speed (mph):	571	573
Max Range (miles):	1800	2426

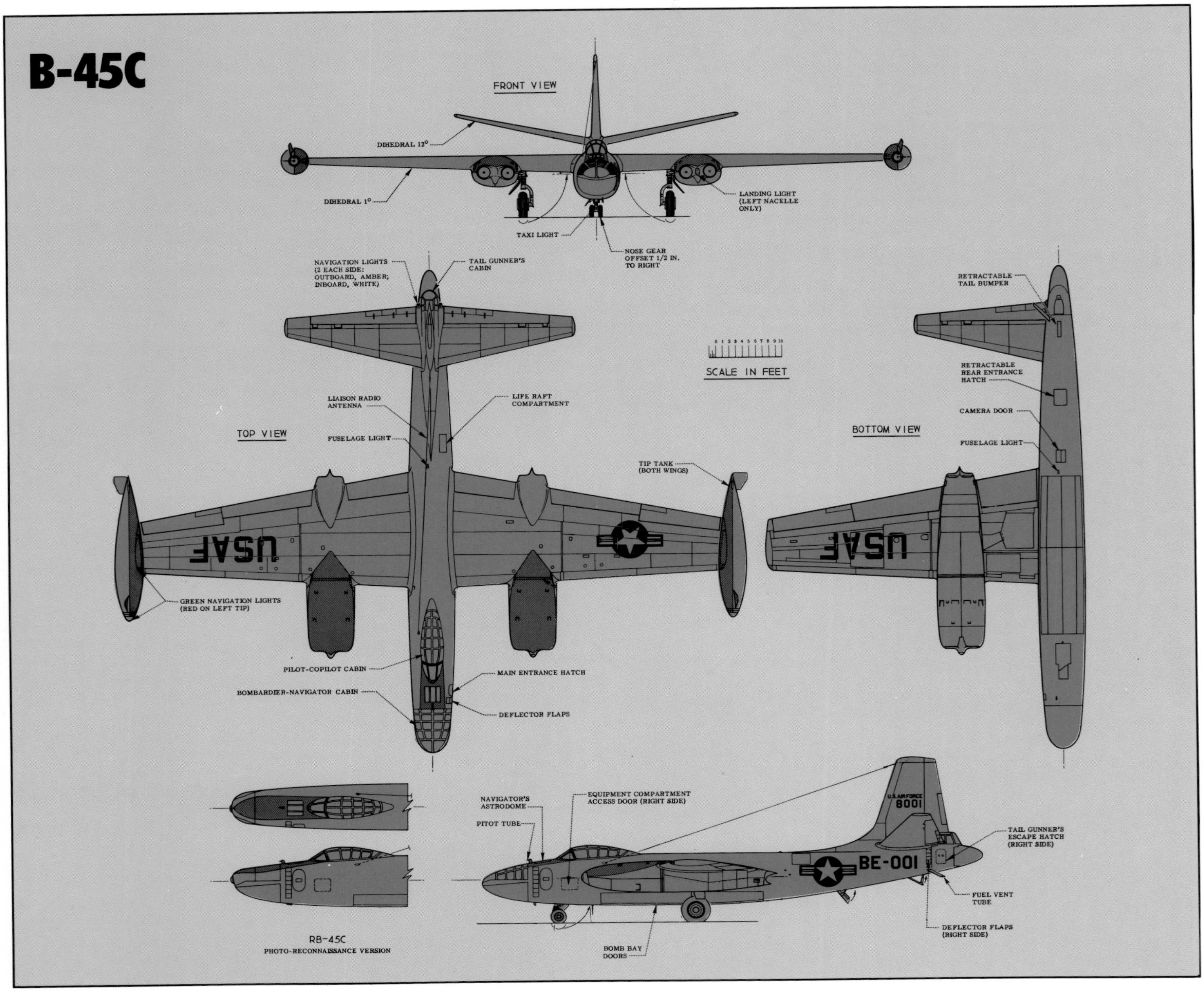

B-45C

FRONT VIEW

DIHEDRAL 12°

DIHEDRAL 1°

LANDING LIGHT (LEFT NACELLE ONLY)

TAXI LIGHT

NOSE GEAR OFFSET 1/2 IN. TO RIGHT

NAVIGATION LIGHTS (2 EACH SIDE; OUTBOARD, AMBER; INBOARD, WHITE)

TAIL GUNNER'S CABIN

RETRACTABLE TAIL BUMPER

RETRACTABLE REAR ENTRANCE HATCH

CAMERA DOOR

LIAISON RADIO ANTENNA

LIFE RAFT COMPARTMENT

TOP VIEW

FUSELAGE LIGHT

SCALE IN FEET

BOTTOM VIEW

FUSELAGE LIGHT

TIP TANK (BOTH WINGS)

USAF

USAF

GREEN NAVIGATION LIGHTS (RED ON LEFT TIP)

PILOT-COPILOT CABIN

MAIN ENTRANCE HATCH

BOMBARDIER-NAVIGATOR CABIN

DEFLECTOR FLAPS

RB-45C
PHOTO-RECONNAISSANCE VERSION

NAVIGATOR'S ASTRODOME

EQUIPMENT COMPARTMENT ACCESS DOOR (RIGHT SIDE)

PITOT TUBE

U.S. AIR FORCE 8001

TAIL GUNNER'S ESCAPE HATCH (RIGHT SIDE)

BE-001

FUEL VENT TUBE

BOMB BAY DOORS

DEFLECTOR FLAPS (RIGHT SIDE)

Above: Using rocket assisted take-off (RATO) packs to augment its own engines, an RB-45C makes a fast airborne leap from the Edwards AFB runway. *Below:* The KB-29 boom operator's view of the second RB-45C during aerial refueling operations at Edwards AFB during June 1951. This moment was recorded in color from another aircraft (see page 71). At that same moment RB-45Cs were at work in Korea.

THE AJ SAVAGE

I n the years immediately following World War II, a conflict evolved which pitted the US Navy against the US Air Force (USAAF before 1947) over the issue of which service could best fulfill America's long range requirements for strategic defense. This was a traditional role that the Navy had held for nearly two centuries. However, with the advent of intercontinental bombers and nuclear weapons, the Air Force now had come to be perceived as the nation's first line of defense.

The Navy had a large fleet of aircraft carriers—including the new 50,000+ ton *Midway* class—but its carrier-based attack bombers were much smaller than the Air Force's land-based bombers. The solution was seen to be the development of an all new class of 'Heavy Attack' aircraft that would be comprised of powerful new bombers as big as USAAF medium bombers.

The first of the new class would be the North American Aviation AJ Savage, a big twin-engined second cousin to the XB-28 and B-45. It was a fast, yet hulking, bird, with folding wingtips to accommodate storage aboard an aircraft carrier's hangar deck. The Savage had a six-ton bomb load, triple that of the B-25 or XB-28.

The initial order for the Savage came in June 1946, with a production series ordered one year later. The XAJ-1 Savage prototype (NA-146) made its first flight on 3 July 1948 with Robert Chilton at the controls. Production of the AJ-1 (NA-156) took place at a leased factory in Columbus, Ohio that had been used during the war to build Curtiss Helldivers.

Above: An early production AJ-1 (NA-156) in flight over the Buckeye State near Columbus. *Below:* An AJ-1 aboard the carrier USS *Coral Sea.*

Above: An AJ-2P reconnaissance aircraft (NA-175) with its distinctive nose.
Below: One of the two XA2J-1 (NA-163) prototypes.

In the meantime, North American proposed a turboprop powered version, which was given the model number NA-163 and ordered by the Navy under the designation XA2J-1. With its Allison T40-A-6 engines driving two massive contra-rotating props, the XA2J-1 made its first flight on 4 January 1952, piloted by Robert Baker and Bud Poage. Ultimately, development problems—with emerging turboprop engine technology in general and with the T40-A-6 in particular—led to the cancellation of the entire XA2J-1 program.

The AJ Savage continued to evolve, however, and the first AJ-2 (NA-184) flew on 18 February 1952. A reconnaissance version was ordered by the Navy under the designation AJ-2P, and first flew on 30 March.

The Savage entered service in September 1949, and carrier operations began in April 1950 aboard the USS *Coral Sea.* During the early 1950s, following the cancellation of the 70,000 ton supercarrier USS *United States* in 1949, the US Navy was forced to be content with smaller carriers than it would have liked. This meant that the Savage was actually *too large* at full squadron strength to operate full-time from carriers as had been originally planned. Thus, the AJ-1 and AJ-2 fleet was to be organized into eight *shore-based* heavy attack squadrons. (The AJ-2Ps went into a pair of photographic squadrons). These shore-based squadrons were then organized into rotating detachments doing temporary duty aboard carriers throughout the world until the early 1960s. By the time that 60,000 ton carriers did enter the fleet in the 1960s, the Savage had been superceded by the jet propelled Douglas A3D Skywarrior.

	AJ-1 Savage	AJ-2 Savage
First Flight:	1949	1953
Wingspan:	71 ft, 5 in	71 ft, 5 in
Length:	63 ft, 1 in	63 ft, 1 in
Height:	21 ft, 5 in	21 ft, 5 in
Engines:	two Pratt & Whitney R-2800-44W Wasps one Allison J33-A-10 turbojet	two Pratt & Whitney R2800-44W Wasps one Allison J33-A-10 turbojet
Engine hp:	2300	2300
Engine Thrust (lb):	4600	4600
Gross Weight (lb):	50,963	50,580
Empty Weight (lb):	30,776	30,776
Max Payload (lb):	12,000	12,000
Crew:	3	3
Operating Altitude (ft):	40,800	41,500
Cruising Speed (mph):	270	260
Top Speed (mph):	449	449
Max Range (miles):	2993	3056

	A3J-1 Vigilante	RA-5C Vigilante
First Flight:	1958	1962
Wingspan:	53 ft	53 ft
Length:	76 ft, 6 in	76 ft, 6 in
Height:	19 ft, 5 in	19 ft, 5 in
Engines:	two General Electric J79-GE-8 turbojets	two General Electric J79-GE-8 turbojets
Engine Thrust (lb):	17,000	17,000
Gross Weight (lb):	56,293	65,589
Empty Weight (lb):	32,714	37,498
Max Payload (lb):	5000	—
Crew:	2	2
Operating Altitude (ft):	43,800	48,400
Cruising Speed (mph):	560	567
Top Speed (mph):	1320	1290
Max Range (miles):	2590	1888

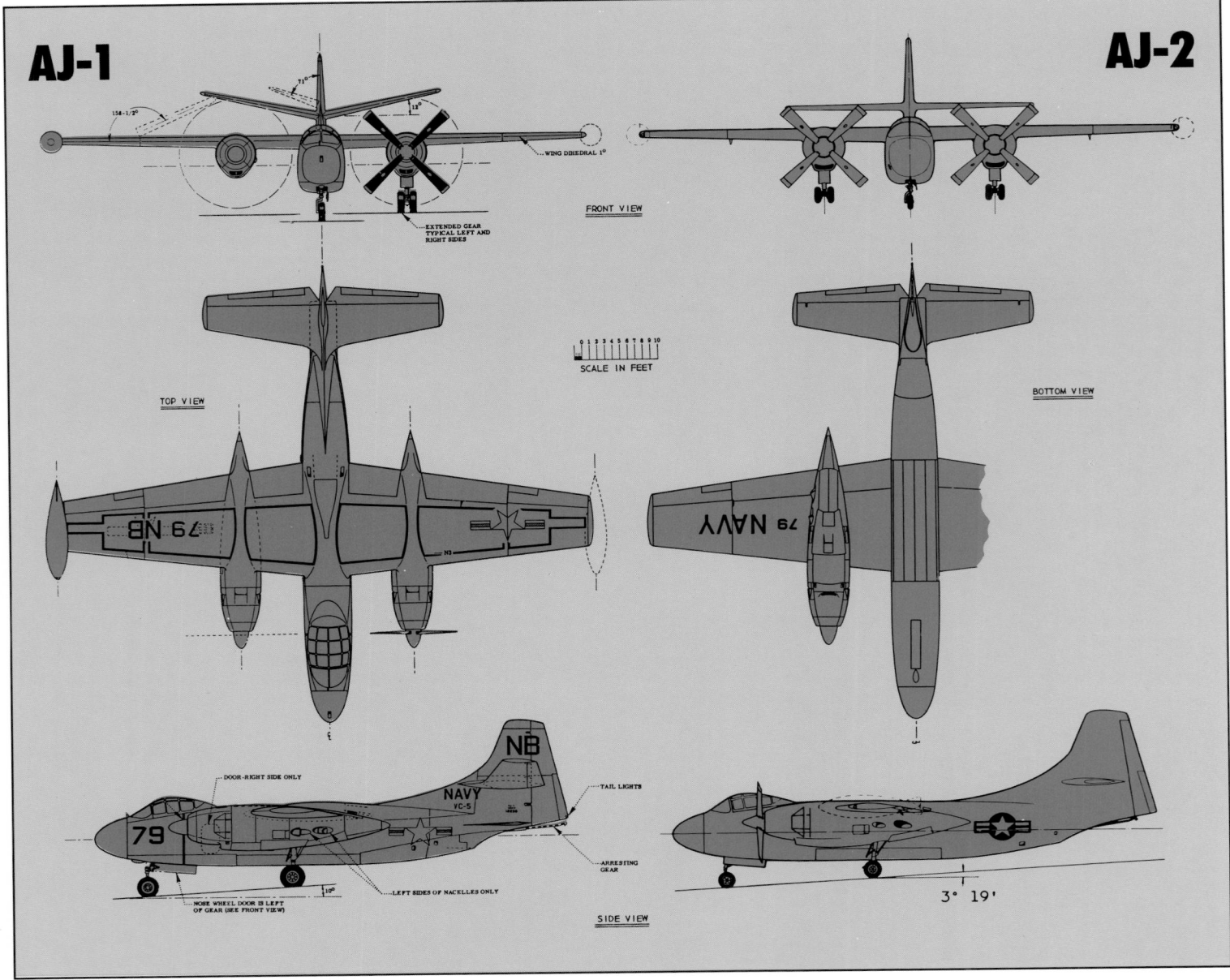

PRODUCTION CLOSE-UP
NAA/ROCKWELL POSTWAR BOMBERS

0   25   50   75   100   150

B-45C

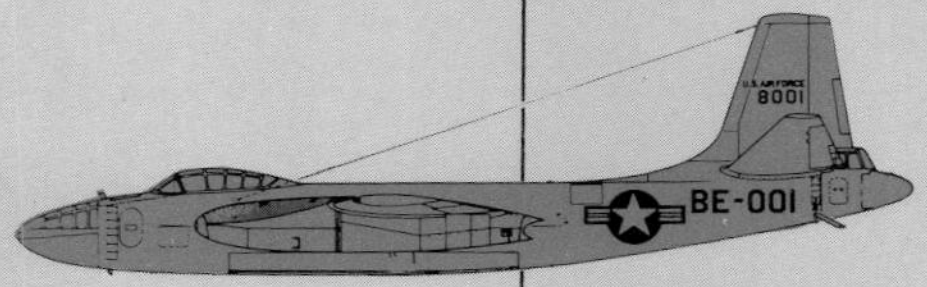

B-45 TORNADO
TOTAL BUILT BY NORTH AMERICAN AVIATION: 143

XB-45 (Model NA-130)   3
B-45A (Model NA-147)   97
B-45C (Model NA-153)   43 (including 33 **RB-45C**s)

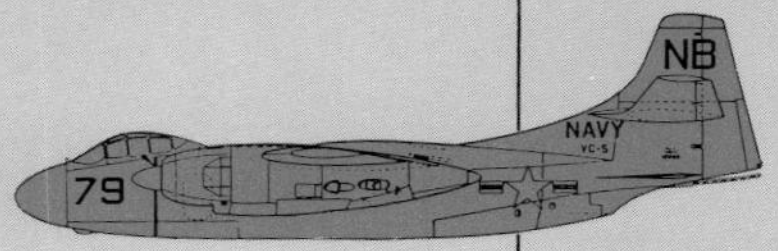

AJ-1

AJ SAVAGE
TOTAL BUILT BY NORTH AMERICAN AVIATION: 145

XAJ-1 (Model NA-146)   3
AJ-1 (Model NA-156)   40 (2 were cancelled)
XA2J-1 (Model NA-163)   2
AJ-2P (Model NA-175)   30
AJ-2 (Model NA-184)   70

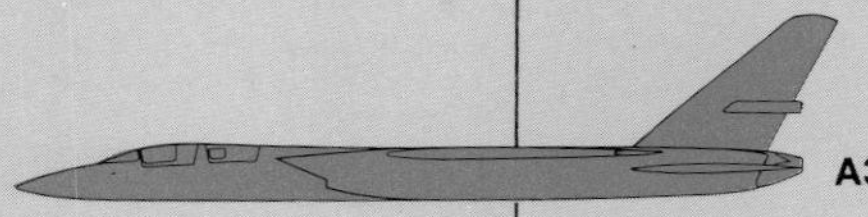

A3J-1

A3J VIGILANTE
TOTAL BUILT BY NORTH AMERICAN AVIATION: 179

A3J-1 (Model NA-247)   59
A3J-2 (Model NA-296)   120

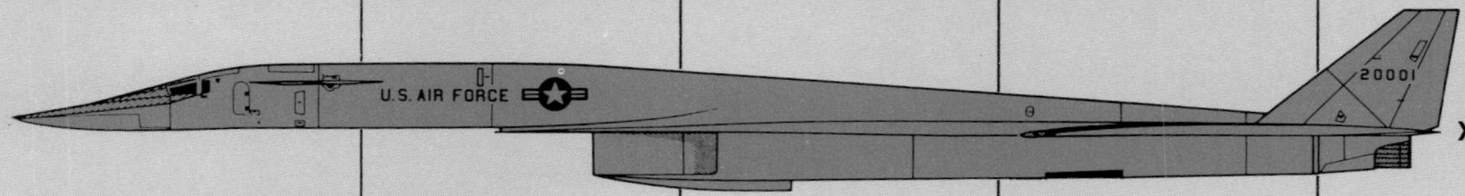

XB-70

XB-70 VALKYRIE

XB-70 (Model NA-278)   2

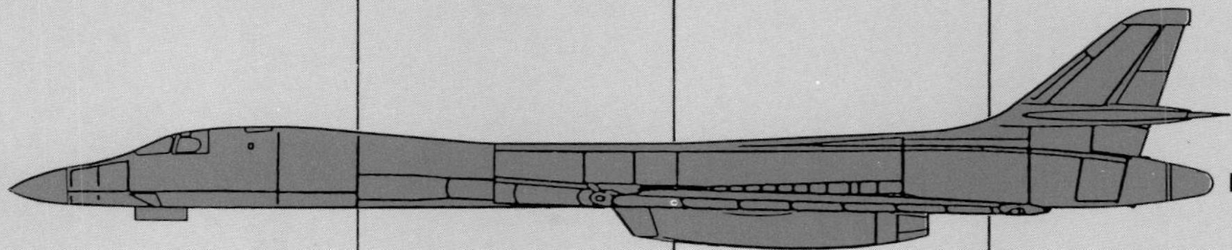

B-1B

B-1
TOTAL BUILT BY ROCKWELL INTERNATIONAL: 104

B-1A   4 (250 cancelled)
B-1B   100

Note: In 1962, all **AJ** series aircraft became **A-2** and all **A3J** series aircraft became **A-5**.

THE A3D VIGILANTE

In July 1955 North American leapfrogged forward to begin development of its NA-233, a new airplane that was to the Douglas A3D what the A3D was to NAA's own AJ—and more. The NA-233 was designed as a Mach 2 strategic bomber that would be capable of operating with heavy attack squadrons aboard the supercarriers that the Navy was scheduled to begin operating in the early 1960s.

The Navy placed its initial order for the new aircraft in August 1956, and the first prototype was flown on 31 August 1958 under the designation A3J-1. Given the name Vigilante, the A3J-1 was ordered into production in January 1959, and entered squadron service in June 1961. Full deployment of the Vigilante came in August 1962 with the inaugural cruise of the Navy's first nuclear aircraft carrier, the 76,000 ton USS *Enterprise*. By this time, the Defense Department nomenclature system had been reorganized and the A3Js were all redesignated as A-5s.

The A-5 series now included the original A-5A (formerly A3J-1) and the A-5B (formerly A3J-2), which was introduced in April 1962. The latter differed from the original Vigilante in that it could carry half again more fuel, thus providing an increase in range capability.

The deployment of the Vigilante aboard the *Enterprise* in 1962 finally gave the US Navy the strategic bombing capability that it had desired since before the end of World War II. The A-5 could carry a 3020 pound Mark 27 or 1885 pound Mark 28 nuclear payload at twice the speed of sound. Ironically, the days of the Navy's strategic bombers were already numbered, and the capability so long sought after would last only two years.

The early 1960s were marked by profound changes within the Defense Department, as Defense Secretary Robert McNamara promulgated the notion that unmanned intercontinental ballistic missiles should become the primary—if not the *only*—weapon in the American

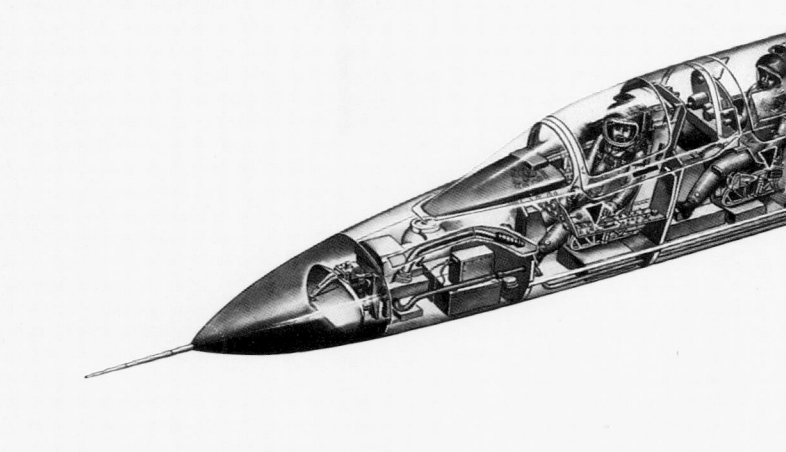

Lower left: Heavy Attack Squadron 7 aboard the USS *Enterprise* received the first operational Vigilantes in 1962. *Above left:* The Vigilante production line. *Above:* A detailed cutaway of the A3J-1. The crew wore pressure suits befitting their roles in this Mach 2 strategic bomber. The space behind the cockpit carried the analog avionics that made the mission possible. Note also the aerial refueling probe folded into the fuselage immediately forward of the pilot's left leg. *Below:* An RA-5C in the paint scheme worn by these aircraft during operations over North Vietnam circa 1972.

strategic nuclear arsenal. Such missiles had been under development for some time in the belief that they would *complement*, rather than *replace*, manned bombers. McNamara saw things differently. For the Air Force, this meant the expansion of the ICBM fleet, but the cancellation of the B-70 bomber and the retirement of the B-58 fleet. For the Navy, it meant the evolution of a new class of nuclear submarine armed with Polaris submarine-launched ballistic missiles (SLBM), but at the same time, the carrier-based, heavy attack squadron would become a thing of the past.

In 1964 the Vigilantes were reconfigured as reconnaissance aircraft under the designation RA-5C. Heavy attack squadrons (VAH) were also redesignated as reconnaissance squadrons (RVAH). The modification to RA-5C standard included the addition of reconnaissance gear, internally mounted in what had formerly been the Vigilante's bomb bay. The changes also included another fuel tank aerodynamically molded into the top of the fuselage and wing reinforcements which permitted the mounting of external underwing pylons, in addition to the two that were already part of the A-5B's configuration. This not only enabled the RA-5C to carry a total of four external fuel tanks to increase its range on reconnaissance missions, but it also allowed the aircraft to retain its *attack* capability through the use of externally mounted bombs and rockets.

The RA-5C conversion came on the eve of the Vietnam War, and the Vigilante squadrons eventually served throughout the war, sustaining 18 combat losses. Finally retired in 1979, the Vigilante remained as the only Mach 2 bomber ever to have served aboard a Navy carrier.

THE SABRE JET AND FURY

In a forlorn stretch of sky above the muddy Yalu River that separates Korea and Manchuria, history was written in streaming contrails by a handful of men and machines. The men were the jet pilots of the US Air Force, competently trained and skilled in handling weapons of war. The machines were F-86 Sabre Jets which, under the control of these men, registered a fantastic record of downing 14 Russian-built MiG-15s for every Sabre Jet lost. The place would come to be called MiG Alley.

What happened over MiG Alley between December 1950 and July 1953 confirmed a place in history for North American Aviation's Sabre Jet, a place which it had already earned in 1948 by becoming the first conventional aircraft to break the sound barrier. The Sabre Jet was possibly the most effective jet fighter in history and one of the true masterpieces from the house of Kindelberger.

EARLY EVOLUTION

Having ended the Second World War with its P-51 Mustang acclaimed as probably the best piston-engined fighter of the conflict, North American Aviation was ready to do the same in the dawning jet age. The first North American design study for a high performance jet fighter was RD-1265, which had been undertaken on 22 November 1944 with the USAAF in mind. The result was North American's fat little straight-winged NA-134. The first customer for the NA-134 was not the USAAF, however, but the US Navy, which ordered three of them on 1 January 1945 under the designation XFJ-1 (Experimental Fighter, North American, first).

The Navy's decision had actually been prompted by their successful carrier trials of the P-51 earlier in the year. The Navy had never bought a NAA fighter before, but they were now keen to have what was seen as a plane that could combine the best characteristics of the Mustang with jet propulsion.

The USAAF ordered three of a longer, trimmer variant, the NA-140, on 18 May under the experimental pursuit designation XP-86. The Navy, meanwhile, had ordered modifications in the NA-134 design and it had evolved into a NA-141 that was, in fact, still closer to the NA-134 than to the USAAF NA-140. On 28 May 1945, the Navy ordered 100 (later reduced to 30) NA-140s under the production designation FJ-1.

An XP-86 mock-up was delivered to the Air Force on 20 June 1945, but even then North American engineers were thinking that the standard straight wing configuration might be obsolete. Theoretical studies on swept wings in Germany dating back to 1940 had postulated that

swept wings could greatly enhance an aircraft's performance as it approached the speed of sound. Since those speeds were still considered impossible, the idea of swept wings attracted little attention outside Germany. Within the Reich, however, a number of swept wing designs evolved hand-in-hand with the advent of jet engines. The Messerschmitt Me-262, the most widely used jet fighter of the war, was designed with slightly swept wings (15 degrees), and this characteristic had added greatly to its performance.

As the war in Europe ended in May, North American's Chief Engineer, Ray Rice, and P-86 Project Aerodynamicist Larry Green got their hands on Messerschmitt's impressive Me-262 transonic wind tunnel data, as well as a captured Me-262, and decided to change the P-86 into a swept wing fighter. This modification, approved by General Bill Craigie of the USAAF Air Research & Development Command on 1 November 1945, proved to be the most important moment in the history of the project, as it transformed the P-86 from just another jet plane into what would become the world's first truly great jet fighter. The difference can be proven by comparing the P-86 (F-86 after 1948) to the Navy's early FJ-series fighters that grew from the same roots, but retained the straight wings.

The XFJ-1 was first flown by Bill Lien on 11 September 1946, and underwent aircraft carrier trials aboard the USS *Boxer* in March 1948. The first XP-86 was delivered to the USAAF on 10 September 1947, eight days before it became the independent US Air Force. The first flight of this prototype came on the first of October, with NAA chief engineering test pilot George Welch in the cockpit.

On 26 April 1948 the XP-86 prototype broke the sound barrier for the first time, although there is some evidence to support the unconfirmed rumors that Welch actually exceeded Mach 1 in the XP-86 prior to Chuck Yeager's official first-ever supersonic flight of 14 October 1947. In any case, by the end of 1947 the XP-86 had more supersonic flight time than the X-1 had! Though it was technically a supersonic fighter, the Air Force later decided to officially restrict the aircraft to Mach .95 (668 mph) at altitudes below 25,000 feet.

The Air Force initially ordered 33 P-86s and 190 P-86Bs with provisions for larger tires, but the latter were canceled in December 1947 and replaced with an increased P-86A order when improved tires were substituted. The first P-86A (North American Model NA-151) made its initial flight on 20 May 1948, and nine days later an additional block of 333 P-86As (North American Model NA-161) were added to the previous order.

The Sabre's designation was officially changed from P-86 to F-86 on

Below: The straight-winged XFJ-1 prototype shortly after its rollout in 1946. *Above:* George Welch at the controls of the first XP-86 over the Mojave Desert during the hot summer of 1947. Soon, the 'P for pursuit' designation would be replaced by 'F for fighter.'

1 June 1948, and by March 1949 the first Air Force F-86A unit—the 94th 'Hat in the Ring' Fighter Squadron at March AFB—was operational. It was this same squadron that was the first to use the appellation 'Sabre Jet' for their F-86s. The name was quickly and universally adopted.

Armament of the F-86 consisted of six .50 caliber machine guns mounted in the nose, but High Velocity Aerial Rockets (HVAR) could also be carried. In September 1948 an F-86A set a world speed record of 671 mph.

With the basic F-86A proving to be such an outstanding fighter, the Air Force proceeded with plans to adapt it for other roles. The first of these was the NA-157, a long-range escort fighter version ordered under the designation F-93 (originally F-86C), and the NA-164 interceptor version, ordered under the designation F-95. Picking up where other jet fighters left off, the YF-93A was also designed to penetrate deeply into enemy territory on high-speed missions. First flown on 24 January 1950, the YF-93A had a solid nose and fuselage-side intakes, but in other respects it resembled the F-86A, upon which it was based. Company test pilot George Welch, an ace wartime pilot with 18 Japanese planes to his credit, was the first to fly the YF-93A. 'A pilot could have been a one-man air force with the YF-93A in the Southwest Pacific air battle,' Welch said after his first flight. A total of 120 F-93s were ordered, but only two flight test aircraft were built due to cuts in the Air Force's long-range fighter program budget. These aircraft were later assigned to the National Advisory Committee on Aeronautics (NACA) Ames Test Center near San Francisco.

With interceptors, however, funding was somewhat easier to come by—especially after the Soviet Union detonated its first nuclear weapon in October 1949. On 7 October, the Air Force ordered two prototype NA-164s and 122 production NA-165s, whose military designation was now changed from YF-95A to YF-86D because there would be less red tape involved in ordering the planes as F-86 developments (which they *really were*) than as 'new type' F-95s. America's first single-seat all-weather interceptor, the radome-nosed F-86D made its initial flight on 22 December 1949.

The basic F-86 Sabre Jet configuration *(top)* compared to the radome-nosed F-86D Sabre Dog *(above)*. Below: The prototype YF-86D (originally YF-95) at Edwards AFB along with the prototype YF-93 (originally YF-86C) early in 1950. The YF-93 (also pictured *at right*) was intended as a long-range escort fighter but the program was cancelled after the first two prototypes were built.

THE SABRE JET AT WAR

When the Korean War began on 25 June 1950, the Mustangs and straight-winged Lockheed F-80 jet fighters that the US Air Force initially deployed were more than adequate to handle the rag-tag inventory of aging aircraft in the inventory of the North Korean air force. On 1 November, however, the situation changed dramatically when Russian-built swept wing MiG-15 jet fighters appeared. An F-80C downed a MiG in history's first all-jet air combat on 8 November, but generally the MiG-15s outclassed anything that the US Air Force had in Korea. For this reason it was fortunate that on that same day the Sabre-equipped Fourth Fighter Interceptor Squadron had been ordered to Korea. The Fourth was picked because it had a large number of pilots with a great deal of air-to-air combat experience in World War II.

In the five weeks that it took the F-86s to be shipped to Korea, the Chinese Communists began a major land offensive, while their MiG-15s seized the air superiority over the battlefield from the Americans.

The Sabres arrived at Kimpo AB near Seoul, South Korea on 13 December and met the enemy for the first time four days later. On that graying December day during the second combat sweep by the Fourth Fighter Group pilots, Lieutenant Colonel Bruce Hinton initiated a pattern which was to last for 32 months. The sharp-shooting wing commander blasted a MiG-15 out of the sky. Two days later the Fourth Fighter Group Sabre pilots downed four more MiGs.

Except for February 1951, when their bases were temporarily overrun by North Korean and Chinese forces, the Sabres flew almost daily combat air patrols from bases at Kimpo, Suwon and Osan in the general vicinity of Seoul. In these patrols, the basic units were four-plane cells flying in 'fingertip' formation—a forward-pointing 'V' with a point man, two planes to the right and one to the left. The Sabres patrolled a 70 mile long area known as 'MiG Alley' that reached northwest from the North Korean capital of Pyongyang to the Yalu

Above and right: Air Force Sabre Jets of the 51st Fighter Interceptor Wing in their characteristic four-plane formations approach MiG Alley. When the F-86F *(left)* reached US Air Force units in Korea in June 1952, it represented a major upgrade from the F-86A types that had just arrived in 1950. Mighty Mouse rockets *(top right)* were a part of the Sabre Jet's armament.

pretty good rate, considering that the average number of Sabres was 184 at any given time. The Fifth Air Force Sabres flew 236 sorties in December 1950; averaged 1024 per month for 1951 (including February, when only *one* was flown due to the bases being overrun); 3279 for 1952; and 5045 per month for the first seven months of 1953.

The last three months of the war — May through July 1953 — saw the three highest numbers of sorties: 6721, 7696 and 5841 respectively. June 1953 also saw 77 MiGs shot down, the highest score of any month of the war. The second place had been September 1952, when 63 MiGs were downed.

In total, the Sabres shot down 792 MiG-15s (96 percent of the MiGs downed by American aircraft) and 18 aircraft of other types. There were 78 Sabres shot down in aerial combat with the MiGs, giving the F-86 a clear ten-to-one superiority over the Soviet-built fighters. In addition to their 810 confirmed kills, the F-86s scored 118 probables and damaged another 814 enemy aircraft.

There were 39 US Air Force pilots who shot down five or more MiGs to become jet aces. Five of these men shot down more than ten: Captain Joseph McConnell (16), Major James Jabara (15), Captain Manuel Fernandez (14 plus a shared victory), Major George Davis (14) and Colonel Royal Baker (13). Of these men only Davis had been an ace during World War II. Jabara, who had scored three and one-half victories in World War II, shot down his fifth MiG on 20 May 1952 to become the first American jet ace.

Major George Davis, an ace in World War II who destroyed seven Japanese aircraft, shot down four MiGs in one day. Captain Dolphin Overton blasted five MiGs in four days to become a jet ace in the shortest time ever. One of the top aces in World War II, with 31 German kills, Colonel Francis S Gabreski downed six and one-half MiGs. (The 'half' was a victory shared with another pilot.) Major William Whisner was an ace in both wars, as were Lieutenant Colonel Vermont Garrison, Major James Hagerstrom, Colonel Harrison Thyng, and the only non-Air Force Sabre Jet ace, Major John Bolt of the US Marine Corps.

River and the Chinese border. For political reasons known only to the Truman Administration, the US Air Force was, at no time during the Korean War, permitted to cross the Yalu River in pursuit of enemy aircraft. Nor were they permitted to bomb the bridges that spanned the Yalu River or the huge MiG base at Antung that was within sight of the Yalu River.

During those 32 months in MiG Alley the F-86 Sabres of the USAF Fifth Air Force flew 87,177 sorties, or individual per-plane missions. This amounted to roughly 22 four-plane patrols per day. This was a

THE LATER SABRE JETS

While the F-86A was clearly superior in most respects to the MiG-15, an improved version was already on the way. The NA-170 was developed in late 1949 at North American by Fred Prill and Ed Kindelberger (nephew of Dutch Kindelberger), and 11 were ordered by the Air Force in January 1950 under the designation F-86E. Outwardly it was more like the F-86A than any other variant of the Sabre. While there were numerous internal improvements, particularly in the control system, the major change introduced was that the F-86E's horizontal stabilizer and elevators moved as a single unit.

The F-86E was endowed with what North American called 'super controls,' which harnessed the power and speed of the new jet and gave it 'a great advantage in maneuverability and control.' According to George Welch, who flew the F-86E on its first flight over Edwards AFB, the added controls 'give the pilot a better grip on the lion he's holding by the tail' when the Sabre's power is unsheathed.

Revolutionary features of the new controls included the 'all-flying tail,' 'artificial feel' and 'irreversible control' systems. The entire horizontal tail surfaces of the F-86E were controllable, giving the airplane better longitudinal control and eliminating the loss of effectiveness of the surfaces due to heavy air loads at extremely high speeds. The 'all-flying tail' consisted of the horizontal stabilizers and elevators which were linked for coordinated movement. (In conventional designs only the elevators are movable by the pilot, with the horizontal stabilizers remaining in a fixed position.)

No longer using conventional power 'boost' to help the pilot move ailerons and horizontal tail surfaces, the F-86E controls were powered completely by an independent source to give more positive control. Conventional boost systems usually supply a greater part of the force

required to move these controls, with the pilot supplying the balance. The pilot's share of power gives him a 'feel' of the controls. With none of the actual air loads or forces acting on the F-86E pilot's stick, a spring-loaded 'artificial feel' system had to be designed to give the pilot a representative sense of the control forces. The 'flying tail' and ailerons of the F-86E were held at given settings—as positioned by the pilot—through an 'irreversible control' system. Conventional controls have a tendency to neutralize—to change position as air loads bear upon them during flight. With the F-86E's controls powered independently—without the aid of conventional boost—the neutralizing effect was eliminated.

The first F-86E was flown on 23 September 1950, and by July 1951 they had begun to arrive in Korea to replace and augment F-86As then in service.

In the meantime, North American had already begun work on the NA-172, a further evolution of the F-86A and F-86E, which entered service with the Air Force as F-86F. The major difference this time was the addition of the General Electric J47-GE-27 engine, which offered a 12 percent improvement in thrust over the J47-GE-13 engine used in the F-86A and F-86E. In addition to the NA-172 models produced by North American at Inglewood, California, the F-86F production run included the virtually identical NA-176, which was built at a former Curtiss plant acquired by North American in Columbus, Ohio. A further F-86F subvariant was a fighter-bomber modification that bore the model numbers NA-191 (when built at Inglewood) and NA-193 (when built at Columbus).

Built to hunt enemy aircraft in the thin air above 40,000 feet or dump bombs from tree-top level on ground targets, the F-86F had a more powerful engine and better radar gunsight than the earlier A and E models. In addition, it had an improved wing and other mechanical

Above: Sabre Jet production at North American's Los Angeles factory in August 1952. *Below:* The first prototype F-86H on Rogers Dry Lake at Edwards AFB in 1953.

refinements. Improvements to the gunsight system increased the accuracy of the Sabre's six .50 caliber machine guns and made the sight easier to maintain in the field, thus redressing an important shortcoming of the earlier Sabres. A new addition to the gunsight, called Manual Pip Control, aided pilots on dive-bombing missions. Like the F-86E, this Sabre had an 'all-flying tail,' with horizontal stabilizer and eleva-tor linked for coordinated movement and better control at high speed. Artificial feel and an irreversible control system were also retained in the F-86F.

The F-86F was first flown on 28 March 1952. It was accepted by the Air Force two days later, and shortly afterward the first shipment was rushed to Korea. The F-86F went into service with US Air Force units in both the United States and Korea in June 1952.

In the midst of production it was discovered that if an extended leading edge replaced the slatted leading edge of the wing the F-86F could make much tighter turns at high altitudes, eliminating one of the advantages that the MiG-15 had over Sabres. This change was made on the F-86Fs that were still at the factory and kits were sent to Korea in sufficient numbers to completely retrofit all the F-86Fs in the field.

Another F-86F field modification came in March 1953, when the six .50 caliber machine guns on eight aircraft were replaced with two to four 20mm cannons. The belt-fed cannons worked well in combat and eventually became generally standard on the subsequent F-86H series, the Navy's FJ Furys and North American's later F-100 Super Sabre fighter.

The idea behind the F-86H, which was first conceived as the NA-187 in March 1951, was to build a Sabre solely dedicated to the fighter-bomber role. The first Inglewood F-86H was first flown on 30 May 1953 by Jim Lynch and the first Columbus-built F-86H flew in September. They were equipped with the Low Altitude Bombing System (LABS) computer and four M-39 20mm guns. These cannons had been developed jointly by the Air Force and the Ford Motor Company. Operating on a completely new principle for aircraft machine guns, the M-39 featured a revolving-drum feed like the famed 'six-shooters' of the old West, and a rate of fire higher than the most advanced .50 caliber machine guns then in use. The F-86H was capable of delivering both conventional and nuclear weapons.

Other special features of the F-86H included hydraulically-operated controls, electrically-operated flaps, a geared elevator, modified wings with a stationary extended leading edge, and a self-sufficient starter system. It also had a clam shell- type cockpit canopy, a companion feature to the improved ejection seat mechanism.

The F-86H went into full production late in 1952. The first two models were produced at NAA's Los Angeles plant, with subsequent production at the company's Columbus plant between September 1953 and 16 March 1956. Perfected after the signing of the Korean Armistice, the F-86H represented a practical application of the fighting, bombing, ground support and aerial reconnaissance knowledge gained through thousands of missions in Korea by its predecessors, versatile F-86As, Es and Fs.

88

F-86F

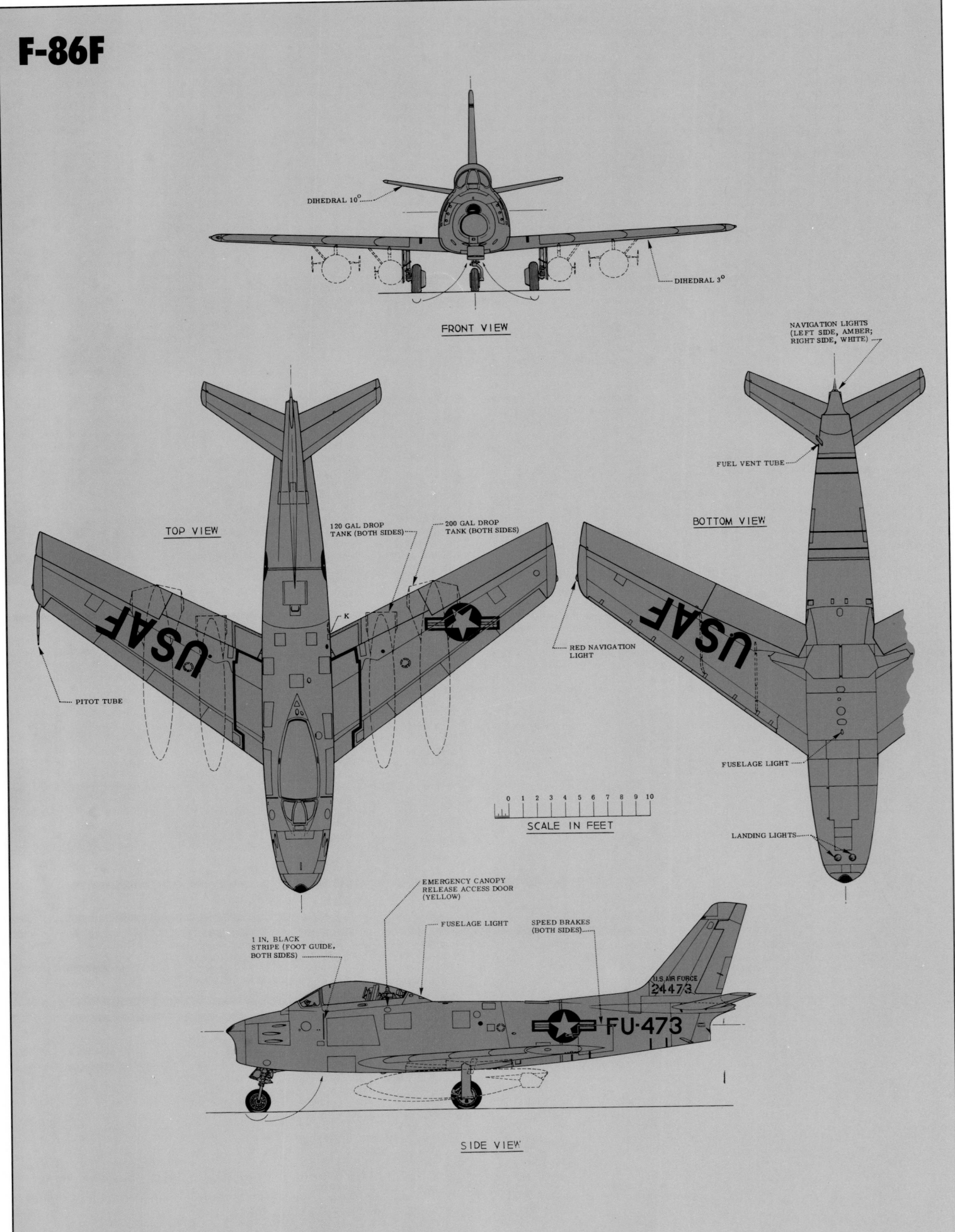

DIHEDRAL 10°

DIHEDRAL 3°

FRONT VIEW

NAVIGATION LIGHTS
(LEFT SIDE, AMBER;
RIGHT SIDE, WHITE)

FUEL VENT TUBE

TOP VIEW

120 GAL DROP
TANK (BOTH SIDES)

200 GAL DROP
TANK (BOTH SIDES)

BOTTOM VIEW

K

USAF

USAF

PITOT TUBE

RED NAVIGATION
LIGHT

FUSELAGE LIGHT

0 1 2 3 4 5 6 7 8 9 10

SCALE IN FEET

LANDING LIGHTS

EMERGENCY CANOPY
RELEASE ACCESS DOOR
(YELLOW)

FUSELAGE LIGHT

SPEED BRAKES
(BOTH SIDES)

1 IN. BLACK
STRIPE (FOOT GUIDE,
BOTH SIDES)

U.S AIR FORCE
24473

FU-473

SIDE VIEW

PRODUCTION CLOSE-UP
F-86 SABRE JET/FJ FURY
TOTAL BUILT BY NORTH AMERICAN AVIATION: 7805

	0	200	400	600	//	2000	3000

XFJ-1 (Model NA-134) — 3
XF-86 (Model NA-140) — 3

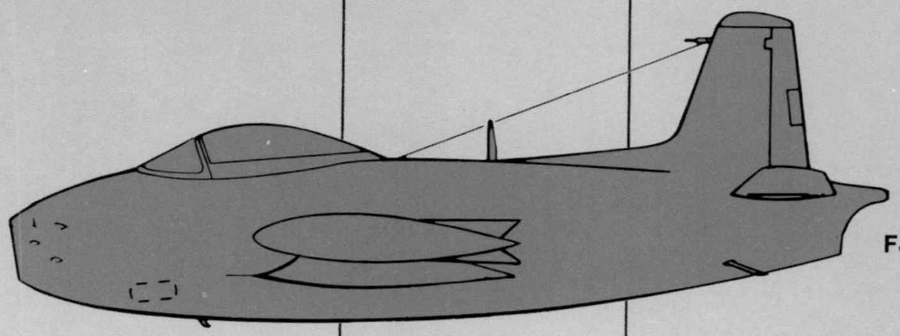

FJ-1

FJ-1 (Model NA-141) — 30 (70 were cancelled)

F-86A

F-86A (Model NA-151) — 554
F-86B (Model NA-152) — 0 (188 on order were completed as F-86A)
F-86C (Model NA-157) — 2 (completed as YF-93; 118 were cancelled)
YF-86D* (Model NA-164) — 2

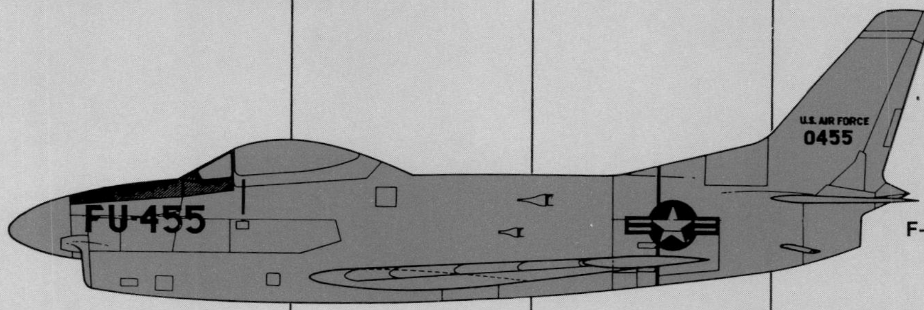

F-86D

F-86D (Model NA-165) — 2504 (including 981 later upgraded to F-86L standard)
F-86J (Model NA-167) — 1 (converted F-86A tested with a Canadian Orena turbojet)
F-86E (Model NA-170) — 456
F-86F (Model NA-172) — 2540 (including a pair of two-seat conversions, NA-204, designated TF-86F)
XFJ-2 (Model NA-179) — 3
FJ-2 (Model NA-181) — 200 (227 were cancelled)
XFJ-2B (Model NA-185) — 1
F-86H (Model NA-187) — 475
FJ-3** (Model NA-194) — 538 (100 were cancelled)
YF-86K (Model NA-205) — 2
FJ-4** (Model NA-208) — 150
FJ-4B** (Model NA-209) — 222 (33 were cancelled)
F-86K (Model NA-213) — 120 (An additional 221 were built in Italy under license from Fiat)
FJ-4F (Model NA-248) — 1 (an FJ-4 retrofitted with a rocket engine)

*Originally designated as YF-95.

**In 1962, under the Defense Department nomenclature merger, FJ-4s became F-1Cs, FJ-4s became F-1Es and FJ-4Bs became AF-1Es. In retrospect, they should have probably been redesignated in the F-86 series rather than creating an F-1 series.

F-86F

NORTH AMERICAN
F-86F *Sabre Jet*

"FLYING TAIL"
ALL CONTROL SURFACES
EXCEPT THE RUDDER
ARE HYDRAULICALLY POWERED

TAIL PIPE

GENERAL ELECTRIC J 47-27 TURBOJET
TWELVE STAGE COMPRESSOR
EIGHT COMBUSTION CHAMBERS
SINGLE STAGE TURBINE

AILERON

LANDING FLAPS

PITOT TUBE
(AIR SPEED)

EJECTOR SEAT

HEAD AND BACK ARMOR

ELECTRICALLY OPERATED CANOPY

BULLET PROOF WINDSHIELD

GUN SIGHT

FUEL TANKS

RADIO

RADAR EQUIPMENT

SIX 50 CAL. MACHINE GUNS
(THREE EACH SIDE)

GUN CAMERA

FU-958

FU-630

The F-86F (NA-172), portrayed in 51st Fighter Interceptor Wing markings by Michael Badrocke, represented the most advanced Sabre Jet to serve during the Korean War. Like the F-86A and F-86E before it, this Sabre was typically armed with six .50 caliber Browning Machine guns, although eight aircraft were experimentally retrofitted with four 20 mm cannons in Korea in 1953. This armament was embraced by the Navy for its FJ Fury series but the idea never caught on with the Air Force.

Other details of the F-86F are pointed out in the photo *below*. The 'flying tail' referred to in this vintage NAA press photo is discussed in detail on pages 86 and 87.

	F-86A Sabre Jet	**F-86F Sabre Jet**
First Flight:	1948	1952
Wingspan:	37 ft, 1 in	37 ft, 1 in
Length:	37 ft, 6 in	37 ft, 6 in
Height:	14 ft, 9 in	14 ft, 9 in
Engine:	General Electric J47-GE-13 turbojet	General Electric J47-GE-27 turbojet
Engine Thrust (lb):	5200	5910
Gross Weight (lb):	15,876	17,921
Empty Weight (lb):	10,093	10,890
Armament:	six .50 cal machine guns two 1000 lb bombs	six .50 cal machine guns
Crew:	1	1
Operating Altitude (ft):	48,000	48,000
Cruising Speed (mph):	533	486
Top Speed (mph):	679	695
Max Range (miles):	1052	1615

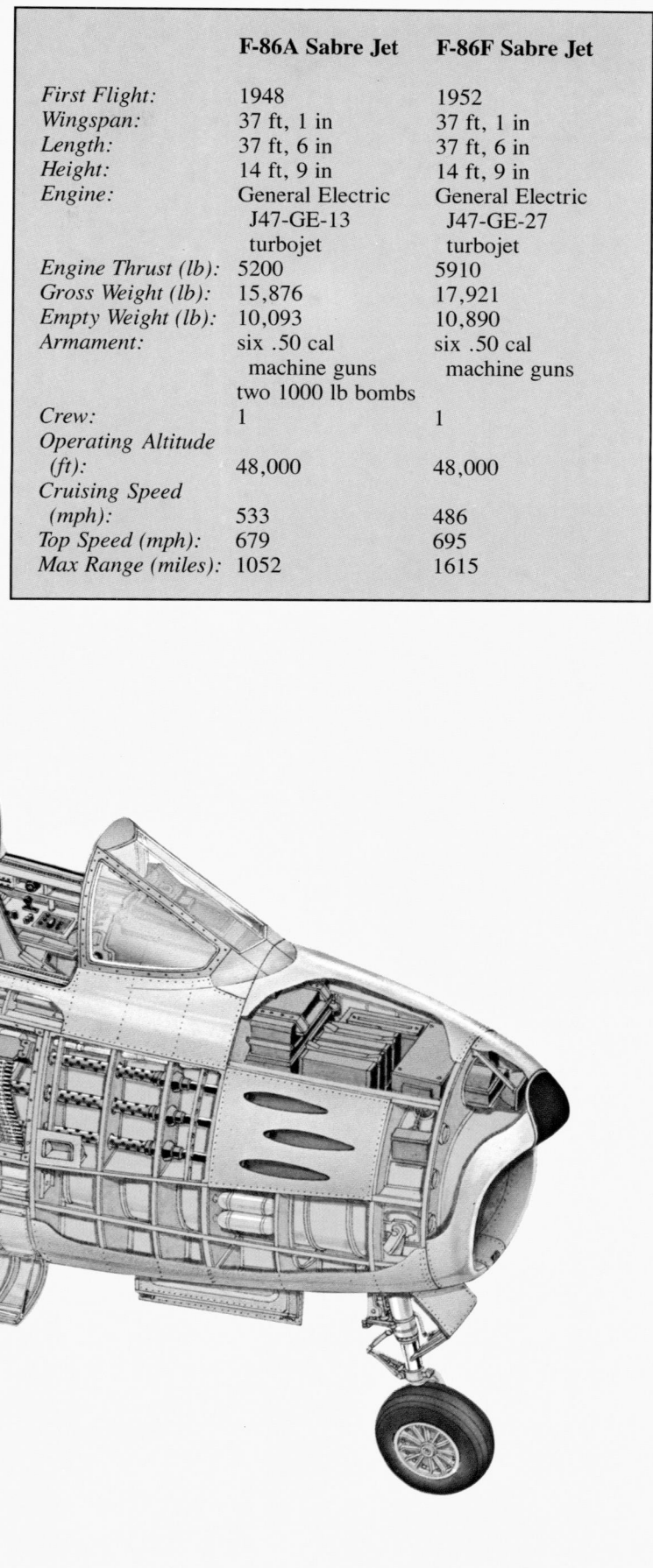

THE SABRE DOGS

While the main trunk of the Sabre Jet's family tree led from the F-86A through the F-86E and F-86F to the F-86H, the interceptor branch that began with the F-86D was still evolving. Known affectionately as 'Sabre Dogs' by their pilots, the F-86D was equipped with the AN/APG-37 radar in its distinctive nose, which was backed up by an AN/APA-84 computer to plot the intercept heading. The 'Dog' carried no guns but instead was armed with twenty-four 2.75-inch 'Mighty Mouse' Folding Fin Aerial Rockets (FFAR) carried in pods and directed by a sophisticated Hughes E-4 fire control system. After 1955 F-86Ds were armed with GAR-1 (later AIM-4) Falcon guided Air Intercept Missiles.

The first F-86D joined the Air Force in March 1951, where it was intended for service with the Air Defense Command (ADC) and never intended for use in Korea. Much faster than the other ADC interceptors—the Northrop F-89 and Lockheed F-94—the F-86D was operational with most ADC squadrons by 1955. This exceptional performance won North American two successive F-86D production contracts in March 1952 and June 1953. Because these orders were supplementary to the original order, new model numbers—NA-190 and NA-202 respectively—were assigned to these aircraft for bookkeeping purposes.

In May 1953 North American began development of its NA-205 project, which led to a simplified F-86D-type interceptor that would be produced under manufacturing license by Fiat in Italy. The project began with two NA-205s, which were actually modified F-86Ds, and followed with 120 NA-213s, which would be produced by North American, and 50 NA-207s for which North American would make the parts for assembly by Fiat. The first of the new type made its debut on 15 July 1954 under the designation F-86K. The F-86K was like the F-86D in most respects, but instead of rockets as its primary armament it carried four 20mm cannons (like the F-86H) that were controlled by the North American-developed MG-4 fire control system.

The final Sabre Dog in the F-86D lineage, the F-86L was not a new plane at all. Rather, it was a series of F-86Ds that were upgraded by North American and redelivered to the Air Force beginning in October 1956. In outward appearance the most noticeable differences between the 'L' and 'D' models were the slightly longer wings and the new wing leading edges. Two cooling ducts were also added to the exterior of the fuselage just aft of the wing. The upgrading included the AN/APR-34 Data Link receiver and AN/APX-25 identification radar. This electronic modernization improved the aircraft's target detection, reduced pilot effort, and simplified ground control. The F-86L was armed, like the F-86D, with 24 'Mighty Mouse' rockets.

By this time the Convair F-102 and F-106 interceptors were replacing the Dogs in Air Defense Command service, so most of the F-86Ls were delivered ultimately to the Air National Guard, where they served until 1962.

The last Sabre Jets to be delivered were the final batch of F-86Fs at the end of December 1956. In the space of nine years North American had produced 554 F-86s, 2506 F-86Ds (of which 981 were converted

	F-86D Sabre Dog	F-86K Sabre Dog
First Flight:	1949	1954
Wingspan:	37 ft, 1 in	37 ft, 1 in
Length:	40 ft, 3 in	40 ft, 11 in
Height:	15 ft	15 ft
Engine:	General Electric J47-GE-17 turbojet	General Electric J47-GE-17B turbojet
Engine Thrust (lb):	5425	5425
Gross Weight (lb):	18,183	18,379
Empty Weight (lb):	13,518	13,811
Armament:	twenty-four 2.75 inch air-to-air rockets	four 20mm cannon two 1000 lb bombs
Crew:	1	1
Operating Altitude (ft):	49,750	49,600
Cruising Speed (mph):	550	550
Top Speed (mph):	692	692
Max Range (miles):	769	744

Below and right: The radome-nosed F-86D Sabre Dog, the US Air Force's first single-seat swept wing interceptor.

F-86D

to F-86L standard), 456 F-86Es, 2540 F-86Fs, 475 F-86Hs, 120 F-86Ks, and parts for 221 F-86Ks to be built in Italy. In addition to these, 1815 Sabres were built by Canadair in Canada, including 30 that were sold to a Sabre-hungry US Air Force at the height of the Korean War! Other companies building the Sabre under license were Commonwealth Aircraft in Australia, which built 111, and Mitsubishi in Japan, which assembled 300 F-86Fs from North American-built parts between 1956 and 1961.

The Sabre Jet turned out to be produced in larger numbers than *any other* American combat aircraft since World War II. In combat with the US Air Force in Korea it achieved an incredible ten-to-one kill ratio, while chalking up 810 aerial victories in three years, compared to 143.5 aerial victories scored by the US Air Force and US Navy F-4s in six years in Vietnam.

Both the F-86A/E/F air superiority fighters and the F-86D interceptors proved to be the best of their type for their time, all of which helped to build the Sabre Jet's legend and make it one of a handful of true classics among American combat aircraft.

THE FJ FURY

Though it was conceived before the Air Force Sabre Jet, the US Navy Fury followed a much later, narrower and shorter evolution. Even though only a handful of the early straight-winged FJ-1 types (NA-141) were built, during 1948 they were the first jets to make operational takeoffs and landings aboard a carrier while at sea. Soon, however, they were superseded by the McDonnell F2H and Grumman F9F aboard the Navy's carriers.

These jets were the leading edge of naval fighter development when the Korean War began, leaving the Navy no swept wing fighter to face the enemy MiG-15. The obvious choice was to order a naval version of the F-86, and this was done in February 1951. The three XFJ-2s

Above: An FJ-1 Fury with tip tanks. *Right:* A brace of US Marine Corps FJ-3s over Japan's Mount Fuji. *Below and below right:* The FJ-3 Fury presented a profile that was similar to that of the F-86E and F-86F, but important distinguishing features included folding wingtips and tall, spindly landing gear for carrier operations. The FJ-3 was also armed with 20mm cannons rather than the Sabre's .50 caliber machine guns.

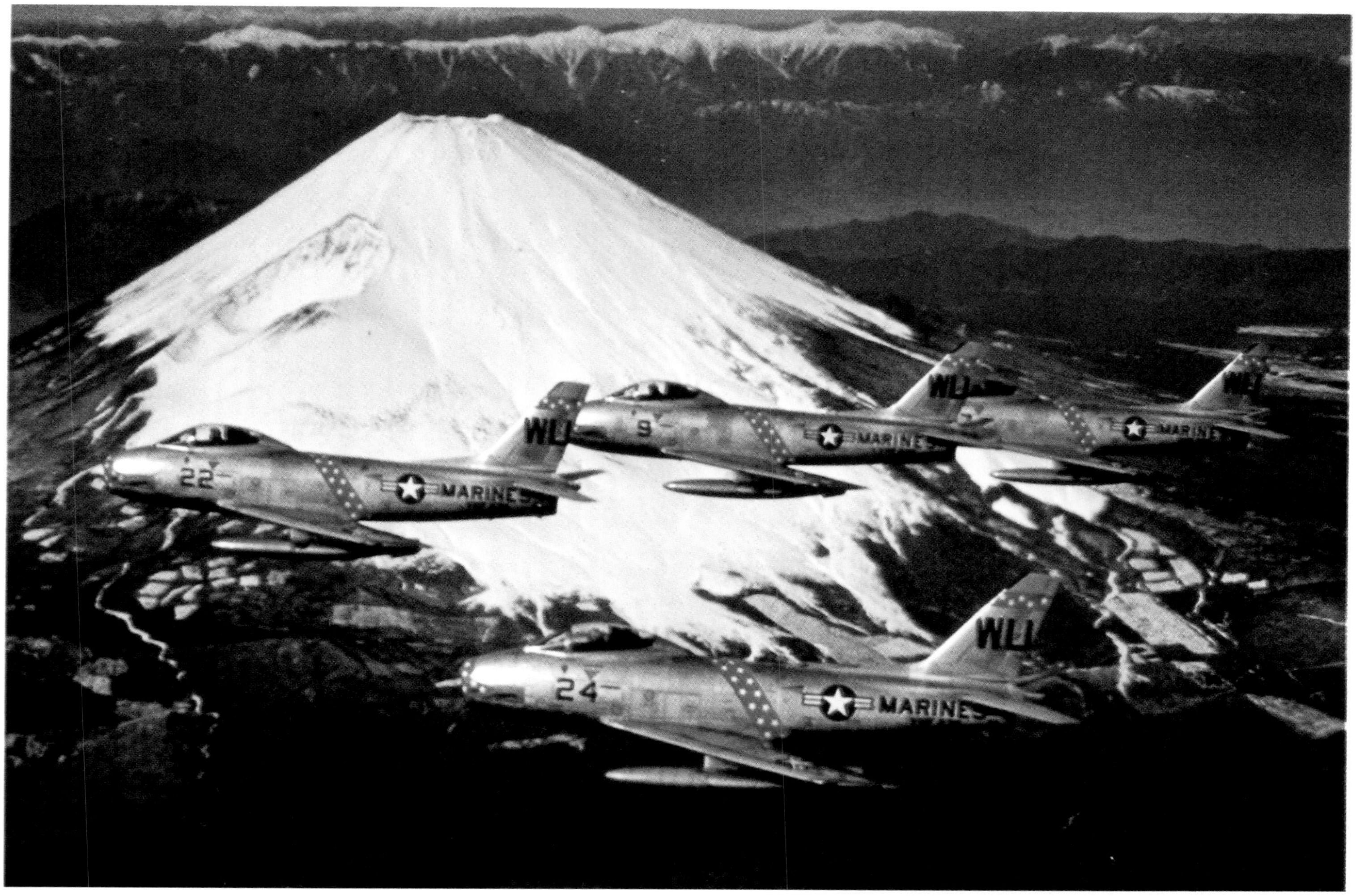
WU
22
MARINES
9
MARINES
WU
MARINES
WU
24
MARINES

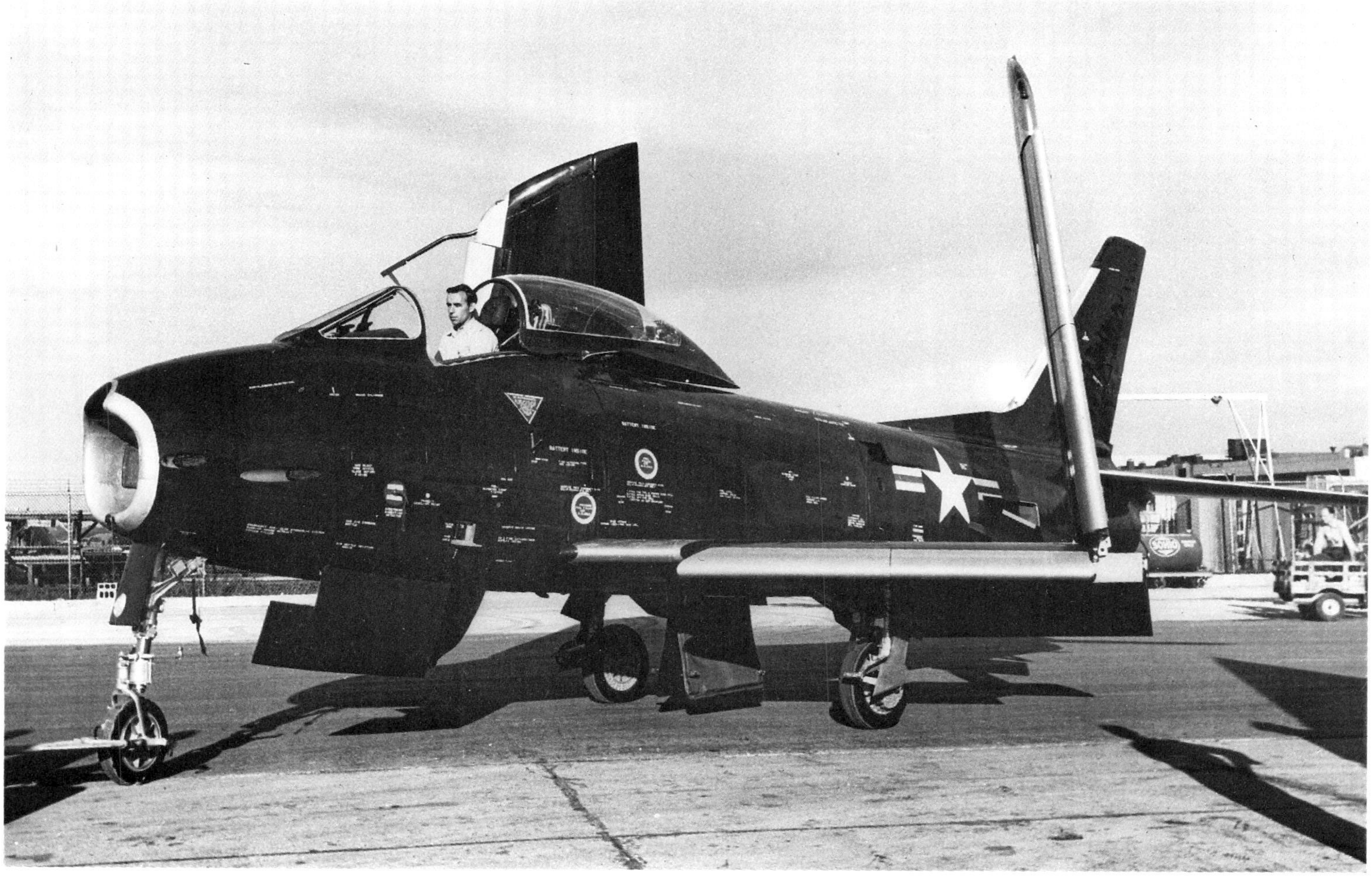

(NA-179) were actually modified F-86Es and led to the FJ-2 (NA-181), which was exactly like the F-86F except for its carrier landing gear, folding wings and four 20mm cannons in the place of the six .50 caliber machine guns favored by the Air Force. There were 200 FJ-2s built—mostly for use by the Marines—but the first of these were not delivered until the last few months of the Korean War, and another 227 were canceled when the war ended.

The FJ-3 (NA-194), which was introduced late in 1953, was similar to the Air Force F-86H. The last 80 of these Furys, delivered in 1956 and designated FJ-3M, were designed to accommodate the ubiquitous AIM-9 Sidewinder air-to-air missile, a capability that had not been shared by the Sabre Jet.

The FJ-4 was the first Fury since the straight-winged FJ-1 that was developed independently of a parallel F-86 type. Like the FJ-3, it had a Sidewinder capability, while its cockpit canopy and a designed wing and nose helped to set it apart from late model Sabres and earlier Furys. The first FJ-4 (NA-208) flew on 28 October 1954 with Richard Wenzell at the controls. Two years later, on 4 December 1956, Wenzell piloted the fighter-bomber variant, FJ-4B (NA-209), on its maiden flight. The latter was produced in larger numbers than the FJ-4, and was deployed into the Navy's Pacific Fleet between 1958 and 1962. It was capable of carrying a two-ton bomb load, as well as a Mk-7 nuclear weapon, or five Bullpup air-to-ground missiles.

	FJ-1 Fury	FJ-4 Fury
First Flight:	1947	1954
Wingspan:	38 ft, 2 in	39 ft, 1 in
Length:	34 ft, 5 in	36 ft, 4 in
Height:	14 ft, 10 in	13 ft, 11 in
Engine:	Allison J35-A-2 turbojet	Wright J65-W-16A turbojet
Engine Thrust (lb):	4000	7700
Gross Weight (lb):	15,115	20,130
Empty Weight (lb):	8843	12,210
Armament:	six .50 cal machine guns	four 20mm cannon 3000 lb external stores
Crew:	1	1
Operating Altitude (ft):	32,000	46,200
Cruising Speed (mph):	432	534
Top Speed (mph):	547	680
Max Range (miles):	1500	1485

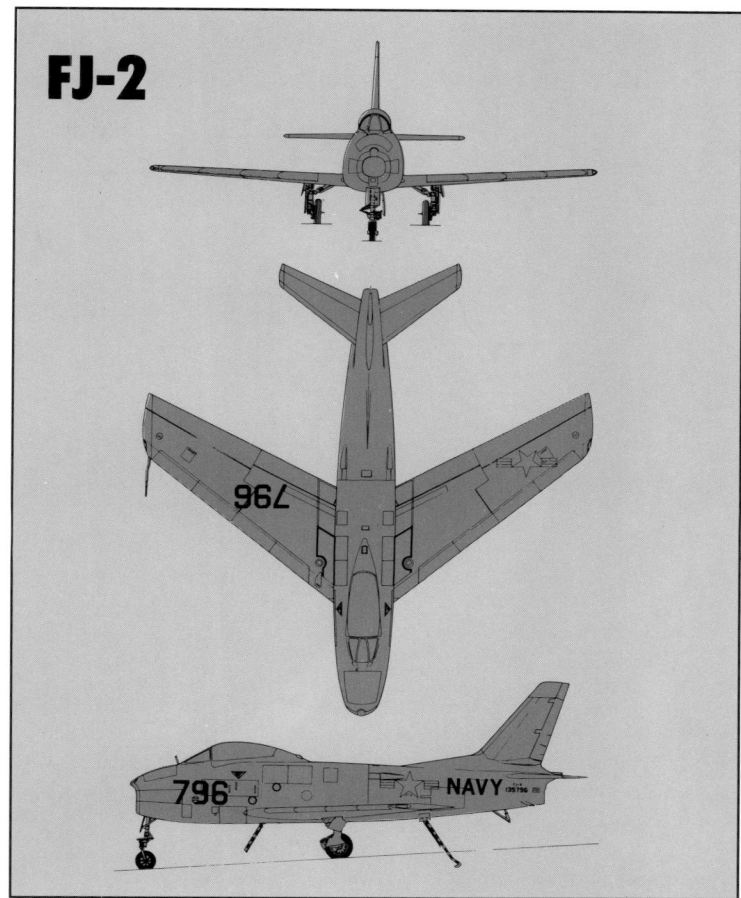

Facing page: An FJ-4 (NA-208) on a test from NAA's Columbus plant. *Below:* One FJ-4 Fury (NA-248) was retrofitted with a Rocketdyne AR-1 rocket engine at the Naval Air Test Center at Patuxent River, Maryland in 1957.

THE FABULOUS FIFTIES

Northmerican Aviation emerged from World War II with an astounding record. Not only had the company produced a total of 42,683 aircraft—more than any other American planemaker—but they had produced the most successful trainer, fighter and medium bomber in American history. From a modest output in 1934-1935, NAA had grown to a company with $50 million in sales in 1939, and went on to double this output in the next two years. In the wartime peak year of 1944, North American's sales neared $700 million. When the war ended in 1945, sales of military aircraft dropped abruptly. In September of that year, NAA's backlog went from 8000 airplanes to 24, its number of employees plummeted from 91,000 to 5000, which prompted the close of its factories in Dallas and Kansas City, and sales revenues returned to prewar levels.

Lee Atwood recalls seeing Dutch Kindelberger 'rifling through a Sears & Roebuck catalog to see if there was a group of items we could produce on a competitive basis. Other [aircraft] companies were considering the manufacture of everything from popcorn machines to coffins. Our decision was to stay with what we knew best—aircraft.'

With only a handful of exceptions, North American would continue to stick with what it knew best, and that would not just be aircraft but, specifically, military aircraft. Immediately after the war, nearly all American aircraft manufacturers dabbled unsuccessfully in the general aircraft market. Almost without exception, none of the postwar efforts by builders of military or large commercial aircraft to make lighter aircraft came to anything. NAA's own effort, the NA-143 Navion, was certainly *not* that exception. First flown on 16 January 1946, the Navion was a four-place luxury aircraft that would have competed directly with the Douglas Cloudstar II and Lockheed's Big Dipper. With the glut of used military aircraft available on the market and the fact that long time general aviation manufacturers were firmly entrenched, none of the newcomers stood a chance of success.

The chart *below* clearly demonstrates North American Aviation's evolution, product proliferation and image of itself in the 1950s.

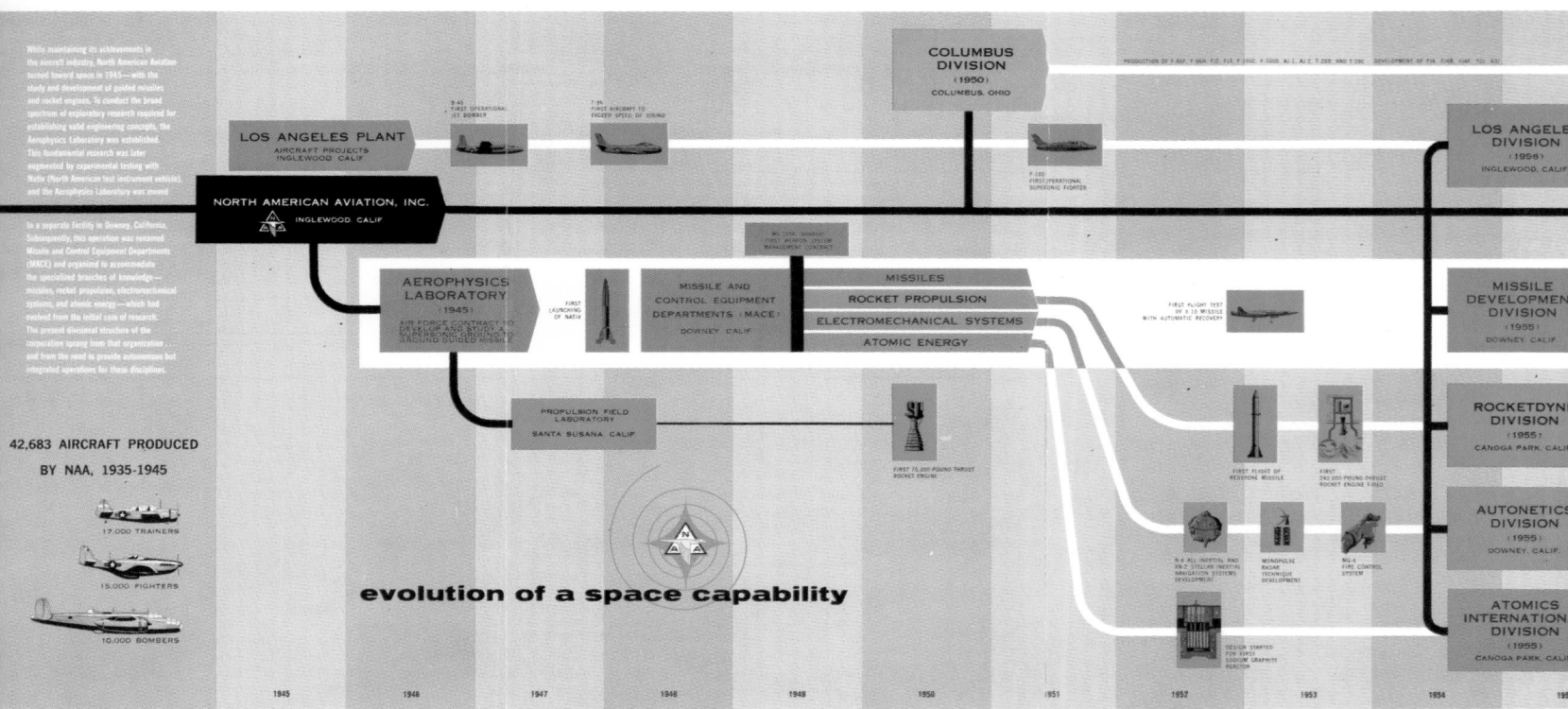

NORTH AMERICAN BECOMES INDEPENDENT

On 3 June 1948 General Motors sold its 29 percent controlling share of North American Aviation stock to the public, and Dutch Kindelberger took over as president and CEO of the company. By 1951 Kindelberger had increased sales back up to over $200 million, and in 1952 they topped $315 million.

By 1948 NAA had opened a new plant in Downey, California, which would eventually become the headquarters of the North American Aviation Missile Division, which later was renamed the North American Aviation Space Division, the site where the Apollo spacecraft were built. Today, Downey still remains the center of Rockwell International's space-related activities.

Two years later, in 1950, North American also began building aircraft in Columbus, Ohio at a factory which had been used to produce Curtiss Helldivers during World War II. The Columbus plant eventually became one of NAA's most important aircraft facilities and the construction site of nearly all the fighters, trainers and heavy attack bombers that the company produced for the Navy during the 1950s and 1960s.

In 1955 the Autonetics, Atomics International, Rocketdyne and the Missile (later Space) Divisions of North American were formed. Autonetics was concerned with advanced electronics projects, such as navigation systems for aircraft, submarines and missiles, and even was involved in the development of an early portable office computer called Recomp 2. Autonetics produced major electronic and microelectronic systems and subsystems for United States defense, including inertial navigation equipment for Minuteman and Peacekeeper ICBMs, as well as radar, and data processing equipment. The division was a pioneer in application of microelectronics technology to these systems. This versatile management and technological base

Above: The NA-143 Navion was NAA's only venture into the world of general aviation. Its lack of success convinced Kindelberger to stick with the kind of high technology activities that would be NAA's hallmark in the 1950's.

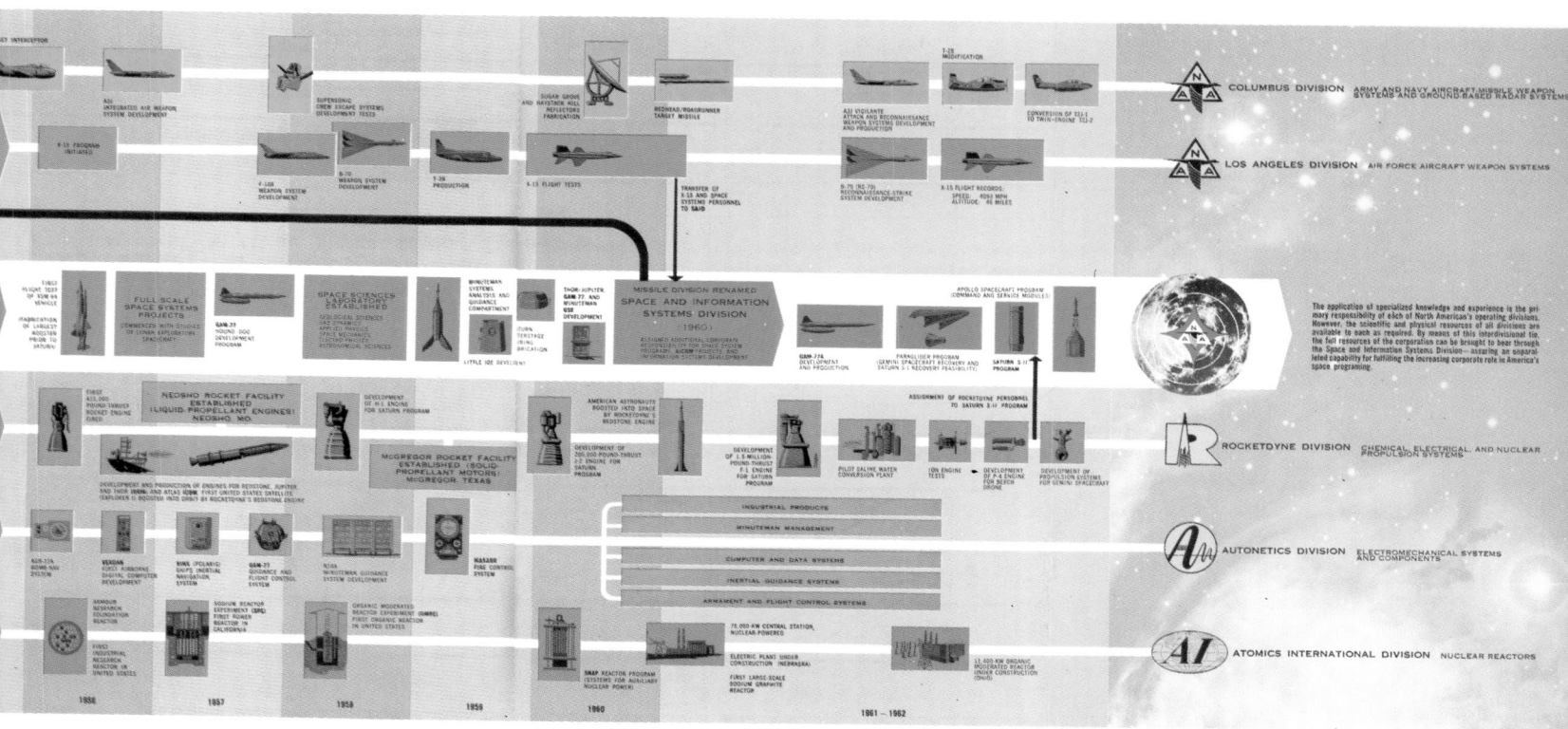

originated in 1946 with a small group of scientists and engineers who developed missile navigation and control equipment. Through the conclusion of several major NAA aircraft programs during the 1950s, by 1960 Autonetics had become the company's largest division, with 26,000 employees at Downey and, later, at Anaheim in Southern California.

The Atomics International Division followed Dutch Kindelberger's view—not uncommon at the time—that nuclear energy would be an important component of future industrial development. Atomics International constructed the first commercial sodium reactor to generate electricity, as well as many other reactors in the United States and Japan, including the L-54 research reactor at the University of Frankfort in Kentucky and the 75,000 kilowatt facility at Hallam, Nebraska. Atomics International also developed the small Systems For Nuclear Auxiliary Power (SNAP) generators that would be used in NASA's deep space probes, such as the Viking Mars lander.

Over the years, the Rocketdyne Division has produced a wide array of rocket engines. In the 1950s these were built for the Air Force's Thor and Atlas ICBMs, as well as for Sidewinder and Sparrow air-to-air missiles. In the 1960s Rocketdyne built the engines for the Saturn 1B and Saturn 5 launch vehicles that would be used throughout the Apollo lunar landing program, in addition to its use in all of the manned Apollo Earth-orbit missions.

The North American Aviation Missiles Division (originally the Missile Development Division) was generated by the Project NATIV experiments that NAA conducted in the late 1940s using captured German V-2s. In turn, these experiments evolved into the X-10 program, which then led to the SM-64 Navajo and later the GAM-77 Hound Dog. In 1960 the Missile Division became the Space Division, a step that ultimately would lead North American to the moon.

Above: Dutch Kindelberger shares a chuckle and an F-100 model with President Eisenhower. Ike invited Dutch to the White House to award him with the Collier Trophy for development of the F-100. *Below:* North American's Los Angeles Division as it appeared in 1957 at a time when the F-107, F-108, X-15 and XB-70 programs were gearing up.

James Howard Kindelberger (1895-1962)

Dutch Kindelberger was a captain of industry who ran North American Aviation like a wing commander would run a fighter wing. He was also a dedicated tinkerer who, in the late 1940s, invented refrigerator magnets and electronic garage door openers for his own convenience. Born in Wheeling, West Virginia on 8 May 1895, the son of steel worker Charles Frederick Kindelberger, Dutch quit high school to follow in his father's footsteps 'throwing pig iron' at the National Tube Company for a dime an hour.

During the first World War he served in the Army Signal Corps as a flying cadet so as not to 'end up in a trench.' After the war, he landed a job with the Glenn Martin Company in Baltimore as a draftsman, where he met Donald Douglas. No one could have predicted at the time that Kindelberger and Douglas would eventually find themselves across the continent in California just a few miles from one another, with each being the head of one of the two largest aircraft companies in the world!

After taking over as head of North American Aviation in 1934, Dutch Kindelberger and Lee Atwood went on to make the company the leading builder of aircraft in the history of the American military establishment. He served as general manager of North American until General Motors sold its interest in 1948, whereupon he became chairman and chief executive officer. He retired as CEO in 1960 at the age of 65 in favor of Lee Atwood, but remained as chairman of the board until his death two years later.

Kindelberger's expertise was management. He saw to it that airplanes were designed with production in mind so that they could be manufactured in the most efficient way possible. He kept his hand on every facet of NAA's operations, specifically the problem areas. 'My day is nothing but trouble,' he would say, 'because the things that are running smoothly don't need my attention.'

Above: Dutch Kindelberger, the steelworker's son turned captain of industry. *Below:* Dutch Kindelberger with Lee Atwood who was his right arm for nearly three decades and his ultimate successor as president (1960-62) and as chairman (1962-1967).

THE X-10/SM-64 NAVAJO

During World War II, German advances in guided missile technology became legendary. Though there had been a wide range of such missiles tested and deployed in the 1944-45 time period, the most notorious were the two 'vengeance weapons.' The V-1 was a subsonic cruise missile (essentially a pilotless jet airplane), while the V-2 was a supersonic, intermediate range ballistic missile. After the war, there was a great deal of interest in this technology, and American and Soviet missiles based on the V-2 eventually led to both ICBMs and spacecraft boosters.

Meanwhile, the characteristics of the V-1 were also of interest. Soon after the defeat of Germany, the USAAF began soliciting proposals from various aircraft builders with an eye toward a successor to the V-1s that had been captured and which were under study. The major concern of the USAAF (US Air Force after 1947) postwar ballistic missile program was *range*. The new missiles, whether they followed in the footsteps of the V-1 or V-2, would have to have a much longer range. With the vertically launched V-2, this was accomplished by mounting a *second* stage—literally another missile—atop the V-2, which would be fired when the V-2—the *first* stage—reached its apogee. This practice proved successful and has been used ever since for both space launches and on ICBMs.

North American Aviation was the first, however, to propose a two-stage cruise missile in which the first stage would be a pilotless airplane that would fly back to its base and land! What would be known generically as the 'Navajo' missile program began in March 1946 as soon as captured German missile data arrived in the United States, but it was not until 1950 that the configuration of the actual Navajo vehicle evolved into its final form. The landing gear equipped Navajo aircraft was ordered under the designation X-10 and delivered for testing in May 1953. The first test flight was successfully conducted in October,

with the X-10 taking off, flying 172 miles and landing under remote control. In its second flight in December 1953, the X-10 achieved supersonic speed for the first time. Though the first seven tests were successful, only 10 of the 13 X-10s that North American built were test flown, and several of these were lost to malfunctions during flight tests over the next two years.

In the meantime, the Air Force decided to proceed with the parallel development of a vertically launched strategic missile, using the Navajo as the *upper* stage. Originally designated B-64 (in bomber nomenclature), these one dozen Navajos were delivered under the surface-to-surface missile designation SM-64. The SM-64 Navajo was notable for a number of reasons. Most obvious was the fact that the cruise missile stage was strapped to the *back* of the larger first stage in the fashion that is familiar today in the Space Shuttle's configuration. Also of note was that the Navajo system's first stage was the most powerful rocket of its era. Capable of delivering 416,000 pounds of thrust, it was more powerful than the Atlas or Titan ICBMs and more powerful than the Redstone, Atlas and Titan variants that were used in the Mercury and Gemini manned space programs.

In 1957, however, the Air Force canceled Navajo in favor of the less complex ICBMs. The X-10 and SM-64 vehicles which remained were later used as aerodynamic test vehicles and as drones. One interesting proposal was put forth by North American Aviation in 1958, which called for using the SM-64's first stage to launch a manned X-15 into Earth orbit. This proposal, made in connection with the Air Force X-20 program, was rejected in favor of the Boeing Dyna-Soar proposal.

Below: An early X-10 test flight over the Edwards AFB test range, circa 1953. *Right:* Just four years later, the X-10 evolved into the SM-64 Navajo vehicle which, had it been taken seriously, could in turn have led to the development of winged spacecraft in the early 1960s.

THE HOUND DOG

Despite the demise of the Navajo, North American cruise missile technology did not lie dormant for long. On 21 August 1957 the company received a contract to develop a single stage, supersonic air launched cruise missile for the Strategic Air Command (SAC) under the designation GAM-77. Nicknamed 'Hound Dog' after the then-popular Elvis Presley song, the new missiles would be carried, two at a time, on the underwing pylons of SAC's B-52s. The Hound Dogs would permit the B-52s to attack targets 700 miles away, and thus to avoid having to fly into the air defenses that might exist around that target. The Hound Dogs were also smaller, harder to track, faster and more maneuverable than the B-52s, thus making an important contribution to the successful completion of the overall mission.

The navigation systems of the B-52 and GAM-77 were integrated, so that the B-52 navigator could cross-check his own data with the automated system in the Hound Dogs. The fuel systems were also integrated and compatible, so that the B-52 could refuel its missiles or borrow fuel from them. The Hound Dog engines could also be used to provide added thrust to the B-52 on takeoff or in emergencies.

The first GAM-77 test flight took place on 23 April 1959, and the Hound Dogs were in service with SAC by the end of the year. The Hound Dog was supposed to eventually have been replaced by the Skybolt air launched missile, but when the latter was canceled in 1962, the Hound Dog remained as an important part of SAC's strike force. Redesignated as AGM-28 in 1963, the Hound Dog went on to equip a maximum of 295 B-52s at the peak of their deployment. In 1972 the Boeing Short Range Attack Missile (SRAM) was introduced as a replacement for the AGM-28. Because the smaller SRAM could be carried internally in the B-52's bomb bay, it presented less aerodynamic drag than the pylon mounted Hound Dogs. The last firing of a Hound Dog during a SAC exercise took place in 1973. The last AGM-28s were removed from service in 1975 and scrapped three years later.

Above: A strategic Air Command B-52 with a Hound Dog slung beneath its starboard wing. The two systems had a symbiotic relationship. They could share fuel and the B-52 jockey could use the GAM-77's engines to augment his own thrust.

Right: A large pack of Hound Dogs await delivery at North American's Space Division factory just off Lakewood Boulevard in Downey, California. The Downey plant was at that time, bubbling with activities that would eventually lead to the Apollo lunar landing program.

Below: You ain't nothin' but a… GAM-77 on a low-level dash over the California high desert. The Hound Dog could outrun the cruise missiles of a quarter century later by a factor of three although its guidance system was somewhat less sophisticated.

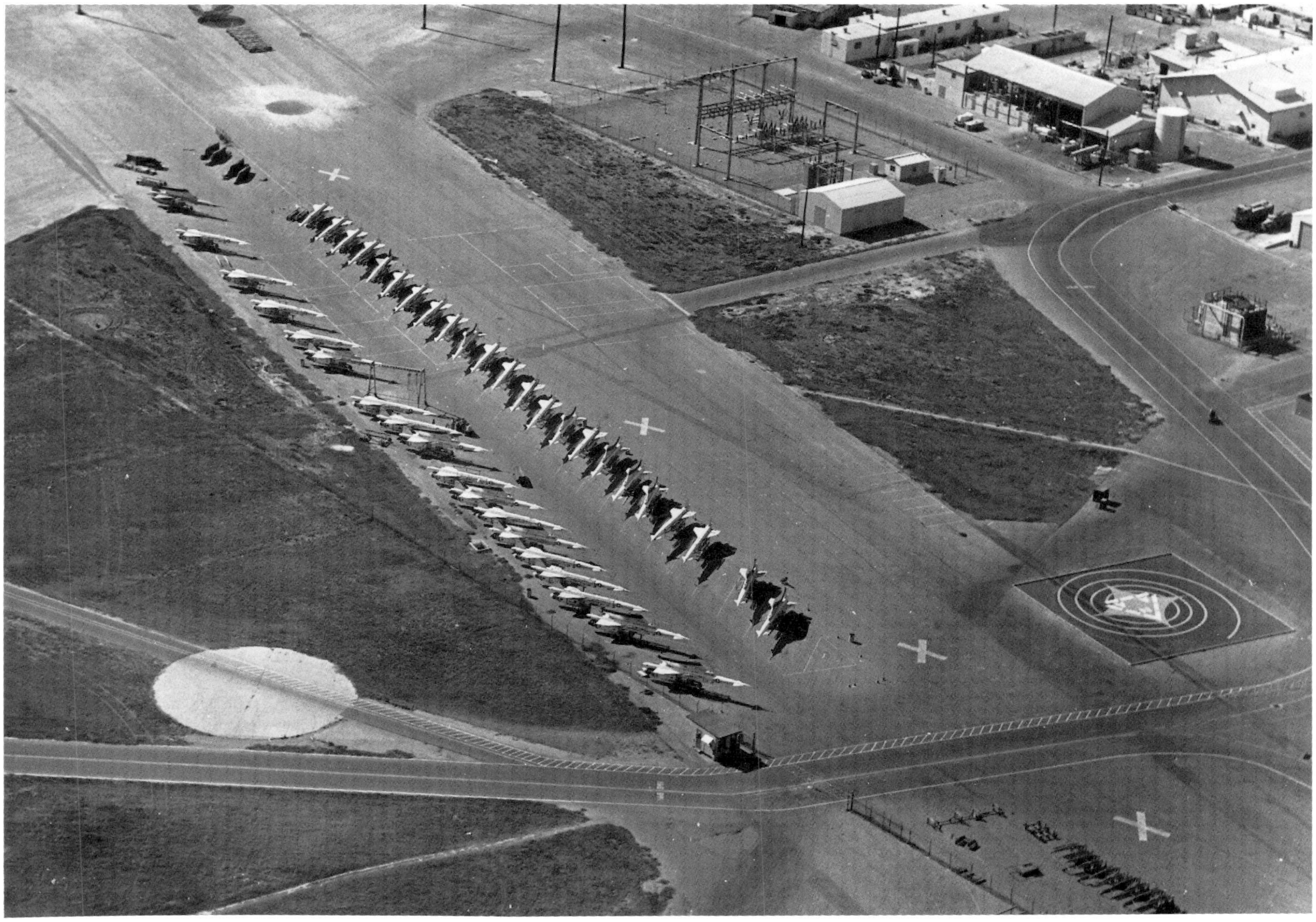

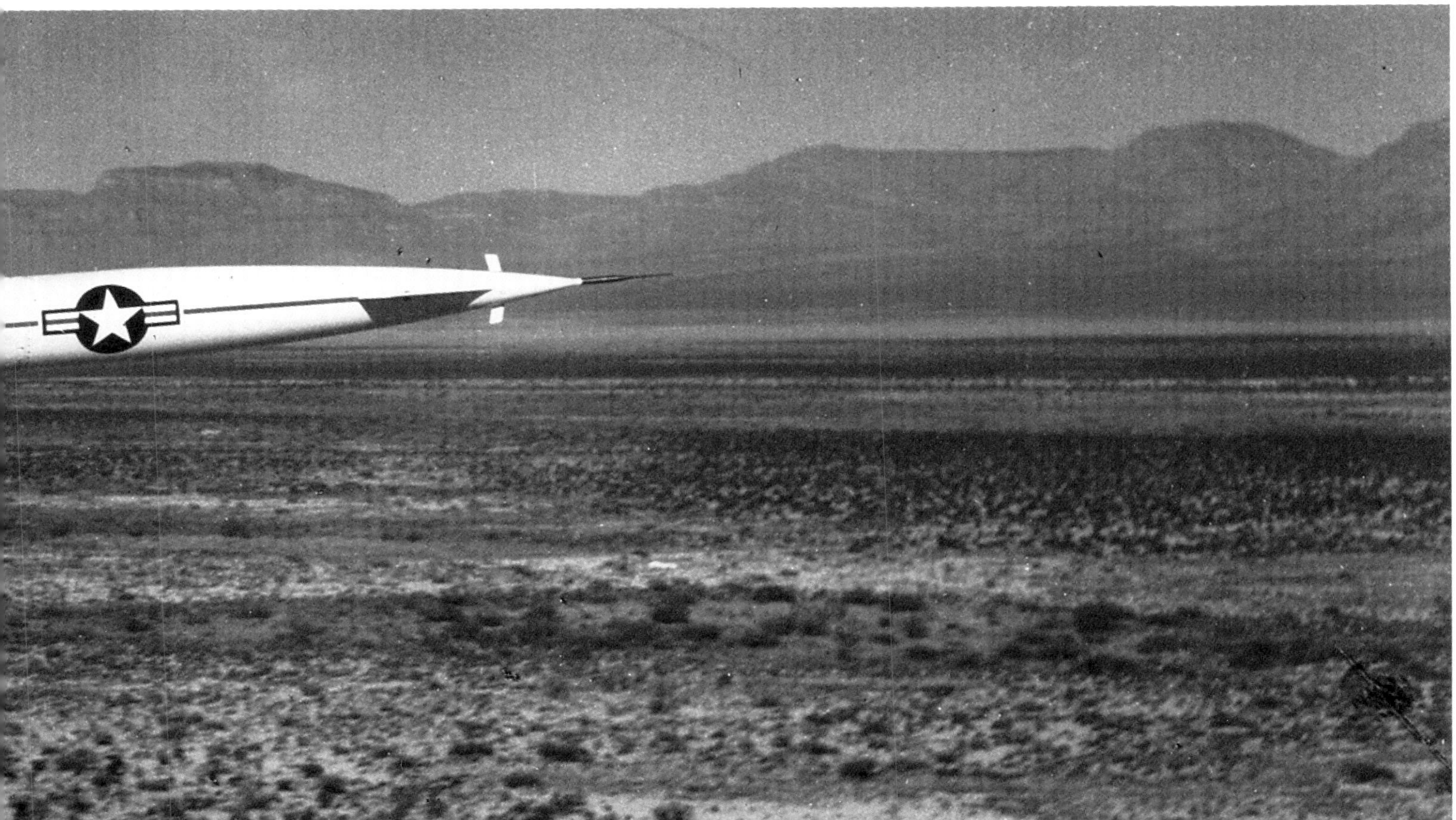

CENTURY FIGHTERS

Having built the premier American fighters in two wars, North American Aviation was set to establish itself as the maker of America's premier *second* generation jet fighters as well. The first generation of jet fighters were those born during, and just after, the Second World War. The second generation would be those born in the early 1950s, and for which their manufacturers would build upon the technological foundation of the first generation aircraft to make the new planes that much more effective.

Within the US Air Force this second generation also had something else in common with the generation it succeeded. Because the second generation coincidentally began with the F-100 designation and ended with the F-108 designation, this group of fighters would always be known as the 'Century Series.'

Most of the manufacturers who had built first generation fighters would eventually build one of the Century Series. Some, like North American and Convair, would build two apiece. North American hadn't built the initial aircraft of the *first* generation, but the F-86 was clearly the *foremost*. However, with the Century birds the company would, in fact, build the *first* one.

THE F-100 SUPER SABRE

When North American started working on a new fighter in January 1951, the choice of name was obvious. With the Sabre currently establishing a remarkable reputation in Korea, the company's next fighter simply would have to be a *Super* Sabre. Developed as NA-188, the titanium-hulled Super Sabre was ordered by the Air Force under the service test designation YF-100A. The order came on 7 December 1951, the tenth anniversary of the Pearl Harbor attack. Coincidentally, the first man to fly the YF-100A would be North American test pilot George Welch, who, as a young USAAF pilot, had been the first man to shoot down a Japanese plane over Pearl Harbor. A NAA test pilot since 1944, Welch also had been the first man to fly the Sabre Jet, as well as nearly all of the subsequent F-86 variants.

Welch's first flight in the YF-100A came on 25 May 1953. Just five months later he flew the first production F-100A. The Air Force had ordered the production series to be developed before the YF-100A had been fully flight tested because they urgently wanted to deploy a completely supersonic successor to the F-86 before the Soviet Union deployed a supersonic successor to the MiG-15. To rush production was a calculated risk, and within it was a serious miscalculation about the directional stability of the aircraft's control surfaces. This ulti-

Above and right: Two views of a late model F-100 Super Sabre on a flight out of the Tactical Air Command's George AFB in California in June 1956. The Super Sabre was conceived as a supersonic successor to the F-86 Sabre Jet, but by the mid-1950s it had evolved into a fighter-bomber. The F-100D, which accounted for well over half of all Super Sabres, were designed, built and flown as fighter bombers.

In this photo, the Super Sabre was a gleaming symbol of the high-tech Air Force of the 1950s—silver against blue!

A decade later, however, the 'Hun' as she came to be known was wearing olive drab to blend in with smokey Asian jungles.

mately resulted in the loss of four Super Sabres during the first year of tests, and subsequently the entire fleet was grounded on 12 October 1954 after George Welch was killed in the crash of an F-100A.

By the spring of 1955 the control surface problem had been resolved and 203 F-100As had been delivered. There were, however, a great many maintenance problems that arose which were related to the complexity of the new components introduced in the F-100 series. This would prove to be a problem with many of the Century Series fighters as the technological advances incorporated into the new planes outdistanced the ability of the Air Force to successfully maintain such sophisticated high technology hardware in the field.

By 1953, however, it was clear that the F-100A would never be an air superiority fighter in the tradition of the P-51 and F-86, and it was at this point that a fork occurred in the Super Sabre's family tree. A highly modified Mach 2 + variant (NA-212), then under development as F-100B, was redesignated as YF-107, while the main stem of F-100 series would consist of Mach 1 fighter-bombers that would enter service with the Air Force's Tactical Air Command (TAC). The first of these was the NA-214, which was ordered in December 1953 as F-100C. The F-100D (NA-223) that followed in October 1954 was similar to the F-100C but had increased wing and tail surfaces, and hence a greater bomb carrying capacity.

The F-100C made its first flight in January 1955 and entered service in July of the same year, quite soon after the completion of the F-100A series. The F-100D was first flown in January 1956, and it was in service by the end of the year. Whereas the F-100A had been armed with 20mm cannons and later Sidewinder air-to-air missiles, the F-100C and F-100D were equipped to carry a 4500 pound conventional or nuclear bomb load, as well as air-to-air or air-to-ground rockets. These two types were also the first to feature provisions for air-to-air refueling. Meanwhile, the Air Force also requested that North Ameri-

Right: The Super Sabre assembly line at Inglewood, California. *Below:* An F-100A.

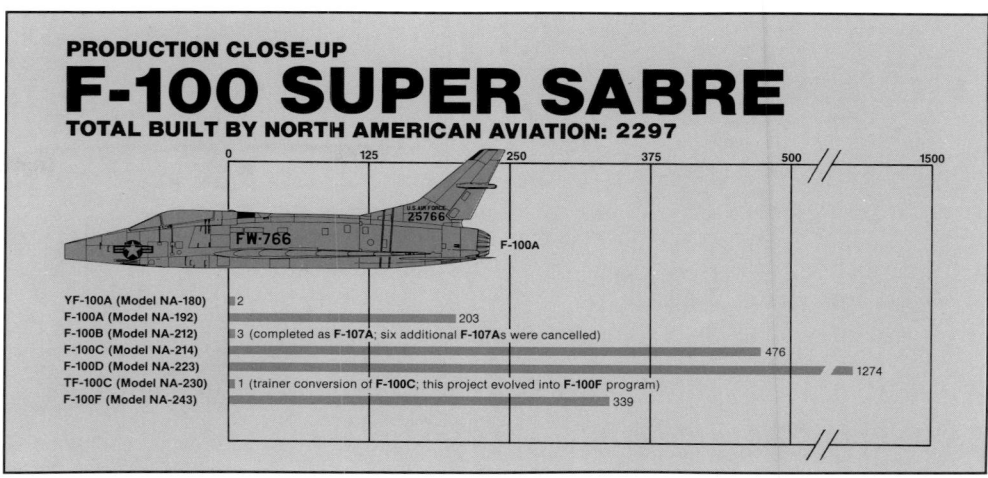

PRODUCTION CLOSE-UP
F-100 SUPER SABRE
TOTAL BUILT BY NORTH AMERICAN AVIATION: 2297

	0	125	250	375	500	1500

FW-766   25766   F-100A

- YF-100A (Model NA-180) 2
- F-100A (Model NA-192) 203
- F-100B (Model NA-212) 3 (completed as F-107A; six additional F-107As were cancelled)
- F-100C (Model NA-214) 476
- F-100D (Model NA-223) 1274
- TF-100C (Model NA-230) 1 (trainer conversion of F-100C; this project evolved into F-100F program)
- F-100F (Model NA-243) 339

F-100D

	F-100A Super Sabre	F-100C Super Sabre	F-100D Super Sabre
First Flight:	1953	1955	1956
Wingspan:	38 ft, 10 in	38 ft, 10 in	38 ft, 10 in
Length:	47 ft, 10 in	47 ft, 10 in	47 ft, 4 in
Height:	15 ft, 6 in	15 ft, 6 in	16 ft, 2 in
Engine:	Pratt & Whitney J57-P-7 turbojet	Pratt & Whitney J57-P-21 turbojet	Pratt & Whitney J57-P-21 turbojet
Engine Thrust (lb):	9700	10,200	10,200
Gross Weight (lb):	28,899	32,615	34,050
Empty Weight (lb):	18,185	19,270	20,638
Armament:	four 20mm M-39 cannon	four 20mm M-39 cannon	four 20mm M-39 cannon
	two 1000 lb bombs	7500 lb external stores	7500 lb external stores
Crew:	1	1	1
Operating Altitude (ft):	44,900	49,100	36,100
Cruising Speed (mph):	589	593	590
Top Speed (mph):	852	924	910
Max Range (miles):	1294	1954	1995

can develop a two-seat training version of the F-100D, later delivered as F-100F.

More than half of the Super Sabres that were built would be F-100Ds. In 1958, just four years after the F-100A first entered service, all of the Super Sabre fleet, except the F-100D, was earmarked for the Air National Guard units. The F-100D, on the other hand, would remain in service with the US Air Force for the next decade, and even longer with several other Allied air forces. Between 1958 and 1960, 203 F-100D and F-100F Sabres went to France, 72 went to Denmark, and Turkey received 87. Meanwhile, the Air Force rebuilt 80 F-100As and transferred them to Taiwan under the military assistance plan. In 1964 North American explored the possibility of establishing an F-100 production center, but the project never materialized.

The F-100D, known familiarly as the 'Hundred' or simply the 'Hun,' first saw active combat duty as a fighter-bomber in 1964 during the first year of the Vietnam War. By 16 May 1964 the entire Plain of Jars region of Laos was under Pathet Lao control. American reconnaissance missions over Laos, codenamed *Yankee Team*, which had been terminated 18 months earlier, were resumed. On 6 June a US Navy reconnaissance plane for *Yankee Team* was shot down by ground fire. On 8 June fourteen Air Force F-100s were dispatched to Danang AB and Takhli RTAFB in Thailand. They made their first strikes against antiaircraft sites in the Plain of Jars on 9 June. On 14 December 1964 the Air Force began *Operation Barrel Roll*, involving F-100 tactical fighter-bomber missions against targets in Laos. This was the beginning of nine years of continuous USAF combat operations in Southeast Asia.

Above: The Super Sabre served for many years as the plane of choice for the US Air Force *Thunderbirds* aerobatic team. *Below:* An F-100C pilot glances back at the photographer in a second F-100C.

Facing page: In May 1958 the Air Force conducted the first zero length launch (ZEL) tests with an F-100D at Edwards AFB, demonstrating a new versatility for manned fighters. Utilizing the thrust of its own engine, plus the power of a 130,000 pound thrust Astrodyne rocket, a combat-loaded Super Sabre roared off a mobile launcher without ever touching the runway. Kicked into the sky with an additional force 10 times more powerful than its own engine, the supersonic jet accelerated to 275 mph in less than four seconds.

The purpose of ZEL is to provide the Air Force with a means of dispersing jet fighters close to the front lines in the event of war and launching them without the use of conventional airfields. Planes such as the F-100 could be towed over rough terrain to a desolate area and made ready for launching in the event of an attack. ZEL might have been used a decade later in Vietnam, but it wasn't.

After several fatal attacks against American personnel in Southeast Asia, the Johnson Administration authorized air attacks on the North only in response to specific attacks in the South. The first of these, codenamed *Flaming Dart*, came in February 1965 when USAF and US Navy aircraft struck the communications center at Ninh Linh in North Vietnam. Chief of Staff General John McConnell convinced the administration that the restrictions inherent in the strictly retaliatory *Flaming Dart* missions made them inadequate from a tactical standpoint. The administration removed the 'strictly retaliatory' requirement, but the objectives of air attacks on the North were still narrowly defined by Defense Secretary Robert McNamara. McNamara's outline, approved by the President, paved the way for a tactical, rather than strategic, air offensive against the North. It would be directed principally at interdicting lines of communication and supply rather than at destroying North Vietnam's ability to wage war. This interdiction campaign would be codenamed *Rolling Thunder*—the longest and largest American air operation in Vietnam.

Rolling Thunder would involve both Navy and Air Force aircraft. Among the latter would be both F-100Ds, as well as a handful of F-100Fs which were converted to 'Wild Weasels.' These nasty-sounding predators were fighter-bombers specifically configured—and equipped with AGM-45 Shrike missiles—to attack enemy radar sites during *Operation Iron Hand*. They were deployed to Korat RTAFB, Thailand in November 1965 and were first used on 3 December. The Super Sabre continued to serve with the Air Force in Vietnam until 1971. At one point, most of the F-100s in the Air Force were in Southeast Asia, and the 3rd Tactical Fighter Wing were using them on more combat missions than were flown by all the P-51s in World War II!

The F-100D followed its older brothers into retirement from active duty with the Air Force in June 1972, but remained with the Air National Guard until November 1979.

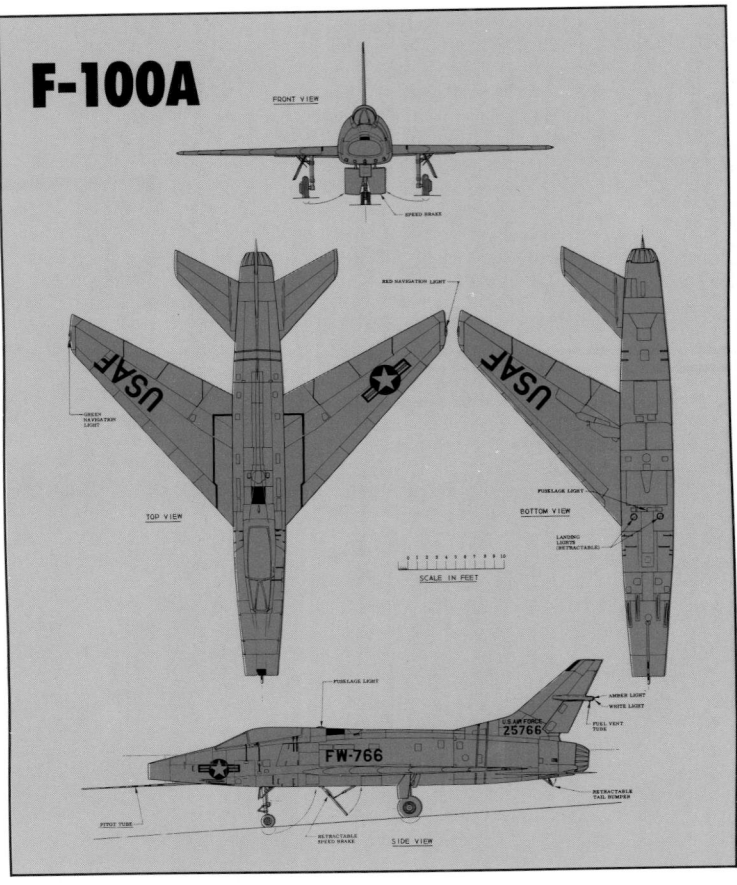

Below: An F-100D drops a pair of 500 pound bombs on a suspected Viet Cong stronghold in South Vietnam in June 1967. *Opposite:* Tactical Air Command F-100Cs *(top)* and an F-100A *(bottom)* with the huge fuel tanks ultimately used on the F-100D.

U.S. AIR FORCE
FW-105
42105
42102
42107
U.S. AIR FORCE

U.S. AIR FORCE
31654
FW-654

THE F-107 SUPER SUPER SABRE

The NA-212 project, which became the YF-107A prototype, began in October 1953 under the designation F-100B. When the configuration of the new airplane changed radically so as to include a fuselage half again longer than that of the F-100A and an intake *above* the cockpit canopy, its designation was changed to YF-107A.

The YF-107A was then developed for the same Air Force requirement that eventually would be satisfied by the Republic F-105 Thunderchief. That requirement stated the need for a fighter-bomber that would be capable of delivering a nuclear payload at Mach 2 speeds. Whereas the F-105 was designed with an internal bomb bay, North American designed the YF-107 to carry its payload in a pod which would be partially recessed into the center bottom of the fuselage. It also incorporated a spoiler system of hinged doors on both the upper and lower wing skins which operated the aerodynamically controlled air passage over and under the wings during high-speed maneuvering. This lateral control method was chosen instead of using conventional ailerons and was considered to be a major advancement of high-speed flight.

The YF-107A was flown for the first time by NAA chief engineering pilot Bob Baker on 10 September 1956. Although the aircraft exceeded Mach 2 in its test, the program was canceled in February 1957 after only three had been built. Ironically, the F-105, which won this particular competition, spent most of its career trucking *conventional* bombs over North Vietnam at *subsonic* speeds.

On 20 November 1957 it was announced that the F-107 had been delivered to the National Advisory Committee for Aeronautics for use in supersonic testing and compilation of research data at NACA's High Speed Flight Station at Edwards AFB, California. NACA studies included (1) investigating control characteristics of an airplane with an all-movable vertical tail, (2) in-flight evaluation of the overhead air inlets for the engine, and (3) a general analysis of flying qualities of the F-107. The latter incorporated what were then new ideas in control systems. North American's use of the all-movable vertical stabilizer had resulted from its previous operational success in the all-movable horizontal stabilizers on the F-86E Sabre Jets, as well as on the F-100 Super Sabre.

These pages: The first of two F-107As during a lazy moment of high altitude flight testing among the thunderheads on a warm summer day in 1957.

Before the year was out, the Air Force would cancel the promising program to sweeten its fiscal year 1959 budget and turn the two F-107As over to NACA (later NASA) for future testing. One of the aircraft still survives—stripped of its racy paint job—at the Pima County Air Museum near Tucson, Arizona.

See specifications table on page 116.

THE F-108 RAPIER

In 1955, with supersonic fighters in service and Mach 2 fighters on the drawing board, the Air Force let it be known that it was planning to take the next logical step toward the development of a Mach 3 interceptor to match the potential development of Mach 3 Soviet bombers. By the end of the year, North American, Lockheed and Northrop had been awarded study contracts to develop proposals for the aircraft then known only as 'Weapons System 202.'

In June 1957, soon after cancellation of the YF-107 program, North American was given a contract to develop their proposal under the designation F-108. The mock-up was presented on 20 January 1959 and the name Rapier was adopted soon after. The name was selected by the Air Defense Command for the F-108 after a contest in which more than 38,000 names were submitted by pilots and airmen throughout the world. North American jet fighters had previously been given names, including Sabre. A 'Rapier' is a narrow, two-edged weapon used for thrusting, and the name 'aptly fits the long range and tremendous striking power of the F-108,' Air Force officials said. Sergeant Charles Wyon, stationed at Ent AFB, Colorado, was awarded a $500 savings bond and a three-day trip to Las Vegas by NAA for submitting the winning name.

Designed to launch a nuclear missile 1000 miles away from its base and be back on the ground half an hour later, the F-108 was described by North American as 'a mobile missile launching platform that moves three times faster than the speed of sound at altitudes above 70,000 feet. It will result in a defense system for the United States that will permit the destruction far offshore of enemy aircraft or missiles approaching from sea level to extremely high altitudes.'

The F-108 was to have been powered by two General Electric J-93 engines and equipped with a new radar and fire control system developed by the Hughes Aircraft Company. Approximately 70 percent of the development and manufacturing would have been performed by several small businesses from coast to coast, but the airplane would have been assembled at North American's Inglewood plant.

In testimony before the Senate Armed Services Committee, Air Force Chief of Staff Thomas White said that manned interceptors were required for long range attack on the enemy and were necessary for identification and air policing. 'In this function nothing has yet been developed with the judgment, flexibility and intelligence of the men in the cockpit,' the general said. He went on to point out that interesting features of the F-108 included its clean aerodynamic design, two engines, construction of stainless steel rather than aluminum, its ability to carry guided missiles with nuclear warheads, and the fact it carried a two man crew. 'The long range radar of the F-108 will have greatly improved capabilities over the radar in our current operational interceptors,' White added.

The F-108 had an overall appearance that was vaguely similar to that of the A3J Vigilante heavy attack bomber that North American was already building for the Navy, and it had many components — such as stainless steel honeycomb construction — in common with NAA's Mach 3 XB-70 Valkyrie.

Unfortunately, like the XB-70, the F-108 also had a huge price tag and a paucity of friends among those who held the government's purse strings. The late 1950s, unlike the earlier part of the decade, were an era of tightened budgets. It was also a time when unmanned missiles presented an ever more serious competition to manned bombers. It was against this backdrop that both the XB-70 and F-108 came under fire. Subsequently, the XB-70 would be cut as a bomber and built only as a test aircraft, and the F-108 wouldn't be built at all.

On 23 September 1959 North American's three decade legacy of building the cream of the Air Force fighter fleet came to an end with a terse statement from the Air Force which stated that: '... The development of the F-108 long range interceptor is being terminated... The decision to discontinue the F-108 development was reached after completion of a study which discloses that the already great and rapidly rising cost and the personnel and material requirements of advanced weapons systems dictates revision of certain existing projects... The F-108 was to be a long range fighter capable of three times the speed of sound (Mach 3). Its development was to precede, but be closely integrated with, that of the Mach 3 B-70 bomber, also being developed by North American. The two weapons systems have a number of major components in common and accordingly a portion of $150 million expended to date on the F-108 has been of direct application and of great value to the B-70 program.'

	YF-107A	YF-108A
First Flight:	1956	none
Wingspan:	36 ft, 7 in	57 ft, 5 in
Length:	61 ft, 8 in	89 ft, 2 in
Height:	19 ft, 6 in	22 ft, 1 in
Engine:	Pratt & Whitney J75-P-9 turbojet	two General Electric J93-GE-3AR turbojets
Engine Thrust (lb):	15,500	20,900
Gross Weight (lb):	39,755	102,533
Empty Weight (lb):	22,696	50,907
Armament:	four 20mm M-39 cannon various external stores	three AIM 47A missiles (formerly GAR-9)
Crew:	1	2
Operating Altitude (ft):	53,200	80,100
Cruising Speed (mph):	598	Mach 3
Top Speed (mph):	1295	1980
Max Range (miles):	2428	2488

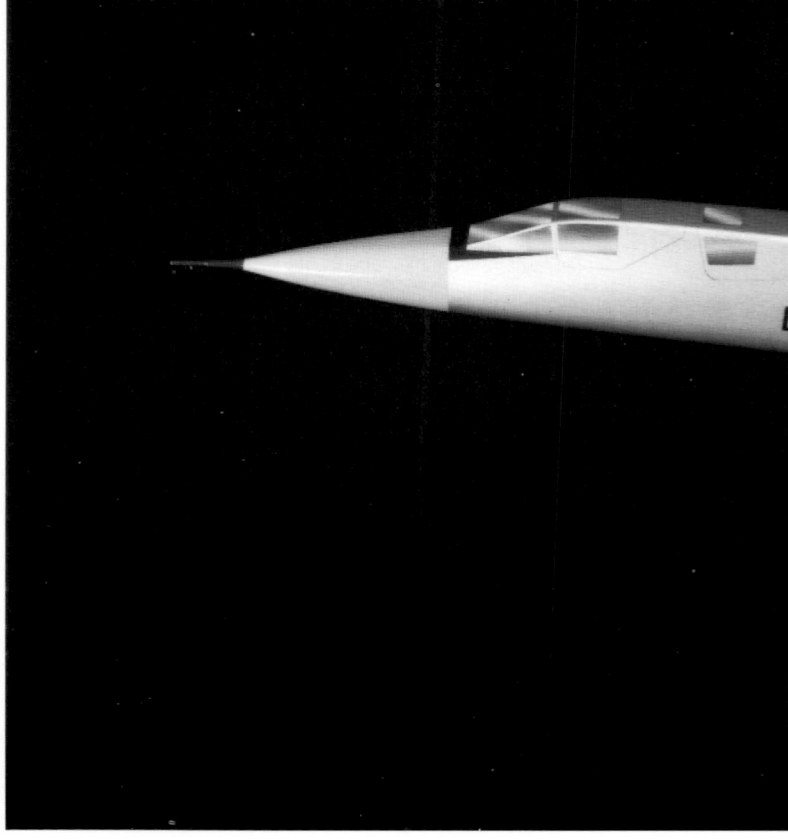

Below: A once-secret model of the F-108 Rapier. *Above:* An artist's conception of Air Defense Command Rapiers on patrol. Three decades later the USSR had Mach 3 Blackjack bombers and the US Air Force had no Rapiers with which to counter them.

THE HYPERSONIC HIGH SIXTIES

Airplanes had existed for 44 years by the time the sound barrier was exceeded for the first time, in October 1947, but only six years elapsed before an airplane flew twice as fast. In October 1967, exactly two decades later, the North American Aviation X-15 hit a speed nearly *seven times* faster!

In light of this accomplishment, it was natural to assume that aircraft cruising at hypersonic speed (three times the speed of sound) would be as common in the 1970s as supersonic aircraft had been in the 1950s. By the late 1950s production aircraft capable of flying twice the speed of sound (Mach 2) were commonplace, and no one company was more clearly in the forefront of exploring the frontier *beyond* Mach 2 than North American (North American Rockwell after 1967). With the exception of Lockheed's YF-12/SR-71 family, North American Aviation had virtually written the book on hypersonic flight activities outside the Soviet Union.

Indeed, as the 1950s came to a close, the sky was no longer the limit and the future for hypersonic winged vehicles appeared quite promising. As things have turned out, however, many of the milestones which North American achieved with its X-15 and XB-70 programs in the 1960s *still remain* as milestones.

THE X-15 PROGRAM

With test pilot Chuck Yeager at the controls, the Bell X-1 exceeded the speed of sound (Mach 1) on 14 October 1947, and on 12 December 1953—again with Yeager as the pilot—the Bell X-1A exceeded twice the speed of sound (Mach 2). Altitude records were also being set at astounding new heights during this era, so it was logical to believe that barriers would continue to be surpassed just as quickly as the sound barrier and the Mach 2 barrier had.

In 1952 the National Advisory Committee on Aeronautics (NACA, which became the National Aeronautics and Space Administration, NASA, on 1 October 1958) directed its laboratories to undertake the project of developing the data necessary to produce a winged, manned aircraft that could be used to investigate the environment of hypersonic speed (above Mach 3) *and* altitudes above 60,000 feet. At the same time, Bell Aircraft, makers of the Air Force X-1 and X-1A, and Douglas Aircraft, makers of the Navy's D-558 series of supersonic research airplanes, were building on the experience to design hypersonic aircraft.

On 9 July 1954 NACA met with the Air Force and Navy to discuss a joint effort, and in December they signed a memorandum of under-

standing, wherein they agreed that the project was 'a matter of national urgency.' Given its expertise in contract management, the Air Force took the lead in the soliciting proposals from various contractors, while NACA's Langley Laboratory continued the theoretical studies, designated Project 1226, that would be used to evaluate the proposals.

By May 1955 proposals had been submitted by Bell, Douglas, Republic and North American Aviation. On 14 June Langley returned its Project 1226 findings, ranking the North American proposal (ESO-7487) ahead of the others, but these findings were not publicly released. In the meantime, not knowing they had won, North American decided that it would like to withdraw from Project 1226 in order to concentrate its efforts on the F-107 and F-108 programs. Of course, when the company got the news that it would be awarded the contract, NAA promptly changed its mind. Given the relative future fates of the three projects, this was quite a fortuitous change of heart!

The Air Force issued a contract on 6 December 1955 calling for the design of a hypersonic research aircraft that would be delivered under the Air Force designation X-15. The NAA team would include engineers Harrison Storms and Charles Feltz, along with test pilot Scott Crossfield.

On 11 June 1956 the Air Force and NACA approved the design, North American model NA-240, and ordered the company to go ahead with three flight-rated X-15 aircraft and a stationary test mock-up. The first X-15 (X-15-1, serial number 56-6670) was rolled out of the company's Los Angeles factory on 15 October 1958. A second one, X-15-2 (serial number 56-6671) followed on 31 January 1959.

A flight routine for the test program was worked out which called for the X-15s to be carried aloft by a specially modified B-52 and then released over the Utah desert, to ignite its engine for the powered portion of the flight. Each test flight would then proceed in a south-westerly direction, ending with a landing at Edwards AFB, California, where the X-15 program would be based. There were several other Air Force test fields between Wendover and Edwards that could be (and *were*) used as emergency landing sites. It had been decided that North American pilot Crossfield—who was participating in the X-15 design as well— would fly all the early evaluation flights before the X-15s were officially turned over to the Air Force and NACA.

The first 'captive' flight, in which Crossfield and the X-15 would remain attached to the B-52, came on 10 March 1959. Crossfield made the program's first, and only, unpowered glide test flight on 8 June 1959 in the X-15-1. His first flight of X-15-2, and the program's first powered flight, came on 17 September, during which Crossfield

Above: The first X-15 (NA-240) as it was rolled out in October 1958. The yellow NASA fin flash would be added two years later.

achieved Mach 2.11 and an altitude of 52,341 feet. Three weeks later he achieved Mach 2.15 on the program's third flight, but four days later X-15-2 suffered an engine failure at Mach 1 and had to make an emergency landing that resulted in serious damage to the aircraft. The aircraft was then returned to North American Aviation to be rebuilt, after which it was put back into service in February 1960 and flown exclusively by Scott Crossfield on nine flights through the end the end of the year. Crossfield made his last flight in the X-15-1 on 23 January 1960, and it was then turned over to NASA by North American on 3 February. Crossfield later was named to direct quality control for North American's Apollo manned space flight activities.

The first person other than Crossfield to fly the X-15-1 was NASA test pilot Joe Walker, who made his inaugural flight on 25 March 1960. Walker set an unofficial world speed record of Mach 3.31 on 4 August. By the end of the year, five other test pilots had flown the X-15, including Neil Armstrong, who later would command the first Apollo mission to land on the moon.

Scott Crossfield's last flight in the X-15-2 was on 6 December 1960, and this aircraft was officially turned over to the government on 8 February 1961. Air Force test pilot Robert White became the first government pilot to fly the X-15-2, two weeks later, on 21 February.

The third and last aircraft, X-15-3, had been rolled out on 30 June 1959, but on 8 June 1960 it was extensively damaged in an explosion during ground testing of its XLR99 rocket engine. Completely rebuilt by North American, the X-15-3 was turned over to NASA on 29 September 1961 and first flown two months later, on 20 December, by NASA pilot Neil Armstrong. This inaugural flight was also the concluding flight of the program for 1961 and the 46th flight of the X-15 program. By this point, X-15s had been flown above 100,000 feet ten times and had achieved a top speed of Mach 5.7 (3900 mph).

The program's most serious nonfatal accident took place during flight 74 on 9 November 1962, when NASA pilot John McKay experienced an engine malfunction in X-15-2 at an altitude of 53,950 feet and attempted to make an emergency landing at Mud Lake, Nevada. Unfortunately, due to the malfunction, he was unable to dump any excess fuel and had to touch down in a grossly overweight condition. A landing gear failure caused the X-15-2 to overturn and hurtle across the lake bed in an inverted position. Miraculously, McKay survived with only three crushed vertebrae and some lung damage, and was able to return to the program in 1963. The aircraft itself was returned to NAA to be completely rebuilt.

In the course of rebuilding it in May 1963, the company decided to undertake a program of extensive modifications to expand the aircraft's 'envelope' of capabilities. The result of the modifications was that X-15-2 became the one and only X-15A. Unveiled on 14 February 1964, the X-15A was tested in captive flight on 15 June and made its first flight (the program's 109th) on 25 June, with Air Force Major Robert Rushworth at the controls. Rushworth reached Mach 4.59 during this flight. Eventually, the X-15A would achieve the program's highest speeds.

For many of its flights, the X-15A was fitted with two large external propellant tanks that were jettisoned at Mach 2. During tests in the

Above: The first X-15 at the moment of release from the B-52 mother ship. *Right:* The cockpit detail and directional rockets in the nose of the second X-15 as seen from the windows of the B-52 mother ship.

	X-15	X-15A-2
First Flight:	1959	1964
Wingspan:	22 ft, 4 in	22 ft, 4 in
Length:	50 ft, 3 in	52 ft, 5 in
Height:	11 ft, 7 in	12 ft, 2 in
Engine:	one Reaction Motors (Thiokol) XLR11	one Reaction Motors (Thiokol) XLR99
Engine Thrust (lb):	16,000	50,000
Launch Weight (lb):	31,275	56,130
Crew:	1	1
Maximum Altitude (ft):	314,750 (1)	354,200 (2)
Top Speed (mph):	4104 (3)	4534 (4)
Max Range (miles):	275	275

(1) achieved on 17 July 1962 (mission 62)
(2) achieved on 22 August 1963 (mission 91)
(3) achieved on 27 June 1962 (mission 59)
(4) achieved on 3 October 1967 (mission 188)

Mach 5+ environment, the X-15A was coated with a white, resin-based MA-255 ablative (heat-absorbing) material. It was in this configuration that Air Force Captain Peter Knight took the X-15A to Mach 6.7, the fastest speed recorded during the program. This record-setting mission occurred on 3 October 1967. It was the 188th flight of the program and the last for the X-15A because of high temperature damage to the white ablative coating and failures within the fuel system.

Two successful flights by the X-15-3 followed this mission, but on 15 November 1967, the program's only fatal accident resulted in the loss of Air Force Major Michael Adams, as well as the X-15-3 aircraft. The aircraft was observed to veer off course at 30,000 feet while traveling at Mach 5.2. The X-15-3 went into a spin and disintegrated in a steep dive when aerodynamic loads on the airframe reached 15 Gs.

With only one aircraft remaining, there were just eight X-15 flights in 1968, compared to 32 in 1965, 20 in 1966 and 15 in 1967. Flown by William Dana for NASA and Colonel Pete Knight for the Air Force, these flights reached top speeds ranging from Mach 4.36 to Mach 5.27, and most were in excess of 200,000 feet.

The program's 199th and final flight came on 24 October 1968, with William Dana as the pilot. There were six attempts during December to make a 200th flight, but each had to be canceled due to weather conditions. At one point, the B-52 mother ship and the X-15-1 had to land at Edwards AFB due to a freak snowstorm.

Overall, in the course of 112 months, the three X-15s had exceeded Mach 5 on 109 flights and set an absolute speed record of Mach 6.7 that has never been equaled by any manned, winged vehicle other than a Space Shuttle Orbiter. During the same period, the X-15s exceeded an altitude of 200,000 feet on 42 occasions, including nine of the program's last 11 flights, and established an absolute altitude record of 354,200 feet (67 miles), which has been surpassed only by orbital spacecraft. Of its 199 flights, 14 were flown by NAA test pilot Scott Crossfield, five by Navy test pilot Commander Forrest Peterson, 89 by five North American test pilots and 91 by five Air Force test pilots.

The legacy of this program is substantial. It is ranked as having been the most successful test series of a purely experimental aircraft in the the history of aviation. It also is considered the single greatest step in the development of data on hypersonic flight, which resulted in a vast trove of information that eventually would be utilized in the future development of manned spacecraft.

At the end of 1968, when the program was officially concluded, the X-15-1 was sent to the Smithsonian Institution, while the X-15A was put on display at the Air Force Museum.

Top: An NAA proposal for a spaceplane based on the X-15 which lost out to the Boeing Dyna-Soar concept in 1960. *Above:* The delta-winged 'X-15B' which would have been the next step if the program had continued. The X-15-3 under the MA-255 ablative coating and equipped with auxiliary fuel tanks. *Bottom:* X-15-3 with Pete Knight at the controls at the start of the 3 October 1967 flight during which he'd achieve a record speed of 4534 mph. *Facing page:* The first X-15 as originally delivered nine years before the record mission below.

THE XB-70 PROGRAM

Developed at a time when Mach 3 flight was still expected to become commonplace, the XB-70 Valkyrie was the first prototype of a planned production series of B-70s designed to cruise routinely at three times the speed of sound.

The Valkyrie was just one more step in a progressive, long range modernization program which the US Air Force's Strategic Air Command (SAC) intended to undertake with its strategic bomber fleet. Its last great *subsonic* bomber was the B-52, which became operational in 1955. Delivery to SAC of the *supersonic* B-58 *(also pictured below)* came in 1960, and the '*triplesonic*' B-70 was expected to follow by the late 1960s. Indeed, this was an era when such an outcome seemed natural and inevitable, made possible by the ongoing technological evolution of the American aerospace industry and the Air Force, which had the money to make it come to life.

The B-70 program began on 23 December 1956, when North American Aviation edged out Boeing to win the $360 million contract. The NAA proposal, NA-278, called for a Mach 3 strategic bomber that would be longer than a B-52 and have a gross weight of 500,000 pounds. It would be capable of outrunning every known interceptor, as well as most of those then on the drawing board. The greatest part of the B-70's weight would be attributable to the airframe being composed of welded stainless steel honeycomb. Aluminum could not be used because of the 600 degree Fahrenheit temperatures encountered at Mach 3. Also, steel, despite its greater weight, was considered to be the optimum material.

The plane's designers were breaking new ground in aircraft design. The results of their work earned the stainless steel honeycomb design an 'Advancement of Research' award from the American Society of Metals. The fuselage was configured to have the same shape as the shock wave it would generate at Mach 3. In this way, the aircraft would take advantage of 'compression lift.' This enormous bulk would be pushed by six boron-fueled YJ93-GE-3 turbojets, which would be assisted by the 'compression lift' principle, a newly discovered anomaly in which the shockwaves created in supersonic flight could provide added lift.

In December 1959, two years after North American had begun work on the first three XB-70 prototypes, Congress cut the program back to *one* aircraft in order to balance the Fiscal Year 1960 budget, but full funding for the program was restored in October 1960 just before the presidential election. However, in March 1961, two months after the Kennedy Administration took office, Defense Secretary Robert McNamara decided to limit the program to the three prototype aircraft then in production and to use them purely as hypersonic research aircraft, delivering none to SAC as strategic bombers. In October 1961 McNamara decided that the XB-70s were to have provisions for the bombardier and navigator deleted from the flight deck of the prototypes, leaving room only for a pilot and copilot.

This flight deck had become a point of pride for North American.

XB-70A Valkyrie	
First Flight:	1964
Wingspan:	105 ft
Length:	185 ft
Height:	30 ft, 8 in
Engines:	six General Electric YJ93-GE-3 turbojets
Engine Thrust (lb):	28,000
Gross Weight (lb):	521,056
Empty Weight (lb):	231,096
Crew:	2*
Operating Altitude (ft):	75,500
Cruising Speed (mph):	1982
Top Speed (mph):	Mach 3 +
Max Range (miles):	4290

* In bomber configuration, four.

Above: A hypersonic family portrait—the first XB-70 along with the X-15-3 on the ramp at Edwards AFB in August 1976. By this time the XB-70 had passed from Air Force to NASA control and was being used to study the characteristics of large supersonic aircraft in support of the National Supersonic Transport program. Soon, this program, like the XB-70 program itself, would fall by the wayside. *Below:* The second XB-70 prototype on a 3 November 1965 test flight dwarfs its B-58 chase plane.

Right: Crowds gather at Palmdale, California for the rollout of the first XB-70 in 1964. *Above:* The big white bird in a 'gear-up' pass over the Palmdale runway.

Pressurized to 800 feet, interior temperatures were kept at 'shirt sleeve' level by a highly efficient air conditioning system. Protection of the crew under all conditions was a basic XB-70 design requirement, so that although the outside environment at 70,000 feet altitude and 200 mph speed was extremely severe, the crew had no need for special clothing or oxygen masks. According to an NAA press release at the time, 'ample roominess, foldout assemblies, and color-coded instrument displays were effectively combined to maintain a work environment of maximum efficiency and comfort.'

Instrument panels were illuminated with white light to improve visibility over the conventional red lighting, and the indications were given in appropriate directions and positions. Ejection *capsules*, rather than conventional ejection seats, were designed to provide special protection to the crew if it became necessary to escape from the aircraft. A pull on a lever would enclose each crewman in his 'clam shell.' The encapsulated shell nature of the system furnished the pressure and breathing oxygen needed during the high altitude portion of a descent. The system also was designed so that the pilot could stay aboard the plane and conduct a descent by means of controls within his pressurized capsule, or he could pull another lever and be rocketed safely away from the plane. The capsule was stabilized to control its attitude and the acceleration applied to the passenger during descent. At 15,000 feet, a parachute would be deployed. Survival equipment, cold-weather clothing, and enough food for several days were stored in the capsule, and in case of a water landing, it would float like a boat, and was equipped with fishing tackle and a life raft.

McNamara was well known for his belief that manned bombers were obsolete and that ICBMs could, by themselves, carry out SAC's strategic deterrent mission. The Air Force disagreed and lobbied hard for the B-70 program. During 1962 they put forth a proposal for a 'Reconnaissance Strike' version (designated RS-70), thus emphasizing the reconnaissance capability that could not be duplicated with an unmanned missile. McNamara was unswayed, and even went so far in March 1963 as to cancel one of the three prototype XB-70s that was still under construction at North American's factory at the Air Force Plant 42 at Palmdale, California near Edwards AFB.

The first XB-70 (tail number 20001) was rolled out a year later, and made its first flight on 21 September 1964, with North American test pilot Alvin White and Air Force Colonel Joe Cotton at the controls. The sleek, arrow-shaped ship was the crest of the aviation technology boom of the postwar period. By the time the second XB-70 (tail number 20207) made its initial flight, on 23 July 1965, a test program was well underway which had the aircraft routinely cruising at Mach 3 for periods of nearly an hour. The maximum distance flown in the test routine would be a 2700 mile circuit, and the longest straight line distance flown was 1190 miles, from Edwards AFB to Carswell AFB in Texas, a flight which took about an hour.

The test program proceeded well until the clear, sunny morning of 8 June 1966. XB-70 number 20207 was high over the Mojave Desert on its 46th flight. It was being escorted by four smaller jets for a picture-taking session conducted by General Electric's engine division, which had built the engines for each of the five aircraft. At the controls were veteran NAA test pilot Al White and Air Force Major Carl Cross, a newcomer to the XB-70 program, but a pilot who had logged 8530 hours, many of them in combat. Just behind the XB-70's starboard wing was a Lockheed F-104 piloted by Joe Walker, a highly regarded test pilot who then held the world's speed record for his 4100 mph flight in NAA's X-15.

At 9:24 am the tail of Walker's plane clipped the big bomber's wingtip. In an instant, the F-104 flipped over and was literally dragged across the top of the XB-70's wings, virtually destroying both of the bigger plane's rudders. As the photographer, nearby in a Lear Jet, recorded the event, Walker's plane disintegrated into a ball of fire. Walker was killed instantly.

The XB-70 continued in perfect, level flight for 16 seconds, then suddenly jerked to the right and went into a violent end-over-end tumble from 25,000 feet. Inside the wildly plummeting XB-70 both White and Cross were desperately trying to engage their complex ejection system to escape from the doomed Valkyrie. White managed to eject, but his arm was severely injured by the 'clam shell' jaws of the ejection capsule. Cross was never able to get his capsule to work, and rode the XB-70 to his death on the desert floor.

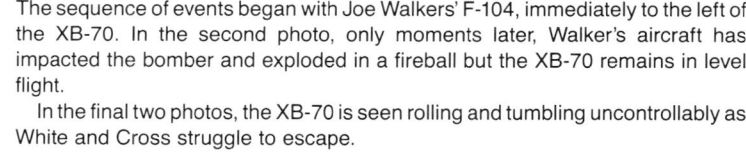

Above: XB-70 pilots confer at the rollout ceremony. From left are Col Joseph Cotton, USAF, co-pilot for the first flight; Van Shephard, Los Angeles Division of North American; Al White, Los Angeles Division, pilot for the first flight and Lt Col Fitzhugh Fulton, USAF. Shephard and Fulton were back-up pilots for White and Cotton.

Opposite: The second XB-70 on the fateful morning of 8 June 1966. *Below:*

The sequence of events began with Joe Walkers' F-104, immediately to the left of the XB-70. In the second photo, only moments later, Walker's aircraft has impacted the bomber and exploded in a fireball but the XB-70 remains in level flight.

In the final two photos, the XB-70 is seen rolling and tumbling uncontrollably as White and Cross struggle to escape.

Above: Its gloss white finish scarred by a 1965 Mach 3 cruise, the first prototype XB-70 returns to Edwards AFB in the company of a B-58 chase plane. The latter was on loan to the test program from the Strategic Air Command, an organization which was scheduled to possess several squadrons of XB-70s, but one whose colors the big Valkyrie would wear only for demonstration purposes.

In terms of speed, these two aircraft represented a class of combat aircraft that were available to the US Air Force in 1964, but whose capability cannot be matched today. The B-58 and XB-70 could cruise at Mach 2 and Mach 3 respectively, while today's strategic bombers can be characterized as 'subsonic' and 'Mach 1 + .'

The first prototype continued in a limited test routine, making its 83rd and last flight on 4 February 1969. The final destination was the Air Force Museum at Wright-Patterson AFB, Ohio, where it remains today. The program logged a total of 252 hours and 38 minutes, with 51 hours and 34 minutes at Mach 3 or above. The project that had produced the world's fastest bomber wound down without ever delivering an operational aircraft to a SAC wing.

In the end, the XB-70 program, like that of the X-15, provided a great deal of useful information that could be utilized in future hypersonic projects. New types of miniaturized, mechanized welding equipment came into being because of the XB-70 program requirements. Such equipment had to be brought to the huge structural parts. One such item was called 'the skate' because it looked much like a roller skate. Developed first as a welding took, its concept was expanded to include cutting and inspection heads. It made it possible to weld, mill and inspect while the work piece remains attached to a guide rail which exactly follows the contour of the structure. The 'skate' would soon be used in the manufacture of both the Apollo spacecraft and the Saturn launch vehicle.

Much of what was learned during the XB-70 design, manufacturing and flight program would have had direct application to development of the American supersonic transport (SST) had the SST actually been built, as planned in the early 1970s. The honeycomb foil developed for the XB-70 later found wide use in the entire aerospace industry and would have been particularly applicable to large commercial aircraft flown at supersonic speeds, where strength and weight are such important factors. In an article on the XB-70, *Time* magazine said, 'The

engineering innovations that were tried in the XB-70 construction may well affect every high-speed airplane built in the foreseeable future.' The American SST, which was at that time perceived as being 'just around the corner,' never appeared.

Ironically, the Russians went on to build what is today the world's fastest interceptor, the MiG-25 Foxbat, because they feared the specter of a Mach 3 American bomber in SAC's arsenal!

THE END OF AN ERA

The end of the XB-70 program marked the point at which the evolution of large, hypersonic aircraft would go into hibernation for a quarter century. When the XB-70 first took shape in the late 1950s and early 1960s, it was confidently predicted that hypersonic flight would be commonplace by the 1970s. Even as the XB-70 was concluding its flight test program, it still was predicted that supersonic transports would be part of everyday commercial aviation by the mid-1970s.

Of course, none of this ever came to pass. Twenty-five years after its first flight, the XB-70 *still* remains the largest hypersonic airplane ever flown. In fact, the only hypersonic aircraft that exist today also date from the 'hypersonic high sixties,' and no airplane has ever taken off horizontally and flown within two Mach numbers of the X-15's top speed. North American Aviation (and after 1967, North American Rockwell) was the key player in the golden age of hypersonic flight, when the American aerospace industry pushed the outside limits of the 'envelope' farther and harder than ever before... or ever since.

Above: This startling early XB-70 design configuration is evidence of the exciting engineering activities that were going on as North American's designers boldly anticipated hypersonic flight.

Below: The first prototype XB-70 Valkyrie taxis out at Edwards AFB prior to its record-breaking Mach 3 flight on 14 October 1965. Even today the XB-70 remains the largest hypersonic airplane ever flown.

Still confident that the burgeoning aerospace technology revolution of the 1950s would continue into the 1970s, NAA's designers produced a vast array of configurations for future projects.

The designs *above* are for hypersonic transports which would have followed the supersonic transports of the 1960s, which was, itself, a victim of the budget-slasher's axe. The cone-shaped spaceplane *at left* was a contemporary of

NAA's X-15 and Boeing's X-20 while being a precursor to Rockwell's Space Shuttle. The same *at right* represents an early lunar landing proposal which envisioned a winged space plane in which astronauts would return to earth to a much more graceful landing than would be possible with Apollo. Eventually, both spaceplanes and lunar landings became reality, but hypersonic transports will be a 21st century phenomena.

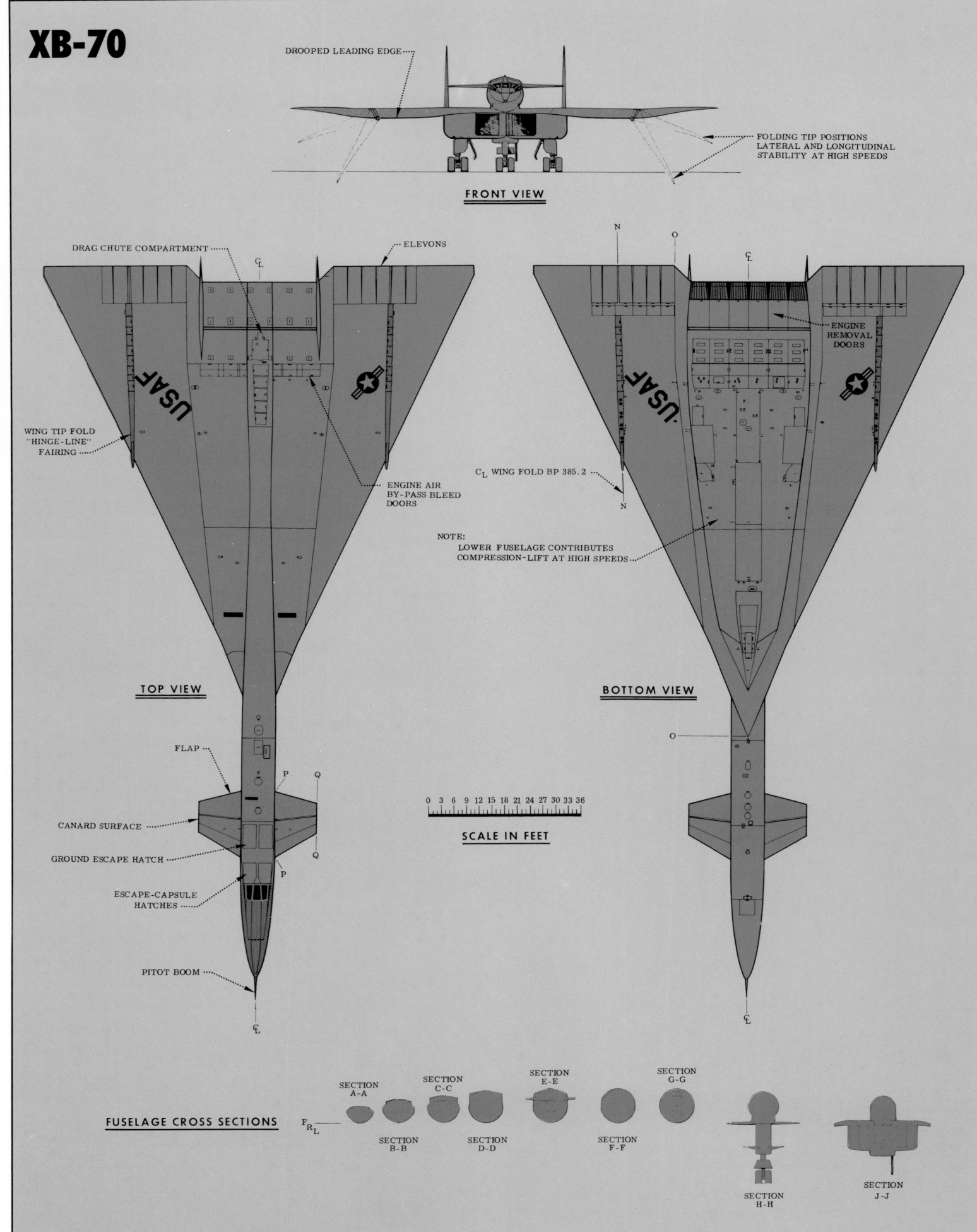

XB-70

DROOPED LEADING EDGE

FOLDING TIP POSITIONS
LATERAL AND LONGITUDINAL
STABILITY AT HIGH SPEEDS

FRONT VIEW

DRAG CHUTE COMPARTMENT

ELEVONS

ENGINE
REMOVAL
DOORS

WING TIP FOLD
"HINGE-LINE"
FAIRING

C_L WING FOLD BP 385.2

ENGINE AIR
BY-PASS BLEED
DOORS

NOTE:
LOWER FUSELAGE CONTRIBUTES
COMPRESSION-LIFT AT HIGH SPEEDS

TOP VIEW

BOTTOM VIEW

FLAP

CANARD SURFACE

GROUND ESCAPE HATCH

ESCAPE-CAPSULE
HATCHES

PITOT BOOM

0 3 6 9 12 15 18 21 24 27 30 33 36

SCALE IN FEET

FUSELAGE CROSS SECTIONS

SECTION
A-A

SECTION
B-B

SECTION
C-C

SECTION
D-D

SECTION
E-E

SECTION
F-F

SECTION
G-G

SECTION
H-H

SECTION
J-J

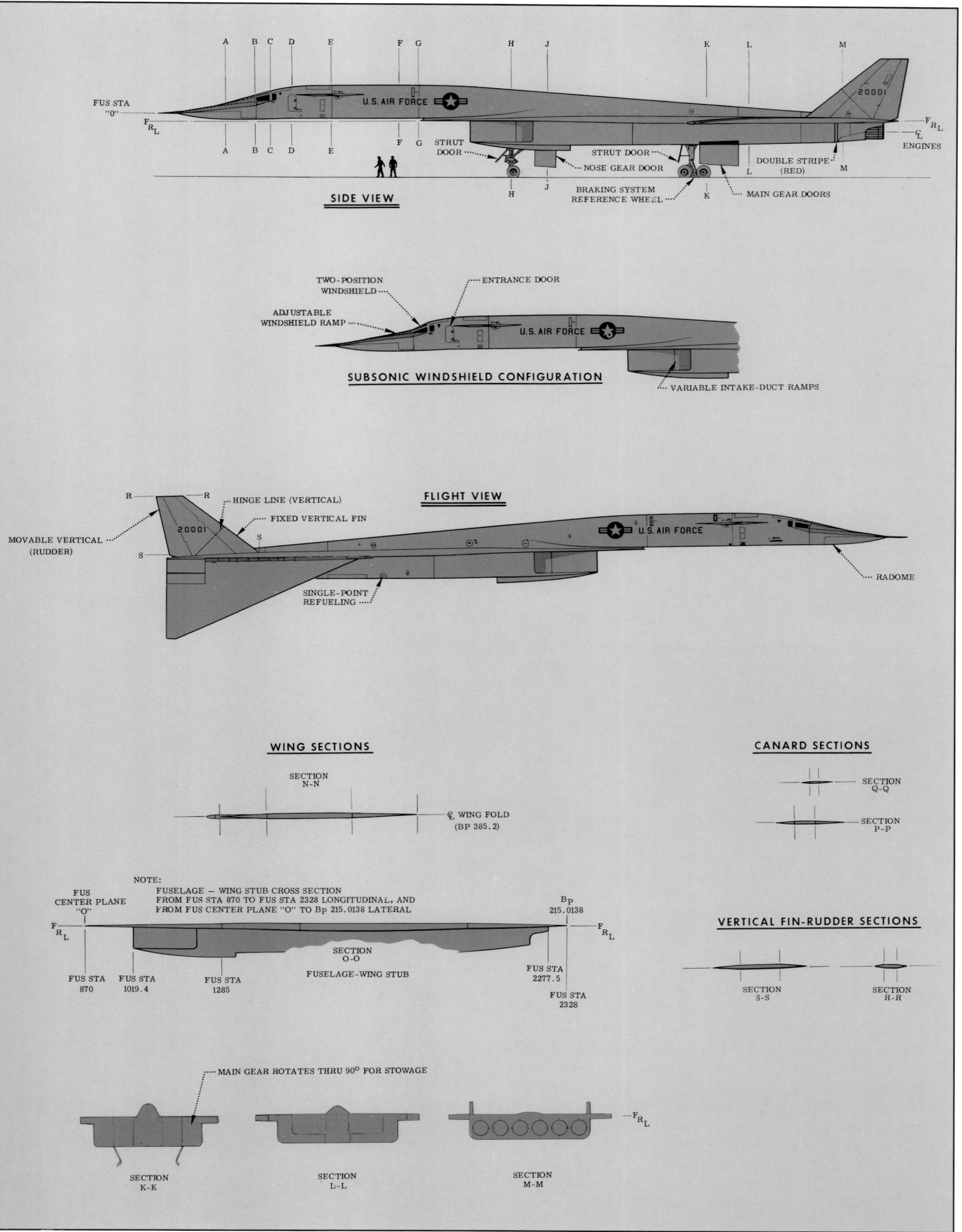

THEY ALSO FLEW

For North American Aviation, the fifties seemed to have been marked primarily by Sabres and Super Sabres, and the sixties by the hypersonic exploits of the X-15 and XB-70—not to mention Apollo! The heritage of the company, however, had been grounded in the world of military trainers and had included, of course, the great T-6 Texan, the tradition of which was continued with a post-World War II generation of trainers. One of these, the T-28, would be adapted as an attack bomber and eventually be used in Vietnam for much the same job as the supersonic F-100 Super Sabre, that ended its career as a fighter bomber. Ultimately, North American's experience with attack aircraft would lead to development of the OV-10 Bronco, which remained in production until the 1980s.

THE T-28 TROJAN

The fabulous success of the Texan during, and even after, World War II made the creation of a successor an obvious move. Developed as the NA-159, this new trainer had approximately the same overall dimensions as those of the Texan, but it also had additional new features, such as a larger canopy, tricycle landing gear and a more powerful engine.

Ordered by the Air Force under the designation T-28A, the first NA-159 flew on 24 September 1949, with JL Zeigler at the controls. Eventually, T-28As would be built for the Air Force, and this series would be supplemented by a Navy order for the nearly identical NA-199. The Navy version was first flown by Bob Hoover on 6 April 1953, and 493 were delivered under the designation T-28B.

Meanwhile, the Navy ordered a variation on the NA-199 to be built with an arrestor hook for carrier landings. This version was developed as NA-225, and 299 of them were built under the T-28C designation. First flown 25 May 1955, the T-28Cs also had a more powerful engine and a greater gross weight.

In the early 1960s, 468 surplus T-28As and T-28Bs were reconfigured to have a ground attack capability, and many were handed over to countries such as Thailand and South Vietnam under the military assistance program. Redesignated as T-28D and AT-28D, these Trojans were given a strengthened undercarriage to accommodate cockpit armor and six underwing pylons. The latter could handle up to two tons of bombs, as well as .50 caliber machine gun pads.

Much of the T-28D conversion work was done by North American's Columbus Division, and this led to the development of the turboprop-powered NA-294. Purchased by the Air Force as YAT-28E, this version actually amounted to only three aircraft, which were converted T-28As with ejection seats, twelve underwing weapons pylons and wingtip mounts for Sidewinder air-to-air missiles. The YAT-28E was first flown in February 1963, but despite the escalating war in Southeast

Above and below: The Air Force T-28A Trojan (NA-159) was the continuation of the long line of piston-engined trainers whose genesis had coincided with that of NAA itself.

The L-17 (NA-154) was the military version of NAA's Navion (NA-143). The Navion failed in the general aviation market place, but Ryan built 120 of them for the US Army under a license arrangement. Designated L-17 (three were designated L-22), they became U-18 in 1962. The family resemblance between the T-28 and Navion is obvious.

Asia, no production order followed. The AT-28D, however, did see a great deal of combat in Southeast Asia throughout the Vietnam War, especially in remote terrain during the years prior to major American involvement.

In 1961 Soviet Premier Nikita Khrushchev proclaimed that communist influence would be spread around the world by means of 'wars of liberation.' With the Viet Cong already active in South Vietnam and Soviet aircraft dropping supplies to communist insurgents in Laos, Southeast Asia seemed ripe for picking by such a war. The Kennedy Administration responded by sending both Army Special Forces and Air Force air commandos to South Vietnam as 'advisors' to help build a South Vietnamese force to resist the Viet Cong guerrillas. The 4400th Combat Crew Training Squadron, known as *Jungle Jim*, was the first US Air Force unit to become involved. After its activation on 14 April, the President authorized deployment of Detachment 2A to Bien Hoa AB near Saigon under the designation First Air Commando Group, codenamed *Farm Gate*. The Group was composed of 151 men with eight T-28Ds, four World War II vintage B-26s and four aging C-47 Skytrains, all marked as South Vietnamese aircraft. It was an unimpressive assortment, but *Farm Gate*'s stated function was to train the South Vietnam Air Force (RVNAF). Given the limited RVNAF capability to fly the missions and the need to train under combat conditions, *Farm Gate* found itself at war.

Through the first half of 1964, the emphasis was on winding *down* American involvement in South Vietnam. In May Secretary of Defense Robert McNamara was in Saigon, where he restated administration policy that US Air Force personnel would be out of the country in 'a matter of months' and that meanwhile, they should limit their activities to providing 'genuine training' only and leave combat operation to the RVNAF. The capabilities of the Second Air Division were wearing thin anyway. The aging prop planes that had come in with *Farm Gate* were starting to fail. On 1 April the last of the B-26s were flown out to Clark AB, their mission assumed by the T-28 fleet. However, T-28 wing failures in combat on 24 March and 9 April led Second Air Division commander Major General JH Moore to note that his division was 'practically out of business.' By the time of the McNamara visit in May the T-28s had largely been replaced by A-1 Skyraiders, with six RVNAF Squadrons scheduled to be equipped with the newer A-1H as the USAF combat squadrons withdrew.

On the night of 2 August 1964 the situation changed decisively. North Vietnamese torpedo boats attacked the USS *Maddox*, an American destroyer, in the Gulf of Tonkin off North Vietnam. The Gulf of Tonkin incident marked the beginning of major American involvement in the Vietnam War. The T-28 fleet remained, but from this point forward they were flown primarily by RVNAF crews.

Above: T-28As on NAA's Columbus, Ohio flight line with Furys, and a Navion in the background. *Below:* A Navy T-28C touches down on a carrier. *Right:* The YAT-28E (NA-284) was a Trojan re-equipped in 1963 with a turboprop engine and heavy attack armament. Only three prototypes were built.

	T-28A Trojan	**T-28C Trojan**
First Flight:	1949	1955
Wingspan:	40 ft, 1 in	40 ft, 7 in
Length:	32 ft	34 ft, 4 in
Height:	12 ft, 8 in	12 ft, 8 in
Engine:	Wright 1300-1 Cyclone	Wright R-1820
Engine hp:	800	1425
Gross Weight:	6365	8247
Crew:	2*	2*
Operating Altitude (ft):	24,000	35,000
Top Speed (mph):	283	346
Range (miles):	1000	1000

* Instructor plus one student.

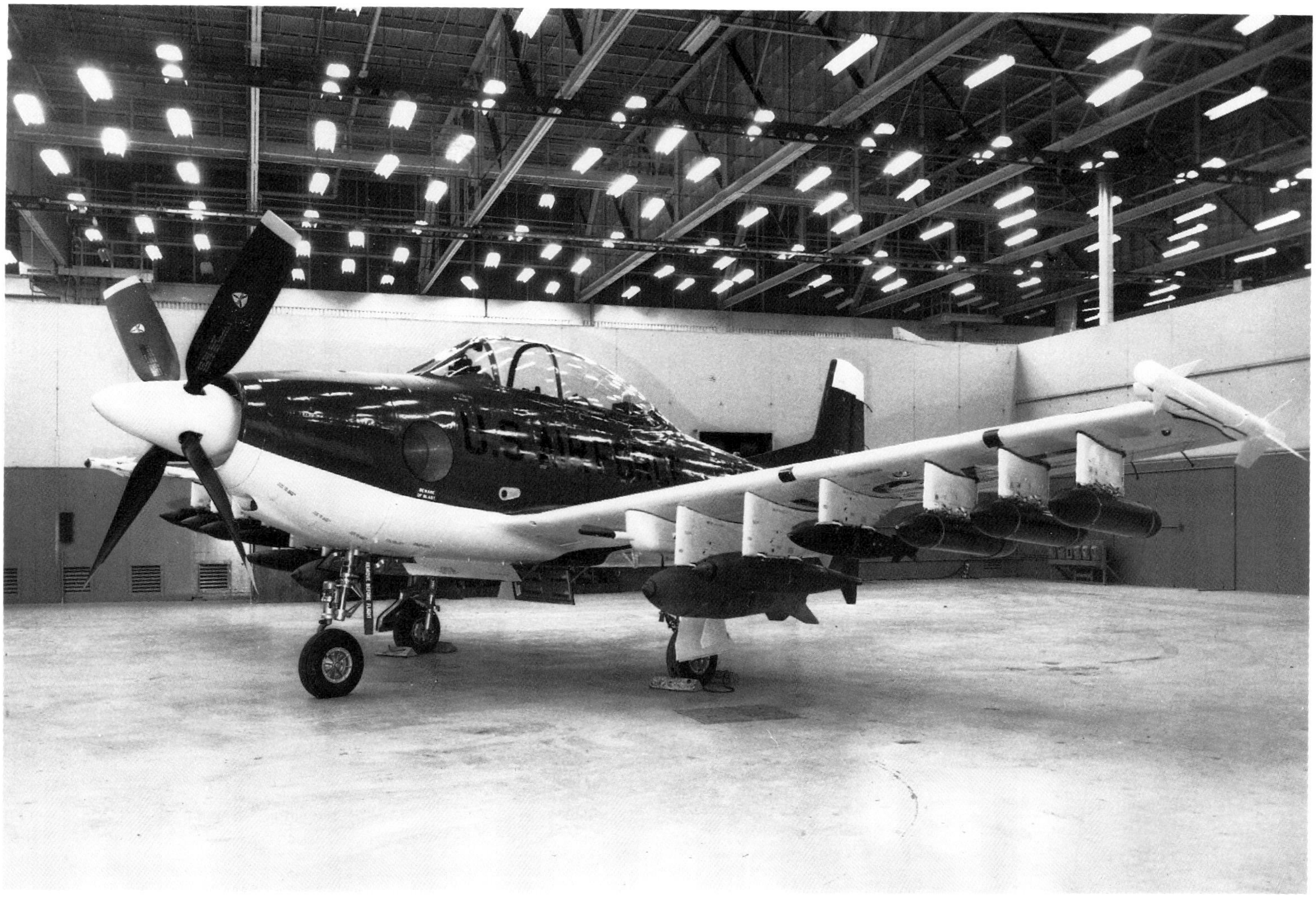

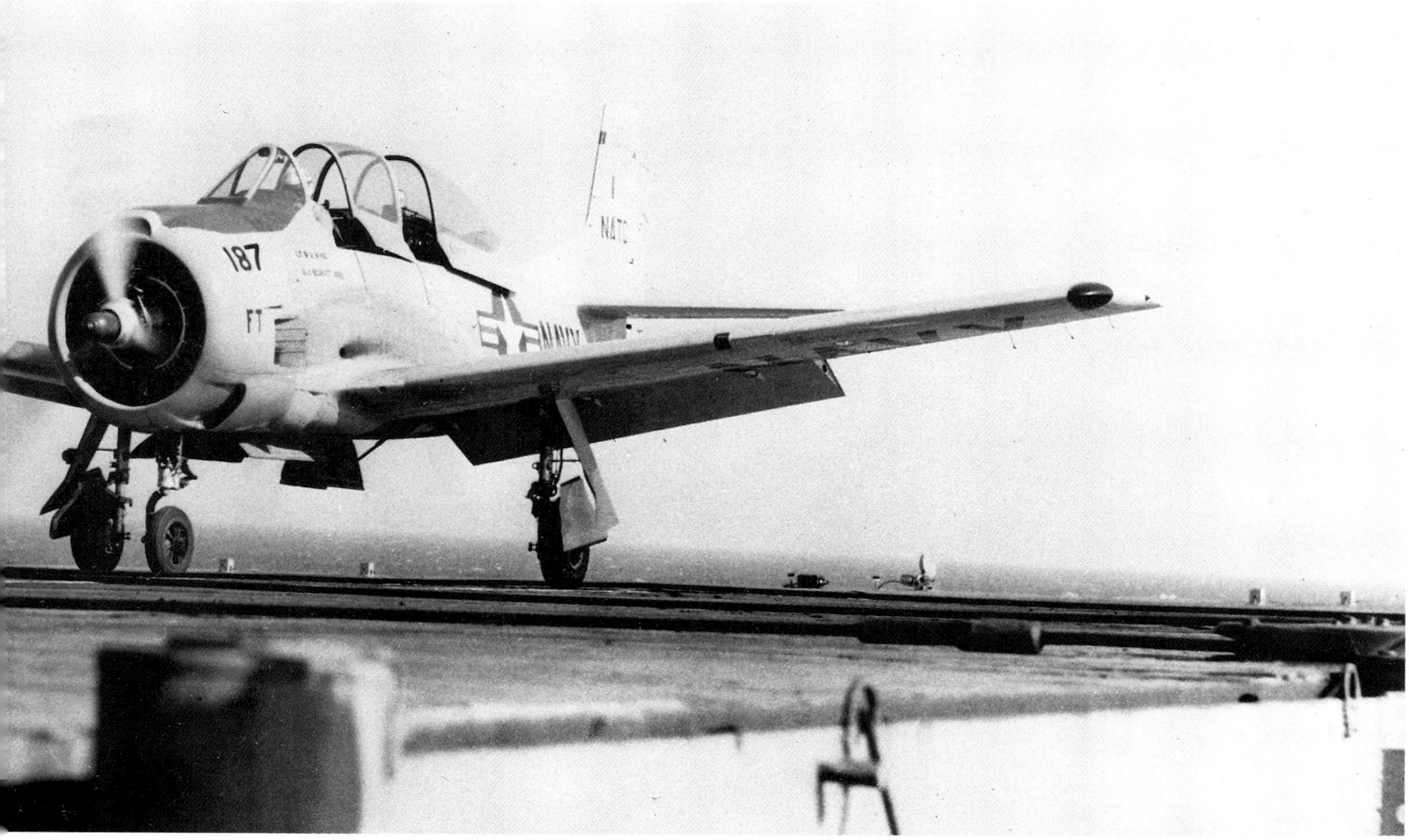
187
FT
NATC

THE T-2 (T2J) BUCKEYE

Northern American Aviation's first jet trainer, the Buckeye, was built at the Columbus, Ohio plant and took its name from the state's nickname. Born in the 'Buckeye State' as the company's NA-241 proposal to fulfill a Navy jet trainer requirement, the project evolved as the NA-249, and was ordered into production under the designation T2J.

Powered by a *single* 3400 pound thrust Westinghouse J-34 engine, the YT2J-1 Buckeye prototype first flew on 31 January 1958 and was followed by 201 T2J-1 production aircraft. An additional 60 aircraft were later canceled to make way for the development of the T2J-2, which was designed with *two* 3000 pound thrust J60 turbojets. In 1962, prior to the delivery of the first TJ-2, the Defense Department nomenclature reorganization took place and it was redesignated as T-2B. The T2J-1s still in service were redesignated as T-2A. A total of 97 T-2Bs were built, followed by 231 T-2Cs, which were similar to the T-2B but powered by two General Electric J85 turbojet engines. The T-2C series also included 12 airplanes exported to Venezuela as T-2D and 40 exported to Greece as T-2E.

The Buckeye would be used for over a quarter of a century by the US Navy and Marine Corps as a land or carrier-based jet trainer. Use of the Buckeye covered the wide spectrum of pilot training, from the student's first flight to advanced training and fighter tactics. The plane featured stepped tandem seating with a clam shell canopy for better visibility and low altitude ejection provisions. Outstanding recognition features were the high mounted horizontal stabilizer and engine compartment, and equipment bays at waist-high maintenance level, located outside the basic structural envelope. A 100-gallon fuel tank was installed on each wingtip, with various armament configurations under each wing. The Buckeye was also equipped with rocket escape systems developed by NAA's Columbus Division. The last Buckeyes were not withdrawn from service until the T-45 Goshawk became operational at the end of the 1980s.

Above and below: Single engined T2J-1 Buckeye trainers (NA-253) in US Navy markings. *Left:* The prototype twin-engined YT2J-2 (NA-280) in high visibility orange. This series of multi-engined Buckeyes were delivered after 1962 as T-2B (NA-288, NA-294 and NA-310).

THE T-39/NA-285 SABRELINER

The idea began as a utility aircraft that could *also* be used as a trainer, and eventually became the only successful commercial program born at North American Aviation. The NA-246 was built as a proposal in response to the Air Force Utility Trainer Experimental (UTX) requirement that called for a six-passenger jet to be used as both a trainer and a utility aircraft. The NA-246 prototype made its first flight on 16 September 1958 at Palmdale, California, and was ordered into production for the USAF Air Training Command under the designation T-39A.

There were a total of 143 T-39As (NA-265) delivered between January 1961 and the end of 1963, with some of them converted to transport aircraft as CT-39A. A subsequent development were six NA-270s delivered to the Air Force as T-39B. These were equipped with NASARR/Doppler radar and were used by the 4524th Combat Crew Training Squadron for F-105 crew training during the Vietnam War.

North American Aviation also developed a naval variant of the NA-265, called NA-277, for the US Navy under the designation T-39D. The T-39D was first flown on 27 December 1961, and 42 aircraft were delivered through 1964. These were used to train radar intercept officers. A strategic bomber radar trainer version for the Air Force, which would have been designated T-39C, was never built.

In 1962 North American decided to develop a *commercial* version of the T-39 for the executive aviation market, under the name Sabreliner. This name was an obvious reference to its greatest military jet and would certainly be a useful marketing tool. North American established a Sabreliner Division to build the new jet, and appointed Remmert-Werner, Inc of St Louis as its sole distributor for the Sabreliner aircraft.

On 23 March 1962 Sabreliner Model NA-265 (T-39A) was awarded FAA Type Certificate A2WE, and by 20 December 1962 both the Sabreliner NA-265-20 (T-39B) and the Sabreliner Model NA-265-30 (T-39D) had been awarded their FAA type certificates. The Sabreliner Model NA-265-40 (commercial Model 40) was certified on 17 April

Above: The fuselage of the first production series US Navy T-39D reached the final assembly line on 17 August 1962. *Below:* The first two US Air Force T-39As were delivered in 1961, while the first commercial Sabreliner *(right)* was certified in 1962.

The NA-265 Sabreliner was North American's only successful commercial aircraft. The Series 40 (NA-265-40) and the larger Series 60 (NA-265-60) that is seen *below*, accounted for most of these sales. First developed in the early 1960s, it was based on the T-39 military trainer. Having developed aircraft itself, NAA turned the commercial marketing of the Sabreliner to Bill Remmert and Bob Werner of Remmert-Werner in St Louis. They, in turn, sold Remmert-Werner back to North American Rockwell in 1968.

Rockwell retained both the manufacturing and marketing functions until 1983 when the Sabreliner Division was sold to Wolsey and Company, who reformed it as the Sabreliner Corporation. At this time, the sale price for the top of the line Series 75 'Silver Sabre' was $1.66 million. The Sabreliner Corporation is still at Lambert Field in St Louis, where Sabreliners have always been built.

Most of the aircraft's customers have been corporate users rather than commercial air carriers. The detail *at left* shows a typical executive configuration as it would have appeared in the 1960s when interior designers favored such brilliant colors.

Below: A Navy T-39D radar trainer touches down. The military versions of the Sabreliner were powered by Pratt & Whitney J60 turbojets.

148

1963, and on 24 October 1963, the first commercial Sabreliner, S/N282-002, was delivered to Pet Milk for a selling price of $989,982.

During 1964 the completion and sale of new Sabreliner aircraft were just getting started, but 19 Model 40s were completed and delivered during the year. By the end of 1966 a total of 73 NA-265-40s had been delivered. On 28 April 1967 the Sabreliner Model NA-265-60 (Model 60) was awarded its FAA airworthiness certificate, and five were sold by the end of the year.

In April 1968, after an unsuccessful merger attempt with Eastern Airlines, Bill Remmert and Bob Werner sold Remmert-Werner to North American Rockwell. Thus, manufacturer and distributor of the Sabreliner aircraft became one corporation. On 27 December 1968 the production of Model 40s (NA-265-40) ended, and on 17 June 1970 the Sabreliner Model NA-265-70 (Model 75) received its FAA type certificate. Within a year, the production of this model was begun at the Los Angeles facility.

On 30 November 1973 the Sabreliner Model NA-265-80 (Model 80) received its FAA type certificate, and on 21 February 1974 the first Model 80, S/N 380-001, was delivered to NL Industries at a price of $1,917,379. By the end of 1974, ten Model 80s had been delivered.

On 8 July 1977 the 500th commercial Sabreliner was delivered to the Proctor & Gamble Company. This total now included 54 Model 80s, seven Model 70s, 124 Model 60s, 212 military T-39s, with the remainder being Model 40s.

The last military Sabreliners included seven Model 40s (NA-282), ordered under the designation CT-39E, and 13 Model 60s (NA-372), ordered under the designation CT-39G. Both are in service with the Navy as fleet tactical support aircraft and are configured in similar fashion to their executive counterparts. The Sabreliners still in service with the Air Force have all been converted from T-39 to a CT-39 configuration and are used by the Air Force's Systems Command and Communications Command to evaluate communications and navigation aids at Air Force bases. The 115 CT-39s that were in service with the Military Airlift Command were phased out in 1986, but the Air Training Command continues to use CT-39s in support of their Instrument Flight Center.

Between 21 and 22 February 1980 a Sabreliner Model 65 (a Model 60 derivative first delivered in 1979) set several long range flight records for its class, including New York to San Francisco (2285 nm in six hours, one minute, 33 seconds at a speed of 436 statute mph); San Francisco to Boston (2361 nm in five hours, one minute, at a speed of

5541 statute mph); and Boston to Paris (3054 nm in six hours, 39 minutes, at a speed of 528 statute mph). On 11 December 1980 the 600th Sabreliner (including 212 military T-39s) was delivered to Standard Oil of California, marking the end of a year that had seen the most deliveries of new Sabreliner aircraft to date. (41 Model 65s were delivered.) During the following year, Rockwell's Sabreliner Division announced an aircraft manufacturing program called Model 40R. The first 40R was delivered to AMP, Inc on 30 September 1981, and a total of six aircraft were also *modified* under the 40R program.

In 1982, with new aircraft production stopped and the future of the Sabreliner Division very uncertain, several reorganizations and manpower reductions went into effect. The primary effort was shifted to selling the remaining 23 used aircraft in inventory and concentrating on Sabreliner service and parts sales. On 1 July 1983 Rockwell International sold its Sabreliner Division to Wolsey and Company, a New York investment company formed in 1980, whereupon Wolsey immediately formed the Sabreliner Corporation, which continues to market the aircraft.

	Sabreliner Series 40 (NA-265-40)	Sabreliner Series 60 (NA-265-60)
First Flight:	1963	1967
Wingspan:	44 ft, 5 in	44 ft, 8 in
Length:	43 ft, 9 in	46 ft, 11 in
Height:	16 ft	16 ft
Engines:	two Pratt & Whitney JT12A-8 turbojets	two Pratt & Whitney JT12A-8 turbojets
Engine thrust (lb):	3300	3300
Gross Weight (lb):	18,650	20,172
Empty Weight (lb):	9,895	11,250
Passengers:	9	8
Crew:	2	2
Operating Altitude (ft):	45,000	39,000
Cruising Speed:	Mach .7	Mach .8
Range (miles):	2100	1800

An Index of Sabreliner (NA-265) Models

NA-246	Original UTX prototype (US Air Force)	NA-308	Sabreliner Series 60 (NA-265-60)	NA-375	Silver Sabre Series 75A (NA-265-75)
NA-265	Initial T-39A (US Air Force)	NA-320	Sabreliner Series 60 (NA-265-60)	NA-376	Conversion drawings, Sabre 75 to 75A
NA-270	T-39B (US Air Force)	NA-327	Sabreliner Series 60 (NA-265-60)		
NA-271	FAA Type Certification for T-39A	NA-336	Sabreliner Series 70 (NA-265-70)	NA-377	Sabreliner Series 60 (NA-265-60)
NA-276	Final T-39As	NA-343	Redesignation of NA-327	NA-378	Silver Sabre Series 75A (NA-265-75)
NA-277	First T-39D (US Navy)	NA-344	Redesignation of NA-336		
NA-282	Sabreliner Series 40 (NA-265-40)	NA-345	Redesignation of NA-320	NA-386	Sabreliner Series 60 (NA-265-60)
NA-285	Final T-39Ds	NA-369	Sabreliner Series 40 (NA-265-40)	NA-390	Sabreliner parts and assemblies
NA-287	Sabreliner Series 50 (NA-265-50) prototype	NA-370	Sabreliner Series 70 (NA-265-70) and Silver Sabre Series 75A (NA-265-75) prototypes	NA-391	Sabreliner parts and assemblies
NA-290	Sabreliner Series 40 (NA-265-40)			NA-392	Sabreliner parts and assemblies
NA-292	Sabreliner Series 40 (NA-265-40)	NA-371	Sabreliner Series (NA-265-60)	NA-402	Sabreliner Series 40A (NA-265-40A)
NA-293	Sabreliner Series 40 (NA-265-40)	NA-372	CT-39G (US Navy)		
NA-297	Sabreliner Series 40 (NA-265-40)	NA-373	Sierra TACAN sets for US Navy Sabreliners	NA-403	Sabre Commander
NA-306	FAA Certification for Sabreliner Series 60 (NA-265-60)	NA-374	Sea Sabre 75A proposal (US Navy and US Coast Guard)	*Types subsequent to 1973:*	
				NA-265-80	Sabreliner Series 80 (NA-265-80)
				NA-265-65	Sabreliner Series 65 (NA-265-65)
				NA-282-65	Sabreliner Series 40EL

THE OV-10 BRONCO

The last aircraft that would be developed by North American Aviation prior to its 1967 merger with Rockwell was developed during the Vietnam War as an entry in the US Navy's design competition for a light armed reconnaissance aeroplane (LARA) specifically suited for counter-insurgency missions. Nine aircraft manufacturers entered the competition, and North American's NA-300 was declared the winning design in August 1964. Seven prototypes were then built by the company's Columbus Aircraft Division, under the designation YOV-10A and the name Bronco. The first of these flew on 16 July 1965.

A number of modifications were made as a result of flight experience with the prototypes. In particular, the wing span was increased by 10 feet; the special, ultra quiet AiResearch T-76 turboprop engines were uprated from 660 shp to 716 shp; and the engine nacelles were moved outboard approximately six inches to reduce noise in the cockpit. A prototype with a lengthened wingspan flew for the first time on 15 August 1966. The seventh prototype had United Aircraft of Canada T74 (PT6A) turboprops for comparative testing.

The OV-10A initial production version was ordered in October 1966 and first flown on 6 August 1967. The US Marine Corps had 114 in service in September 1969, of which 18 were on loan to the US Navy. Those aircraft were used in Vietnam for light armed reconnaissance, helicopter escort and forward air control duties. At the same time the US Air Force ordered 157 OV-10As for use in forward air control roles, as well as for limited quick-response ground support.

Production of the OV-10A ended in April 1969, but 15 aircraft were modified by LTV Electrosystems under the USAF *Pave Nail* program to permit their use in a night forward air control and strike designation role in 1971. Equipment installed in the *Pave Nail* program included a stabilizer night periscopic sight, a combination laser range finder and target illuminator, a Loran receiver and a Lear Siegler Loran coordinate converter. This combination of equipment generates an offset

The OV-10A of the 1960s *(above)* differed from the OV-10D of the 1980s *(right)* in terms of avionics and armament.

vector to enable an accompanying strike aircraft to attack the target or, alternatively, illuminate the target, enabling a laser-seeking missile to home on to it. These specially configured aircraft were deactivated in 1974 after the war by removal of the special equipment.

Beginning in the late 1960s five OV-10A derivatives were sold to four foreign air forces, commencing with six delivered to the Federal German Luftwaffe for target towing under the designation OV-10B. Another German Bronco, designated OV-10B(Z), was structurally similar to the OV-10B, except that a General Electric J85-GE-4 turbo-jet engine of 2950 pounds (1338 kg) thrust was mounted above the wing on a pylon that is attached to existing hoisting points to increase performance for target towing duties. Twelve were ordered by the Federal German government and first flown on 21 September 1970. The jet pods were fitted by Rhein Flugzebau following the prototype installation by Rockwell. Further sales of the Bronco under the defense Department's Military Sales Program in the mid-1970s included 32 OV-10Cs sold to Thailand, 16 OV-10Es sold to Venezuela and 16 sold to Indonesia as OV-10F.

Meanwhile, the US Marine Corps undertook the modification of many of its OV-10As to OV-10D standard as Night Observation/ Gunships (NOGS). Distinguishing features of the YOV-10D Night Observation Gunship System are a 20mm gun turret mounted beneath the aft fuselage and a forward looking infrared (FLIR) sensor installed beneath the extended nose. A laser target designator is incorporated within the FLIR sensor turret. Two wing pylons are installed at the Sidewinder missile wing stations which are capable of carrying a variety of rocket pods, flare pods and free-fall stores. In 1974 Rockwell received a US Navy contract to establish and test the production OV-10D configuration. In addition to retention of the basic weapon system capability, the OV-10D incorporates an uprated 1040 shp propulsion system, and 100-gallon fuel drop tanks on the wing pylons when extended radius/loiter time is required. In August 1988, the Navy gave Rockwell a contract to upgrade an additional 42 OV-10As to OV-10D standard.

In addition to the OV-10As and OV-10Ds in service with the Navy and Marines, the Air Force maintains over 70 OV-10As in service with the 22nd Tactical Air Support Squadron at Wheeler AFB, Hawaii.

For a relatively small aircraft, the Bronco is a very potent attack plane. Under its wings it has four weapon-attach points, each with a capacity of 600 pounds and a fifth attachment point with a capacity of 1200 pounds under the center fuselage. Two 7.62mm M60C machine guns can be carried in each position. Provisions for carrying one Sidewinder missile on each wing and various stores with a wing pylon kit, such as rocket pods, flare pods and free-fall ordnance are included, up to a maximum weapon load of 3600 pounds.

	OV-10A Bronco	OV-10E Bronco
First Flight:	1967	1973
Wingspan:	40 ft	40 ft
Length:	41 ft, 7 in	41 ft, 7 in
Height:	15 ft, 1 in	15 ft, 1 in
Engines:	two AiResearch T-76-G-10/12	two AiResearch T-76-410/411
Engine hp:	715	715
Gross Weight (lb):	8000	14,466
Empty Weight (lb):	4850	6893
Armament:	4800 lb external stores	four M60 7.62mm machine guns plus external stores
Crew:	2	2
Operating Altitude (ft):	25,900	30,000
Cruising Speed (mph):	207	210
Top Speed (mph):	284	288
Max Range (miles):	1427	1382

Below: A US Marine Corps North American OV-10A Bronco, circa 1967.

OV-10A

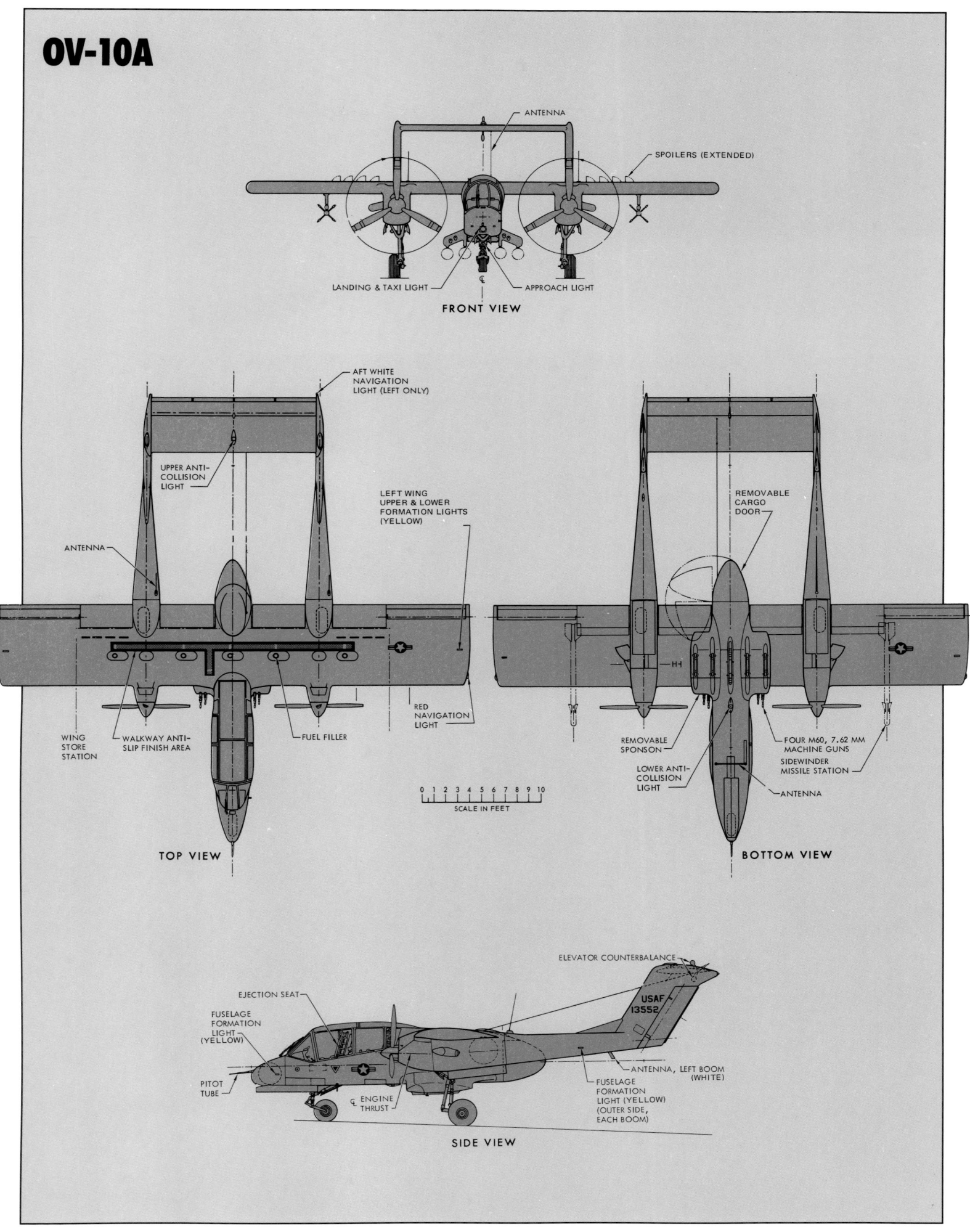

FRONT VIEW

ANTENNA

SPOILERS (EXTENDED)

LANDING & TAXI LIGHT

APPROACH LIGHT

TOP VIEW

AFT WHITE NAVIGATION LIGHT (LEFT ONLY)

UPPER ANTI-COLLISION LIGHT

LEFT WING UPPER & LOWER FORMATION LIGHTS (YELLOW)

ANTENNA

WING STORE STATION

WALKWAY ANTI-SLIP FINISH AREA

FUEL FILLER

RED NAVIGATION LIGHT

BOTTOM VIEW

REMOVABLE CARGO DOOR

REMOVABLE SPONSON

LOWER ANTI-COLLISION LIGHT

ANTENNA

FOUR M60, 7.62 MM MACHINE GUNS

SIDEWINDER MISSILE STATION

0 1 2 3 4 5 6 7 8 9 10
SCALE IN FEET

SIDE VIEW

ELEVATOR COUNTERBALANCE

EJECTION SEAT

FUSELAGE FORMATION LIGHT (YELLOW)

PITOT TUBE

ENGINE THRUST

USAF 13552

ANTENNA, LEFT BOOM (WHITE)

FUSELAGE FORMATION LIGHT (YELLOW) (OUTER SIDE, EACH BOOM)

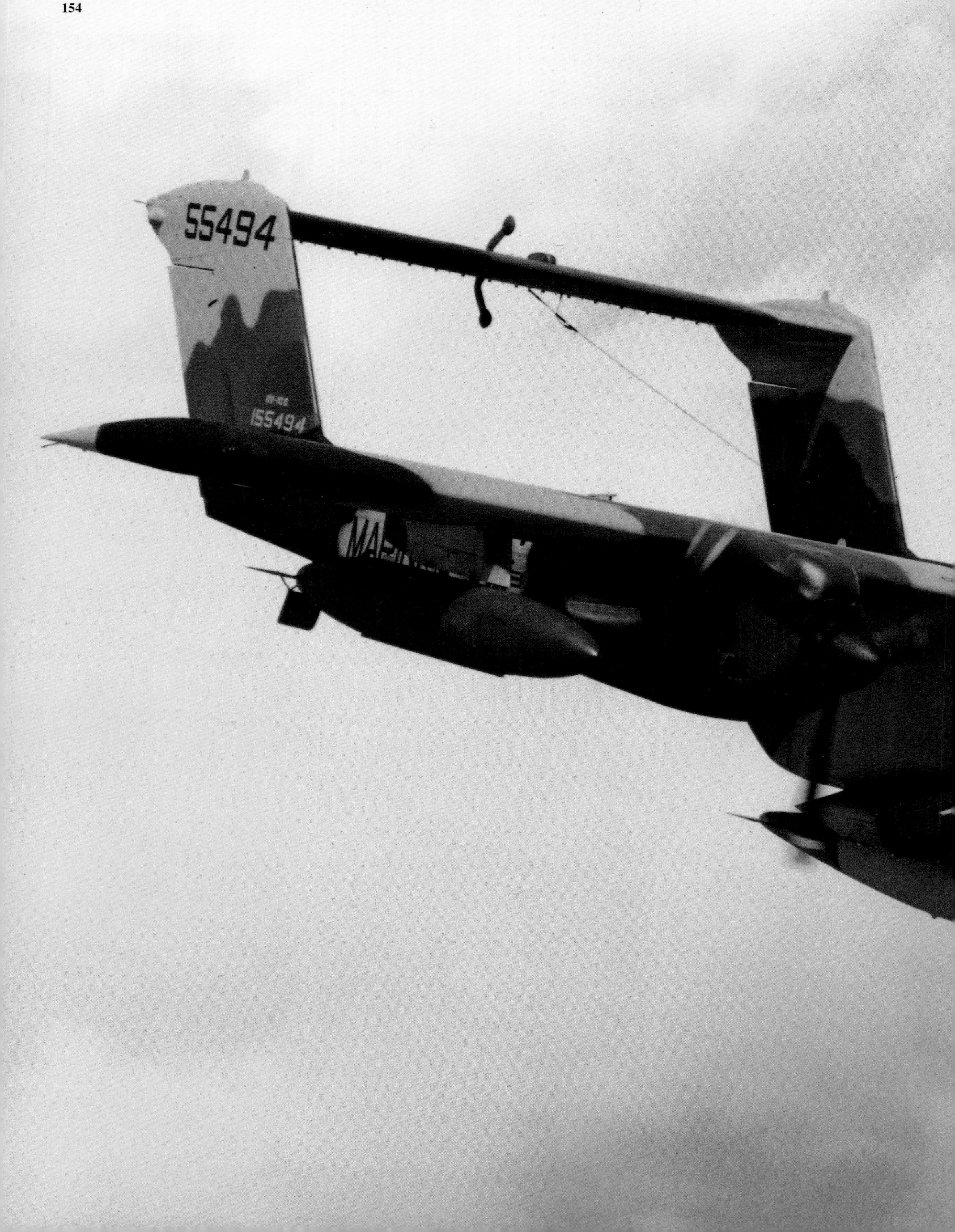
55494
155494

Below: In August 1988, Rockwell and the Department of the Navy signed a contract to upgrade 42 Marine Corps OV-10A to OV-10D configuration at Rockwell's Palmdale Aircraft Assembly Complex. This conversion involved giving the aircraft larger engines, new avionics, (including a forward-looking infrared radar) and a reconfigured cockpit. A number of modifications were performed to extend the OV-10's service life, including the strengthening of its structure. In addition, 14 service life extension program (SLEP) kits were supplied to the Navy to convert an additional 14 OV-10Ds to the D (SLEP) configuration at the Navy's Depot at Cherry Point, North Carolina.

Contract value for the first 15 aircraft factory conversions and seven SLEP kits was estimated at approximately $48 million, with delivery of the first 15 OV-10D conversions planned for early 1991.

PROJECT APOLLO

On 12 April 1961, after centuries of dreaming of such a day, the first member of the human race traveled into space. Soviet cosmonaut Yuri Gagarin completed one orbit of the Earth and returned in triumph. Less than one month later, on 5 May, Alan Shepard became the first American astronaut in space, and the race was on.

The race to where?

President John F Kennedy left little doubt three weeks after Shepard's flight, when he stood before Congress and declared, 'I believe this nation should commit itself to achieving the goal—before this decade is out—of landing a man on the moon and returning him safely to Earth.'

THE SCOPE OF THE PROJECT

What Kennedy envisioned was nothing short of the most incredible feat of engineering ever undertaken. Only two human beings had been in space by that time, and he wanted to commit the nation to design and develop the vehicle and systems to support a crew on a half-million mile roundtrip through uncharted outer space. 'No single space project,' Kennedy continued, 'will be more exciting, or more impressive to mankind, or more important to the long-range exploration of space; and none will be so difficult or so expensive to accomplish.'

He was so right. However, the bold venture *was* accomplished, and North American Aviation built the spacecraft that did it.

McDonnell Aircraft of St Louis—like North American Aviation, a noted builder of high performance fighters—had earlier won the NASA contract to build the Mercury spacecraft which would be used on America's first six manned space missions between May 1961 and May 1963. McDonnell had also gotten the contract for the follow-on spacecraft, a two-man ship called Gemini, and was in the forefront of the bidding for the lucrative and prestigious contract for Apollo. Nevertheless, North American's earlier experience with the X-15 and the Air Force's 'Man In Space Soonest' (MISS) program (which was canceled in favor of NASA's Mercury project) helped North American edge out their competitor from St Louis.

The contract for the Apollo spacecraft was issued to North American Aviation on 28 November 1961 after only two Mercury space flights had been completed. Thus, the whole NASA manned space program was geared, at an early stage, toward becoming a massive practice routine for future Apollo lunar missions. The Mercury flights had studied man's ability to survive and function in space for up to 34 hours.

The ten Earth-orbiting Gemini missions, flown between March 1965 and November 1966, studied the astronauts' ability to live and work in space for much more extended periods of time. The Gemini program accomplished a rendezvous between two manned spacecraft, as well as practicing rendezvous and docking procedures with an unmanned Agena 'docking target.' The latter was directly related to a maneuver that Apollo astronauts would ultimately have to perform in *lunar* orbit. In December 1965 Gemini 7 established an endurance record of 330.5 hours (two weeks), which simulated the length of time that it would take for a roundtrip to the moon with a week's stay. This mission, in fact, *exceeded* the duration of any of the Apollo missions.

As the Mercury and Gemini flights were taking place, North American Aviation's Space Division was working on the enormous task of designing Apollo to meet the deadline set by President Kennedy. The challenge, as North American viewed it, was 'to create an artificial world: a world large and complex enough to supply all the needs of three men for two weeks.' This 'world' had to contain all of the life-sustaining elements of Earth—food, air, shelter—as well as many special complex extras (navigation, propulsion, communications). Perhaps the greatest challenge was that of reliability. Everything had to work, and *keep* working no matter what the circumstances. Unlike the previous manned space programs in which crewmen could return to Earth almost within minutes if an emergency arose, it could be as much as three days before the Apollo crew could get back to Earth from the moon.

Above: The bell-shaped McDonnell Mercury *(left)* and Gemini *(right)* space capsules that were used for America's first 16 manned space missions between 1961 and 1966. *Right:* The Rockwell Apollo spacecraft CSM-011 was delivered to NASA at the Kennedy Space Center in June 1966 for an unmanned test flight two months later.

Basically, the NASA requirement was for a system containing (a) a booster rocket; (b) a spacecraft; and (c) a lunar landing craft. The purpose of the system would be to simply send a three-man crew *to* the moon, and into orbit *around* it. Two of the three men would then travel to the surface of the moon in the 'lunar lander,' while the third remained in orbit in the spacecraft. The system then would have to provide up to 35 hours on the moon, return the two moon explorers to the orbiting spacecraft, and return all three safely to Earth. The entire trip, from launch to Earth landing, was expected to last between eight and 10 days (including six days roundtrip flight time), although the Apollo spacecraft would be designed for 14-day operation to give a wide margin of safety.

By the peak of the Apollo's development, in 1966, there were 350,000 people at 20,000 companies involved. North American (which would become North American Rockwell a year later) had the central spacecraft contract worth $3.3 billion alone. Rockwell's Rocketdyne Division had the contract for the engines for the huge Saturn 5 rocket, which would launch Apollo, and Grumman Aircraft had the contract for the lunar landing vehicle.

THE APOLLO SPACECRAFT

Apollo was a three-part vehicle. First, there was the two-part spacecraft, which was built by North American Rockwell. It was composed of a cone-shaped Command Module (CM) in which the three astronauts would travel to and from the moon and re-enter the Earth's atmosphere. Behind the CM was the barrel-shaped Service Module (SM), which contained the service propulsion rocket engine to insert the CM/SM into lunar orbit (transfer from the ellipse of lunar approach to an orbit around the moon and reduce the craft's velocity with respect to the moon from 5600 to 3600 miles per hour), as well as electrical systems and supplies of oxygen, fuel and water to support the spacecraft and its crew. The CM was Apollo's 'dormitory' and 'cab,' while the SM was its 'engine' and 'physical plant.' The service propulsion rocket engine also injected the CSM into trajectory for return to Earth, increasing its velocity from 3600 to 5600 mph. Except during the time of the CM's re-entry into the Earth's atmosphere at the end of a flight, the CM and the SM were always joined into a single spacecraft unit known as the Command/Service Module (CSM).

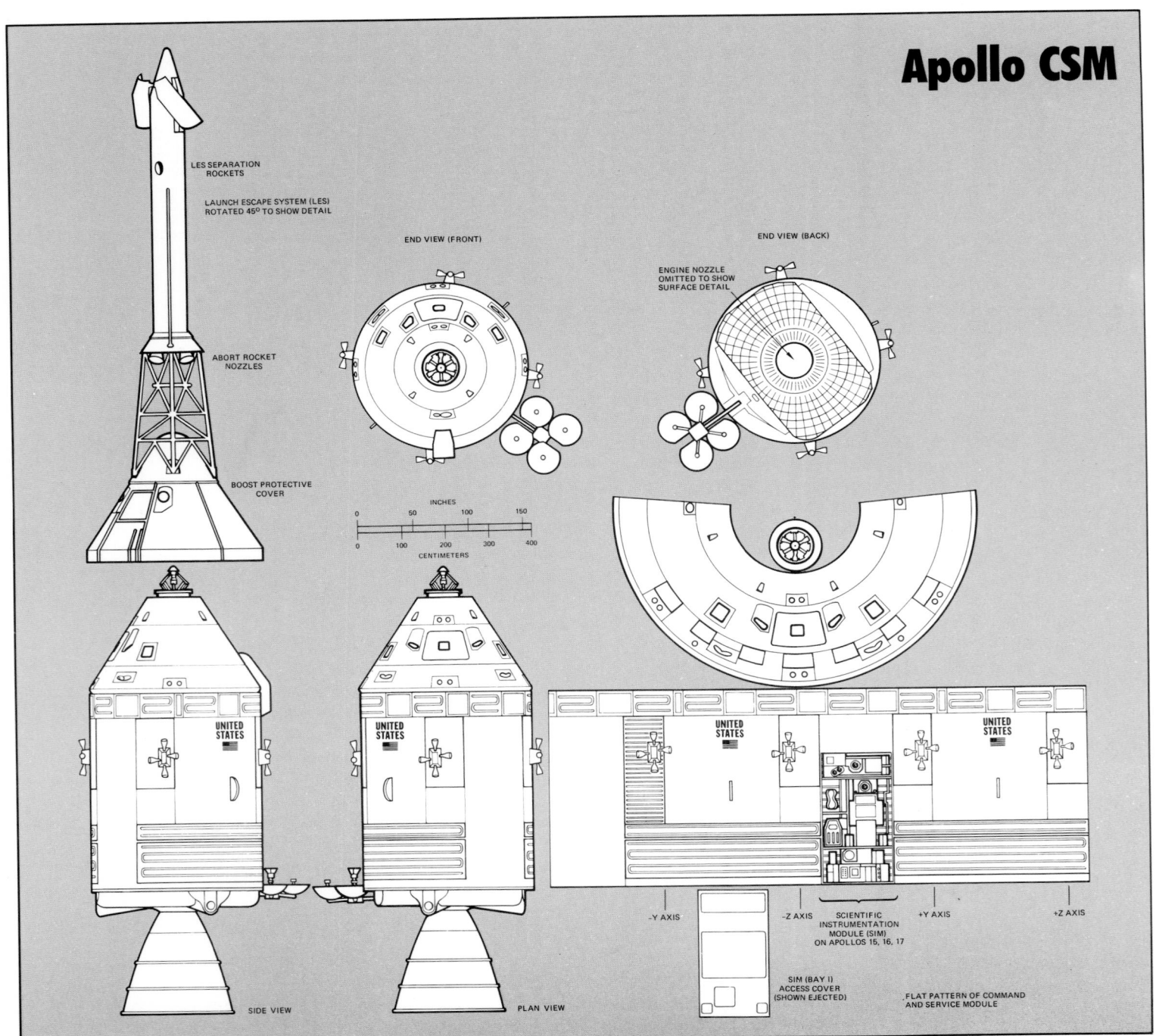

Above: The delivery of the new Apollo CSM-101 to Kennedy Space Center in August 1968. Compare this photo to the drawings *at left and right*.

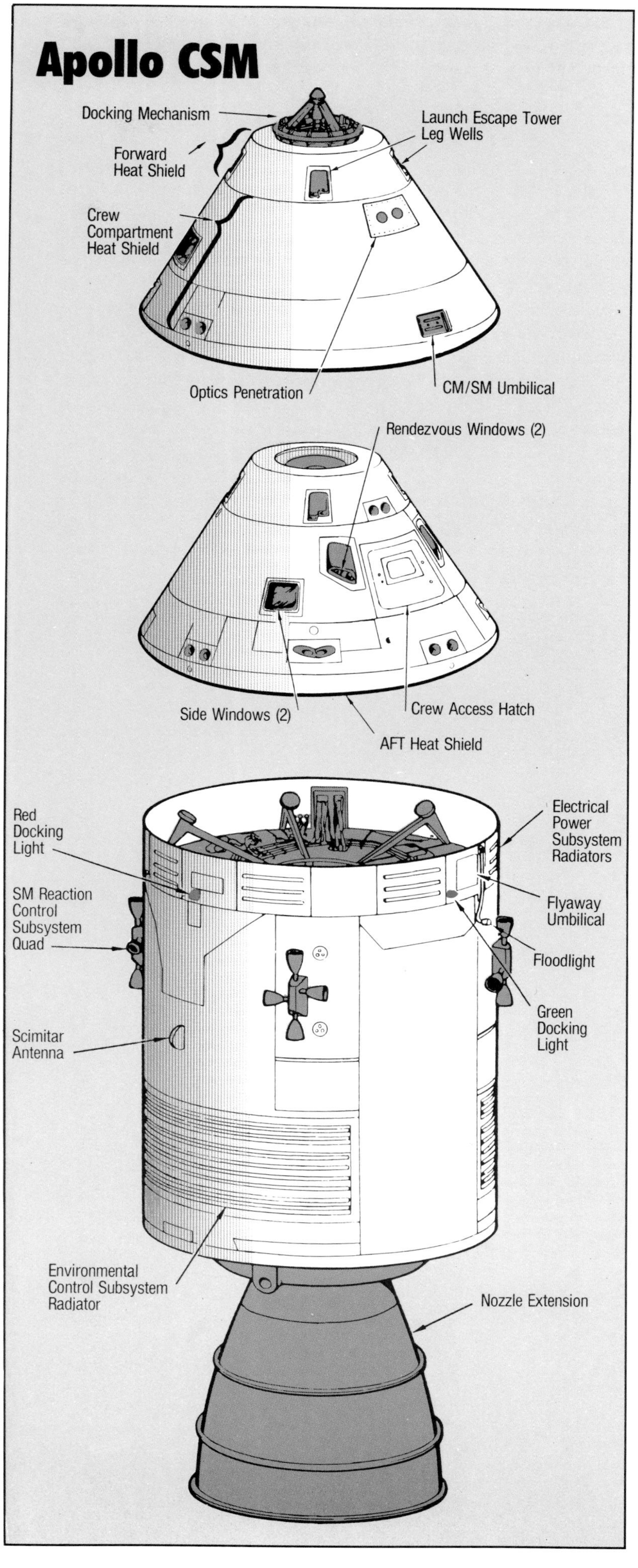

Apollo CSM

- Docking Mechanism
- Launch Escape Tower Leg Wells
- Forward Heat Shield
- Crew Compartment Heat Shield
- Optics Penetration
- CM/SM Umbilical

- Rendezvous Windows (2)
- Side Windows (2)
- Crew Access Hatch
- AFT Heat Shield

- Red Docking Light
- SM Reaction Control Subsystem Quad
- Scimitar Antenna
- Environmental Control Subsystem Radiator
- Electrical Power Subsystem Radiators
- Flyaway Umbilical
- Floodlight
- Green Docking Light
- Nozzle Extension

The Grumman Lunar Excursion Module (LEM, or LM) was to be carried into Earth orbit packed into an adapter 'sleeve' (also built by North American Rockwell) that was located atop the Saturn 5 below the CSM. After the third stage, the booster was to be reignited for translunar injection, and during intitial translunar coast the 'sleeve' would be jettisoned from the third stage (S-IVB) and CSM. The CSM would then turn around and extract the LM from the S-IVB. The astronauts in the CSM would then rendezvous with the unmanned LM and attach it to the 'nose' of the CSM. The LM would be carried to the moon attached thusly to the CSM. Once in lunar orbit, two of the astronauts would transfer to the LM for the roundtrip to the lunar surface. As such, the LM carried completely separate and adequate stocks of oxygen and other supplies. The LM would, in turn, be discarded after use, and all three astronauts would return to the Earth in the CSM, jettison the SM, and re-enter the atmosphere in the CM.

North American Rockwell's contract included 45 CSMs, of which 24 were Block 1, first generation spacecraft. The first manned mission was intended to have been in CM Number 012, but when it was destroyed by fire in January 1967, the Block 2 spacecraft were developed and the Block 1 spacecraft were relegated to testing. Of these, six were actually tested in unmanned space flights, of which two (Apollo 4 and Apollo 6) featured the entire CSM unit.

Of the 21 Block 2 CSMs, three were used for ground testing prior to any manned flights, and two others were used for manned Earth orbit

flights prior to the lunar missions. There were nine CSMs that achieved manned lunar orbit, six of which supported actual lunar landings. An additional four CSMs would be used for Earth orbit missions after the last lunar mission, and three Block 2 CSMs were not used. These were not maintained in flight-ready condition and will never be used.

In addition to the 45 CSMs, North American Rockwell built four mission simulators, five trainers, 23 full-scale mock-ups for design studies and 30 'boiler plate' engineering test CSMs, which were essentially 'empty' CSM shells that were used for launch, impact, recovery and dynamic tests during the 1963 to 1965 development period.

PROJECT DEVELOPMENT

The initial design phase of the Apollo spacecraft was completed in less than a year and the first 'boiler plate' CM (BP-1) was delivered to NASA on 7 September 1962. The first low-altitude flight test of a boiler plate (BP-6) was conducted on 12 March 1963, and two months later, on 28 May, the BP-13 was placed into orbit from Cape Kennedy. By the time of the first manned mission of the Gemini program in March 1965, six unmanned Apollo boiler plate CMs or SMs had already been launched and testing of the launch escape system was underway.

On 26 February 1966 NASA conducted the first unmanned space flight of an actual fully configured Apollo spacecraft. The purpose of

the test was to determine the system's ability to withstand entry temperatures, determine adequacy of the CM for manned entry from low orbit, to test command and service module reaction control engines and to test the service module engine firing and restart capability. Recovery was made in the south Atlantic, 5300 miles downrange from the Kennedy Space Center, near Ascension Island.

A second successful test was run on 25 August, in which the CSM was sent into space for most of one orbit and recovered in the Pacific. These tests paved the way for what was to have been the start of manned Apollo flights.

There were to be three manned, Earth-orbit evaluation flights during 1967, beginning on 21 February. The crew that was selected for the Apollo 1 mission included Ed White, a veteran of Gemini 4 (and the first American to walk in space) along with Roger Chaffee. The third member of the crew—and the mission commander—was Virgil 'Gus' Grissom, who had flown in space on the second Mercury flight in 1961 and had commanded the first Gemini mission in 1965.

On 27 January 1967, three weeks before the launch, the crew were in Apollo 1 conducting a routine ground test when a flash fire broke out.

'We've got a fire in the cockpit,' screamed Grissom as White began trying to open the hatch. The fire spread quickly in the pure oxygen atmosphere of the capsule, and it soon became a blazing inferno. Chaffee's words were the last recorded from the crew: 'We've got a bad fire, let's get out, we're burning up.'

Fighting their way through the smoke, NASA, as well as North American, technicians reached the capsule and finally removed the hatches. Five minutes had passed since the fire had started. All three men were dead. Though badly burned by the fire, the three men's fate was sealed by the suffocating smoke.

In the aftermath of the disaster, NASA put the entire Apollo program on hold until the cause of the fire could be fully investigated and the problems eliminated. As the prime contractor for the CSM, the bulk of this chore fell to Rockwell. They redesigned the interior of the spacecraft, from the hatch to the wiring. Some thought was given to using an atmosphere of nitrogen plus oxygen like that of the Earth's atmosphere and like that used aboard Soviet spacecraft, but this idea was rejected. However, by redesigning the wiring and fireproofing the interior, it was felt that a future disaster could be avoided. Most important—at least symbolically—was the redesigned outward-opening hatch that took five rather than 90 seconds to open.

The fire had cost NASA three of its best astronauts, but it also had cost the Apollo program more than a year of delay. Instead of three manned and two unmanned flights during 1967, only one unmanned flight was made. This test, which took place on 9 November and which was designated Apollo 4, involved the first use of the Saturn 5 launch vehicle, as well as the first *orbital* flight of a CSM. Just two years remained in the decade. If Kennedy's goal for the American space program was to be met, everything had to move ahead flawlessly.

Far left: NAA engineers Charles Feltz and Robert Templeton inspect the first full scale Apollo CM mockup in April 1962. *Left:* CSM-009 is hoisted up the gantry for its February 1966 unmanned flight. The conical adapter sleeve below the CSM would be used to house the LM during the manned operational launches.

Above from top: Gus Grissom, Ed White and Roger Chaffee shortly before their deaths on 27 January 1967 in the tragic fire that destroyed the Apollo 1 Spacecraft.

The first unmanned test in space of the LM came with Apollo 5 on 22 January 1968, and the redesigned CSM was tested in space again on 4 April during Apollo 6. By the end of April, NASA had decided that no further unmanned Apollo space flights were necessary to evaluate the system before putting the program back on track.

APOLLO TO THE MOON

The long-awaited first manned Apollo flight, designated Apollo 7, was launched on 11 October 1968, 21 months behind schedule. The crew for the flight was Walter Schirra (like the late Grissom, one of the original Mercury seven), Walter Cunningham and Donn Eisele. They conducted a rendezvous with the Saturn 4B upper stage of their Saturn 1B launch vehicle in the same manner that the Gemini astronauts had rendezvoused with the Agena two years earlier. They then carried out exhaustive tests of the spacecraft's system under operational conditions. Schirra came down with a head cold that the others caught, and this led to a decision not to wear helmets during re-entry to keep the pressure on their ear drums equalized as cabin pressure changed during descent. The only long-term effect from this was that Schirra showed up in television commercials 17 years later using the incident to advertise a cold remedy.

A disastrous setback had been overcome and the American space program was back on the road to the moon. By this time, however, the Soviet lunar program was moving ahead rapidly. In September 1968, one month before Apollo 7, the Soviets had sent an unmanned Zond spacecraft, similar to their Soyuz-type manned craft, to the vicinity of the moon and back.

Apollo 8 was launched atop a Saturn 5 on 21 December 1968, less than two months after the splashdown of Apollo 7. Aboard the CSM were Frank Borman, James Lovell and William Anders. Ten hours and 55 minutes after launch they were out of Earth orbit and conducting their first midcourse correction enroute to the moon.

One minute short of 69 hours, Apollo 8 reached and swung around the back side of the moon. Nine minutes later the CSM's engines were fired and the spacecraft was placed into lunar orbit.

Apollo 8 made 10 lunar orbits in 20 hours, during which time no one aboard gave any thought to sleep as they photographed the lunar surface and conducted surveys that could be used in planning subsequent landings.

Three days later, at 146 hours and 31 minutes, the CM separated from the SM and plunged into the Earth's atmosphere at 24,696 mph. Borman, Lovell and Anders splashed down in the Pacific on 27 December 1968 after a 147-hour, half-million-mile journey. Soviet Premier Brezshnev sent his congratulations and announced that his country had 'no intention' of sending a man to the moon. The Soviets *had* been working feverishly to that end, but they now recognized that the race was lost and it would be better in the long run to drop out rather than come in second. The American space program clearly had momentum.

The next step in the Apollo program was the March 1969 Earth-orbit mission of Apollo 9, which would be the first time that a manned CSM

was accompanied by an LM. As such, the Apollo 9 mission also involved the first rendezvous and docking in space between a CSM and the LM vehicle which would actually land on the moon. The Apollo 9 crew also set the precedent of naming the CSM and LM. The names they chose—*Gumdrop* for the CSM and *Spider* for the LM—were particularly descriptive of the shapes of the two craft.

During the course of the five-day mission, the Apollo 9 crew conducted numerous tests with *Gumdrop* and *Spider*, including docking and redocking numerous times. At one point, James McDivitt and Russell Schweichart 'flew' *Spider* 133 miles from David Scott in *Gumdrop* and simulated the process of the rendezvous of an LM with a CSM after a lunar landing.

Two months later the crew of Apollo 10 combined the experiences of the two earlier missions by practicing the rendezvous between CSM and LM *while in lunar orbit*! At one point Tom Stafford and Gene Cernan detached from the CSM *Charlie Brown* and flew the LM *Snoopy* to within ten miles of the lunar surface.

Apollo 10 marked the end of seven years of step-by-step planning and rehearsals. Only eight months were left in the decade during which President Kennedy had pledged the nation to landing a man on the moon.

Below left: The crew of Apollo 7 (with Wally Schirra in the foreground) aboard CSM-101 prior to the first Apollo manned spaceflight. *Right:* CSM-109 was delivered to Kennedy Space Center in 1970. *Below:* The breathtaking earthrise as first witnessed by the Apollo 8 crew on Christmas eve in 1968.

Apollo 11 was launched on 16 July 1969 and reached lunar orbit 70 hours and 50 minutes later. After spending a day checking their equipment, astronauts Neil Armstrong and Edwin Aldrin detached the LM *Eagle* from the CSM *Columbia* and began the two-and-one-half hour descent to the musty, gray surface below. Then, with NASA control and Houston telling them that they had only 30 seconds of fuel remaining for the landing, Aldrin brought *Eagle* slowly down.

Said Armstrong, 'Forward... drifting right... contact light. Okay engine stop... descent engine override off. Engine arm off.'

Sensing that history had just been made, Houston replied, 'We copy you down, *Eagle*.'

Over the quarter million miles of space came Armstrong's confirmation, 'Houston, Tranquillity Base here... the *Eagle* has landed.'

'Roger, Tranquillity,' said Houston Control, 'we copy you on the ground. You've got a bunch of guys about to turn blue. We're breathing again. Thanks a lot!'

'Thank you,' replied the crew of the *Eagle* from mankind's first fragile outpost on another celestial body.

The Apollo 11 LM landed in the moon's Sea of Tranquillity on 20 July 1969, 102 hours and 45 minutes after leaving the Earth. Nearly seven hours later, Armstrong opened the *Eagle*'s hatch and made his way down the LM's ladder to the ground.

'I'm at the foot of the ladder,' he said. 'The LM footpads are only depressed in the surface about one or two inches, although the surface appears to be very, very fine grained. As you get close to it, it's almost like powder. I'm going to step off the LM now. That's one small step for man... one giant leap for mankind.'

Neil Armstrong was 109 hours and 24 minutes from planet Earth, but the dreams of centuries were fulfilled in his single step. Mankind had walked upon the moon.

With the words 'magnificent desolation' on his lips, Edwin Aldrin followed Armstrong down the ladder. They set up a television camera about 30 feet from *Eagle*, gathered samples and walked up to 300 feet from the landing site they'd dubbed 'Tranquillity Base.' Their first outing on the lunar surface lasted about two and one-half hours. The entire first visit to the moon lasted 21 hours and 36 minutes and included seven hours of sleep for the two men. (One wonders how they *could* sleep!)

The Apollo 12 mission, launched on 14 November 1969, followed essentially the same pattern as Apollo 11, but with a longer stay on the

Above: The heat-scarred Apollo 11 CSM is recovered in the Pacific after the milestone lunar mission. *Right:* The Apollo 13 launch with the CSM dwarfed by the huge Saturn 5. The chart *at far right* details the number of Apollo and Saturn components that were produced by North American Rockwell or its Rocketdyne subsidiary.

Saturn 5/Apollo

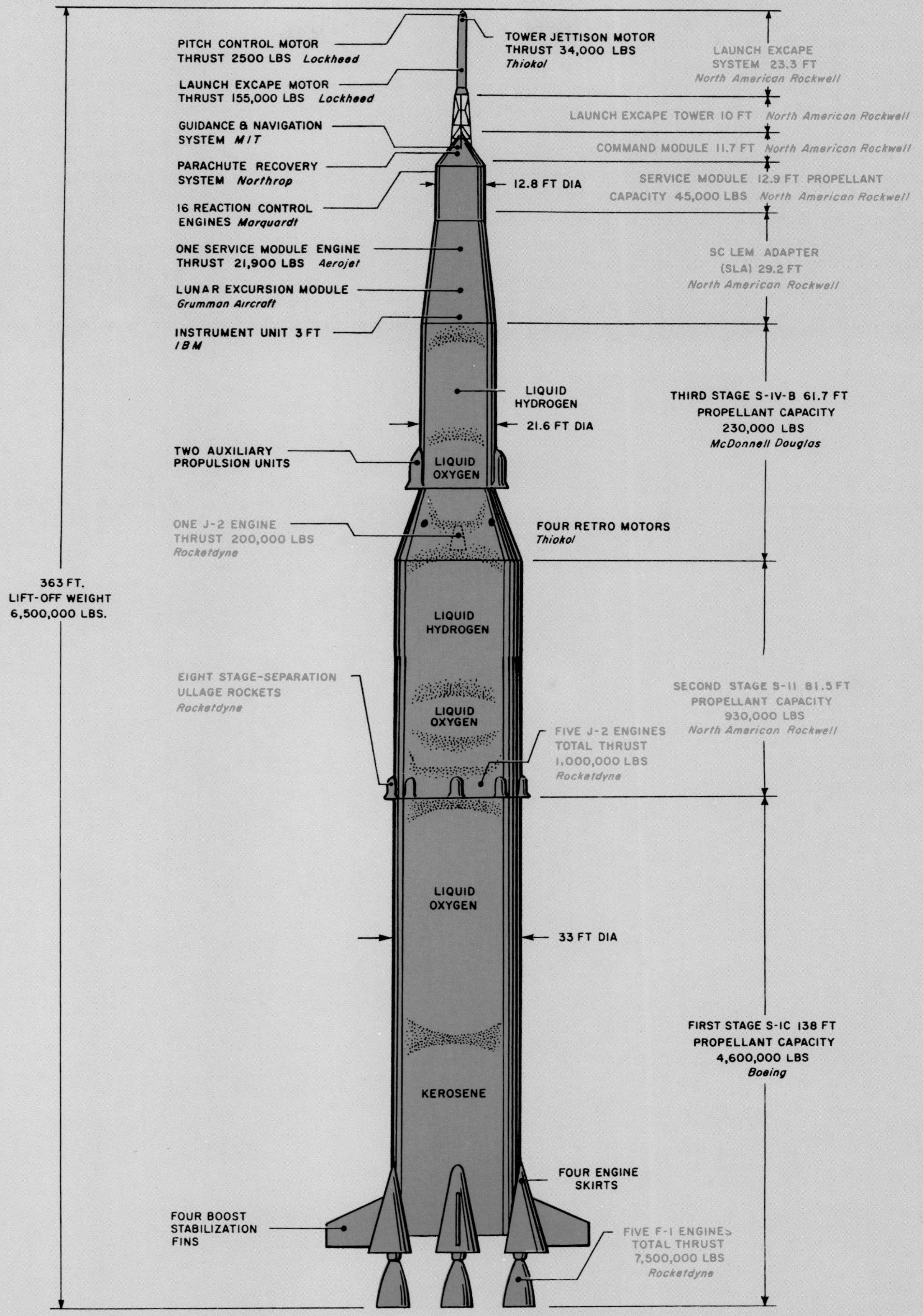

PITCH CONTROL MOTOR
THRUST 2500 LBS *Lockheed*

TOWER JETTISON MOTOR
THRUST 34,000 LBS
Thiokol

LAUNCH EXCAPE
SYSTEM 23.3 FT
North American Rockwell

LAUNCH EXCAPE MOTOR
THRUST 155,000 LBS *Lockheed*

GUIDANCE & NAVIGATION
SYSTEM *MIT*

LAUNCH EXCAPE TOWER 10 FT *North American Rockwell*

PARACHUTE RECOVERY
SYSTEM *Northrop*

COMMAND MODULE 11.7 FT *North American Rockwell*

12.8 FT DIA

SERVICE MODULE 12.9 FT PROPELLANT
CAPACITY 45,000 LBS *North American Rockwell*

16 REACTION CONTROL
ENGINES *Marquardt*

ONE SERVICE MODULE ENGINE
THRUST 21,900 LBS *Aerojet*

SC LEM ADAPTER
(SLA) 29.2 FT
North American Rockwell

LUNAR EXCURSION MODULE
Grumman Aircraft

INSTRUMENT UNIT 3 FT
IBM

LIQUID
HYDROGEN

THIRD STAGE S-IV-B 61.7 FT
PROPELLANT CAPACITY
230,000 LBS
McDonnell Douglas

21.6 FT DIA

TWO AUXILIARY
PROPULSION UNITS

LIQUID
OXYGEN

ONE J-2 ENGINE
THRUST 200,000 LBS
Rocketdyne

FOUR RETRO MOTORS
Thiokol

363 FT.
LIFT-OFF WEIGHT
6,500,000 LBS.

LIQUID
HYDROGEN

EIGHT STAGE-SEPARATION
ULLAGE ROCKETS
Rocketdyne

LIQUID
OXYGEN

SECOND STAGE S-II 81.5 FT
PROPELLANT CAPACITY
930,000 LBS
North American Rockwell

FIVE J-2 ENGINES
TOTAL THRUST
1,000,000 LBS
Rocketdyne

LIQUID
OXYGEN

33 FT DIA

FIRST STAGE S-IC 138 FT
PROPELLANT CAPACITY
4,600,000 LBS
Boeing

KEROSENE

FOUR BOOST
STABILIZATION
FINS

FOUR ENGINE
SKIRTS

FIVE F-1 ENGINES
TOTAL THRUST
7,500,000 LBS
Rocketdyne

lunar surface. The mission also assured that not one, but two, American crews would walk upon the moon before the end of the 1960s.

The Apollo 13 mission, which came three months into the new decade, almost turned out to be another major disaster. The crew aboard the CSM *Odyssey* was nearly 56 hours into the mission and nearing the moon when a loud blast suddenly rocked the spacecraft. The Number 2 oxygen tank in the service module had just exploded as the result of an electrical short circuit and precious oxygen began leaking into space from both Number 1 and Number 2 tanks. Had the spark occurred anywhere but in airless outer space, an electrical fire would have resulted that would have destroyed the spacecraft.

Because of the loss of oxygen and electrical power to the CSM, the mission and even the survival of the crew was in question. There was certainly no longer enough oxygen to sustain a moon landing, so that part of the mission was quickly abandoned. Beyond this, however, lurked the fear that there might not be enough oxygen to get the crew back to Earth alive. The crew was forced to essentially 'turn off' the

CM and abandon it for the undamaged LM. Using the oxygen stored there, they turned the LM *Aquarius* into a 'lifeboat.'

Because the SM had been severely damaged in the explosion, its power could not be used to slow the spacecraft and turn it around. Therefore, Apollo 13 had to continue to coast to the moon under its then-present momentum and use the lunar gravity to swing the craft around and hurl it back to Earth.

Five hours after the explosion, John Swigert, James Lovell and Fred Haise reached the moon, completed a half-orbit turn around it and set a course for home, praying that the oxygen in *Aquarius* would be enough.

Back on Earth, people around the world watched and prayed as NASA and Rockwell engineers worked out the calculations that they

The Apollo CSM in lunar orbit: Apollo 15's CSM-12 *Endeavor (right)* and Apollo 17's CSM-114 *America (below)*, probably the last manned spacecraft to fly in lunar orbit in the twentieth century.

hoped would give the crew the margin they would need to get home alive. Any number of things could have gone wrong. The men in the *Aquarius* could have simply run out of oxygen. *Aquarius* was designed to support two men on the moon for a day and a half, but now it had to support three men for more than three days. If the oxygen was ample, then there was the problem of the electricity failing and the men freezing to death. Finally, and in many ways most frightening of all, was the prospect of the engines malfunctioning during the required midcourse correction. If that happened, the crew would pass near the Earth and hurtle into the emptiness of space, lost forever among the stars.

The midcourse correction went smoothly after all, but the powered-down spacecraft got colder and colder. The craft was still 18 hours from Earth orbit and near freezing when calculations determined that it was close enough to Earth for the astronauts to return to *Odyssey* and begin bringing the power back up. The astronauts had conserved the resources of the *Odyssey* by tapping into the LM's environmental control system. By doing this, they had ensured enough electrical power for 24 hours and enough water for drinking and cooling the spacecraft's systems for eight hours after that.

Eighteen hours later, and four long days after the explosion, the crew fired the CM's thrusters and they worked. They sealed the passageway between *Aquarius* and *Odyssey* and said farewell to their lifeboat. Less than an hour later, the CM plunged into Earth's atmosphere and 14 hours and 55 minutes after they'd left Earth, Lovell, Haise and Swigert were bobbing in the Pacific Ocean and savoring the sweet smell of Earth's atmosphere.

Once again, the Apollo program was put on hold while Rockwell and NASA engineers went to work troubleshooting the problem and redesigning the SM. Modifications and safety features added up to nearly half a ton of increased gross weight, but the program was back on track within a year, and Apollo 14 was launched on 31 January 1971.

Apollo 15, launched on 26 July 1971, was the first of three Apollo J-series missions. It was capable of staying longer on the lunar surface and equipped for more extensive scientific studies in the areas of lunar surface science, lunar orbital science and operational engineering. In

APOLLO CSM/LM MISSIONS

Mission Designation	Dates	Duration (Hours)	Crew*	Lunar Samples Collected (lbs)	Lunar Landing Site
Block 1 Spacecraft (unmanned)					
CSM-009 test	26 February 1966		None	—	—
CSM-011 test	25 August 1966		None	—	—
Apollo 1	21 February 1967	0	Gus Grissom, Roger Chaffee, Ed White	None	(Capsule and crew lost 27 January 1967)
Apollo 4	9 November 1967		None	—	—
Apollo 5	22 January 1968		None	—	—
Apollo 6	4 April 1968		None	—	—
Block 2 Spacecraft (manned)					
Apollo 7	11-22 October 1968	260	Wally Shirra, Donn Eisele, Walter Cunningham	None	(Earth orbit only)
Apollo 8	21-27 December 1968	147	Frank Borman, James Lovell, William Anders	None	(Lunar orbit only)
Apollo 9	3-13 March 1969	241	James McDivitt, David Scott, Russell Schweickart	None	(Earth orbit only)
Apollo 10	18-26 May 1969	192	Tom Stafford, John Young, Gene Cernan	None	(Lunar orbit only)
Apollo 11	16-23 July 1969	195	Neil Armstrong, Michael Collins, Edwin Aldrin	44	Sea of Tranquillity
Apollo 12	14-24 November 1969	245	Charles Conrad, Richard Gordon, Alan Bean	75	Sea of Storms
Apollo 13	11-17 April 1970	143	James Lovell, John Swigert, Fred Haise	None	(Mission aborted)
Apollo 14	31 January-9 February 1971	216	Alan Shepard, Stuart Roosa, Edgar Mitchell	94	Fra Mauro Crater
Block 2 Spacecraft: Apollo J (manned)					
Apollo 15	26 July-7 August 1971	295	David Scott, Alfred Worden, James Irwin	173	Hadley-Appenine region
Apollo 16	16-27 April 1972	266	John Young, Thomas Mattingly, Charles Duke	209	Descartes region
Apollo 17	7-19 December 1972	302	Gene Cernan, Ronald Evans, Harrison Schmitt	250	Taurus-Littrow region
Block 2 Spacecraft: Apollo/Skylab missions (manned)					
Apollo/Skylab 2	25 May-22 June 1973	673	Charles Conrad, Joseph Kerwin, Paul Weitz	—	—
Apollo/Skylab 3	28 July-25 September 1973	1427	Alan Bean, Owen Garriott, Jack Lousma	—	—
Apollo/Skylab 4	16 November 1973-8 February 1974	2017	Gerald Carr, Robert Gibson, William Pogue	—	—
Block 2 Spacecraft: Apollo-Soyuz Test Project (manned)					
ASTP	15-24 July 1975	217	Tom Stafford, Vance Brand, Deke Slayton	—	—

*Mission Commanders are listed first, CSM pilots second through Apollo 17, LM pilots third through Apollo 17. Those LM pilots listed third on Apollo 11, 12 and 14-17, as well as the respective mission commanders, walked upon the lunar surface.

the equipment bay of the LM, the Apollo J also carried the four-wheeled, 462 pound Lunar Roving Vehicle (LVR). The 'Rover' was capable of carrying two astronauts for up to 50 miles at speeds of 8.7 mph. While this was not the kind of speed that would amaze the drivers on earthly freeways, it greatly expanded the areas of the lunar surface that could be explored.

The final two Apollo J missions came in 1972 and marked the end of mankind's exploration of the moon for probably the rest of the century. Like the other post-Apollo 14 flights, Apollo 16 and Apollo 17 went exactly as planned, with each mission extending the crew's duration on the lunar surface.

THE POST-LUNAR APOLLO

NASA had originally intended to continue the lunar landing program through Apollo 20 in 1974. There were certainly enough qualified astronauts and a sufficient number of flight-rated Apollo spacecraft and Saturn 5 launch vehicles available. However, the cost of running the missions was simply more than NASA could afford. The Apollo program had cost $25 billion and had successfully landed twelve men on the lunar surface, so it was time to move forward.

The next step in NASA's overall plan for manned space flight involved an Earth-orbiting space station. The plan had once involved a 100-person, continuously staffed station that would be in place by the mid-1970s. With the high cost of the Vietnam War and of the Johnson administration's 'Great Society' welfare boondoggle, however, NASA's grand space station—like the continued lunar missions—was no longer economically viable. The compromise was Skylab, a three-man, 100-ton station built by McDonnell Douglas. The major part of Skylab—its orbital workshop and crew quarters—were fashioned from the third stage (S-IVB) of a Saturn launch vehicle. The remaining Apollo CSMs would become an important part of the Skylab program, as they would be used to transfer crews to and from the space station where they would live and work for up to four months.

Skylab itself was launched on 14 May 1973 in the last operational use of a Saturn 5 rocket, the launch vehicle that had been used on all

APOLLO CSM/LM SPECIFICATIONS

Mission Designation	Rockwell CSM Serial Number	Code Name (CSM)	Weight with Fuel (SM)	Weight with Fuel (CM)	Grumman LM Serial Number	Code Name (LM)	Weight with Fuel (LM)
Block 1 Spacecraft (unmanned)							
CSM-009 test	CSM-009	—	55,000	12,000	—	—	—
CSM-011 test	CSM-011	—	55,000	12,000	—	—	—
Apollo 4	CSM-017	—	55,000	12,000	LTA-1R	—	29,500 (dummy)
Apollo 5	no CSM	no CSM	no CSM	no CSM	LM-1	—	31,700
Apollo 6	CSM-020	—	42,600	12,500	LTA-2R	—	26,000
Block 2 Spacecraft (manned)							
Apollo 7	CSM-101	—	49,730	12,659	—	—	None
Apollo 8	CSM-103	—	51,258	12,392	LTA-B	—	ballast only
Apollo 9	CSM-104	Gumdrop	36,159	12,405	LM-3	Spider	32,021
Apollo 10	CSM-106	Charlie Brown	51,371	12,277	LM-4	Snoopy	30,849
Apollo 11	CSM-107	Columbia	51,243	12,250	LM-5	Eagle	33,205
Apollo 12	CSM-108	Yankee Clipper	51,105	12,365	LM-6	Intrepid	33,325
Apollo 13	CSM-109	Odyssey	51,099	12,327	LM-7	Aquarius	32,124
Apollo 14	CSM-110	Kitty Hawk	51,744	12,694	LM-8	Antares	33,680
Block 2 Spacecraft: Apollo J (manned)							
Apollo 15	CSM-112	Endeavor	54,044	12,774	LM-10	Falcon	36,230
Apollo 16	CSM-113	Casper	54,044	12,874	LM-11	Orion	36,218
Apollo 17	CSM-114	America	54,044	12,800	LM-12	Challenger	36,262
Block 2 Spacecraft: Apollo/Skylab missions (manned)							
Apollo/Skylab 2	CSM-116	—	17,000	13,200	—	—	None
Apollo/Skylab 3	CSM-117	—	17,000	13,200	—	—	None
Apollo/Skylab 4	CSM-118	—	17,000	13,200	—	—	None
Block 2 Spacecraft: Apollo-Soyuz Test Project							
ASTP	CSM-119	Apollo	17,676	13,105	—	—	None

previous Apollo lunar flights. The first crew was supposed to have been launched immediately, but one of Skylab's solar arrays was severely damaged in its launch and there was some doubt whether the station could function without it. The crew was launched eleven days after, when it was determined that Skylab would be habitable.

Between May 1973 and February 1974, three crews spent 28, 59 and 84 days on three visits to Skylab. In each case, their Apollo CSM proved functional after being 'parked' in a powered-down condition for their entire stay. During the second Skylab mission, astronauts Jack Lousma, Dr Owen Garriott and Apollo 12 veteran Alan Bean discovered a problem with the thrusters on their SM. NASA considered the immediate launch of another Apollo CSM on a rescue mission, but, realizing that the crew could survive for months aboard Skylab, they decided to give the astronauts time to execute a repair themselves, which they did.

The final Apollo Skylab mission set a new record for manned duration in space of over 2017 hours, but despite the optimism at the time, it was the end of an era. No American crew would come close to equaling that record for the balance of the century, yet it would be matched many times over by Soviet cosmonauts aboard their Salyut and Mir space stations in the decade to come.

It was symbolic of the era of superpower detente—and of Soviet ascendancy in space—that the last mission flown by Apollo spacecraft involved a rendezvous between Soviets and Americans in space. The idea for a joint mission was agreed upon in principle during the 1972 summit between Leonid Brezshnev and Richard Nixon, and engineering teams from both sides met soon afterward to design a docking module and system. Astronauts and cosmonauts paid visits to one another's space centers and toured one another's spacecraft in anticipation of what would be called the Apollo-Soyuz Test Project (ASTP).

Below: An artist's conception of Apollo CSM-119 during its historic 1975 rendezvous with the Soviet Soyuz 19. *Facing page:* Apollo 17 Commander Gene Cernan on the lunar surface in December 1972. Rockwell had built enough CSMs for three more landings, but Apollo 17 would be the last. *Overleaf:* The Apollo 16 CSM *Casper* after its return to earth.

On 15 July 1975 the last Apollo spacecraft was launched from the Kennedy Space Center, crewed by veteran Apollo astronaut Tom Stafford, along with Vance Brand and Deke Slayton. Slayton, who had been picked as one of the original Mercury astronauts 14 years earlier, had, ironically, never flown in space before. Seven hours before the Apollo ASTP launch, the USSR had launched their Soyuz 19 spacecraft from the Baikonur Cosmodrome, with veteran cosmonauts Valeri Kubasov and Alexei Leonov aboard.

The historic rendezvous and docking of the two ships took place two days later, on 17 July. The first international handshake in space was followed by a congenial series of visits to the two craft over a period of four days. Soyuz 19 returned to Earth on 21 July, but the Apollo ASTP craft remained in space for another three days.

Their return to Earth on 24 July marked the successful conclusion of 15 manned Apollo missions spanning a period of eight years. The Apollo spacecraft had not worked flawlessly, but everyone that had taken a crew into space had gotten them home alive. Most remarkable, of course, was that the system had gone from an idea to a flight-ready craft in just six years, and the North American/Rockwell Apollo CSM had taken 27 human beings on flybys of the moon and two dozen of them into lunar orbit! It was an astounding system whose tremendous feat will not be equaled in this century.

There were proposals to run one Earth-orbit manned mission a year through 1978 just to keep the United States active in space until the Space Shuttle came on line, but this scheme was abandoned as being too costly for the dwindling resources of the American space agency. Three CSMs still remained, but they were 'all dressed up, with nowhere to go.' Long before the Apollo-Soyuz Test Project, indeed long before Apollo 17, Rockwell and NASA had begun to dismantle the vast infrastructure and pool of engineering and management expertise that had made the Apollo lunar landings possible. The mold, so to speak, had been broken. People began to marvel at Apollo the way they had once marveled at the Egyptian pyramids. Indeed, Apollo will certainly stand as one of the wonders of the twentieth century, if not of all time.

THE B-1 PROGRAM

After the inglorious demise of the XB-70 program, the Strategic Air Command (SAC) was left with no potential successor for the B-52. SAC's original plan had been to begin augmenting and replacing the B-52 with production B-70s by the end of the 1960s. This would not now be possible, and it was certainly fortunate that Boeing's B-52 was the airplane it was, for it has had to remain in service three times longer than expected. The Air Force got more than its money's worth, while Boeing was paid the tribute of having the B-52 likely to continue in useful service until the 1990s.

A new aircraft to augment and replace the B-52 was luckily not needed in the 1960s, but it was certainly true that such a plane would be needed *some day*. That day turned out to be the mid-1980s, and the airplane was the Rockwell B-1.

EARLY DEVELOPMENT

The idea which eventually evolved into the B-1 began as the Advanced Manned Strategic Aircraft (AMSA) project in 1962. At that time, the XB-70 was clearly doomed by Defense Secretary Robert McNamara's desire to rely more and more on ICBMs for SAC's strategic capability. The Air Force knew that they would eventually need a *manned* strategic aircraft, and AMSA was a research and development project that would keep the idea alive, even if it would progress at a slower pace than they would have liked.

The Air Force published their AMSA requirements in 1965 and indicated that they wanted the new aircraft to be operational at squadron strength by 1980. After having entertained AMSA proposals from several manufacturers, the Air Force finally settled on the Los Angeles Division of North American Rockwell (now North American Aircraft Operations Division of Rockwell International).

Under the Defense Department nomenclature reorganization, all combat aircraft numbering was restarted at one. The new AMSA bomber was, of course, designated B-1. It is an interesting point of trivia that in the twenty years preceding 1972, 40 bomber projects received 'B' designations (including 19 that actually went into service), while in the same length of time since 1962 there was only one, the B-1.

A contract was issued on 6 June 1970, calling for five flight-test aircraft and two non-flying airframes to be used in instructional tests. General Electric, the engine contractor, was asked to build 40 F101 turbofan engines, which translated as one complete replacement set for each of the five prototypes. This initial order was reduced in January

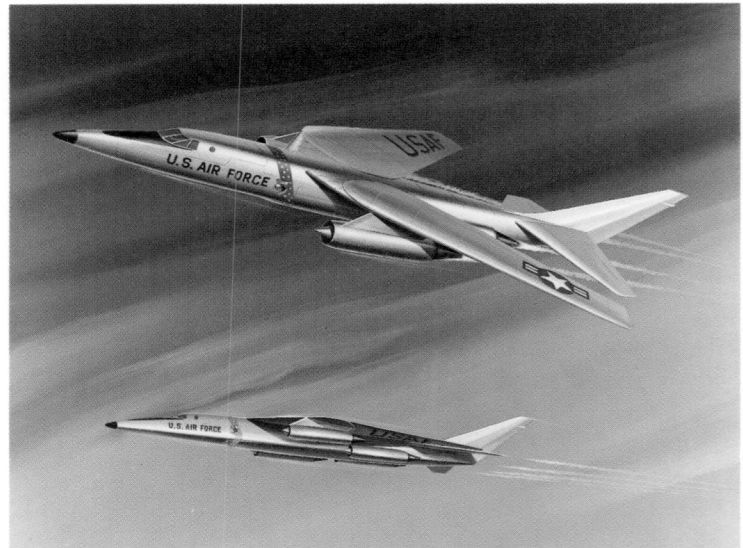

Above: Compare these early Rockwell artist's conceptions of the AMSA to the views of the B-1A on pages 178-179. The size and basic configuration was established early, but the wing form and engine placement changed a number of times before a final choice was made.

Facing page: Initially, the B-1As (like the XB-70s) were painted gloss white to reflect heat from a nuclear blast, but during low-level bombing tests in the 1970s, two of them were repainted in the desert camouflage scheme seen here.

1971 to three flight-test aircraft, one non-flying airframe, and 27 engines. At the same time, the constantly evolving design for the new plane was frozen and production began.

The actual assembly of the first of what was intended to be 250 B-1s began at the Air Force's Plant 42 at Palmdale, California on 15 March 1972. This aircraft rolled out on 26 October 1974 and made its maiden flight on 23 December. The second B-1 prototype (the avionics systems test aircraft) did not fly until 14 June 1976, three months after the first flight of the third prototype on 26 March.

By the time that Democrat Jimmy Carter replaced Republican Gerald Ford in the White House in January 1977, it was clear that the three B-1 prototypes had flown into a turbulent storm of controversy from which they would not emerge unscathed. Carter had campaigned for the presidency on a platform of reducing defense spending, particularly spending on strategic weapons, and the B-1 program was a prime target.

When he moved into the Oval Office, the new President inherited two production contracts that had been issued in December 1976, for two groups of B-1s, totaling 11 aircraft. Nevertheless, he made good on

his campaign promises and canceled the B-1 production program on 30 June 1977. The initial test phase, along with completion of a fourth prototype, was allowed to continue, however.

Over the next 46 months, until the prescribed end of the B-1 test phase, the first three prototypes made 79, 60 and 138 test flights respectively, totaling 1516 hours of flying time. During this period, the second prototype achieved a top speed of Mach 2.22 on 5 October 1978. The fourth prototype, which joined the program on 14 February 1979, logged 378 hours during 70 flights before the program ended in April 1981.

By this time, the Carter administration had been replaced by the more defense-conscious administration of Ronald Reagan, who was willing to address the need for a replacement for the aging B-52 fleet. Several options were studied under the Long Range Combat Aircraft (LRCA) evaluation program, including developing an advanced version of the FB-111 strategic fighter-bomber, and waiting 10 years for the arrival for the Northrop B-2 Advanced Technology Bomber (ATB, or 'Stealth'). In the end, the best choice seemed to be a strategic bomber that was *already* under development.

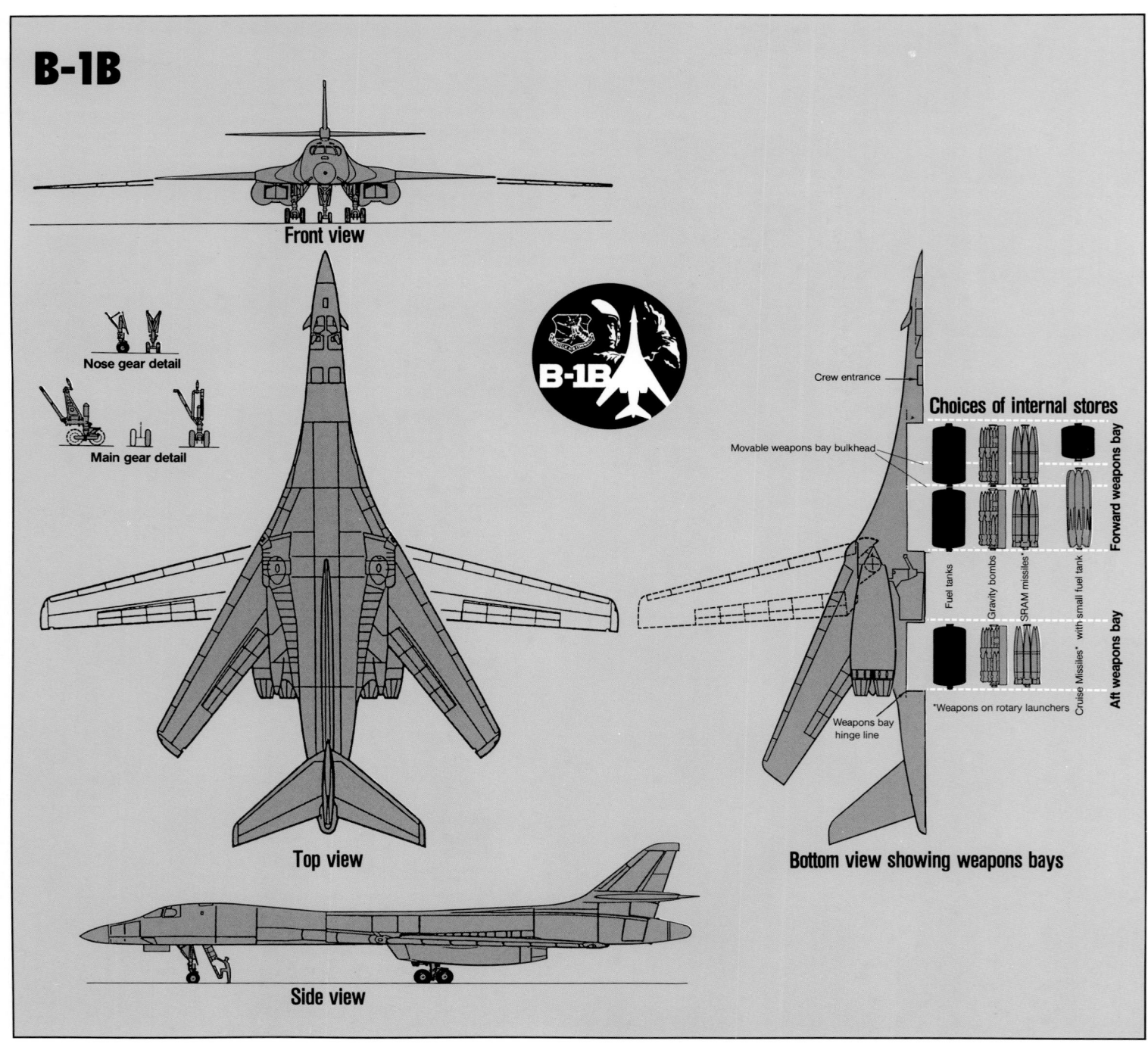

THE PROGRAM REVIVED

On 2 October 1981 President Reagan officially asked Rockwell to develop a new version of the B-1 which would retain the original's general appearance, while incorporating the state-of-the-art avionics and 'Stealth' technology that had evolved during the 10 years since the original B-1 design had been frozen. The new aircraft would be designated B-1B, while the original four B-1 aircraft were redesignated B-1A.

Since it would take Rockwell three years to rebuild the assembly line and construct a new airframe from the ground up, the first step in B-1B development would be the modification of the second and fourth B-1As to B-1B standard. This would allow the avionics systems of the B-1B to be tested several years before the first new airframe was ready.

The number four B-1A prototype, painted in three-tone desert camouflage markings, paid a visit to the 1982 Farnborough Air Show in England, where it was the star attraction. The white number two B-1A prototype joined the B-1B test program in March 1983, with a huge '*B-1B*' painted on its tail in red, white and blue. The third proto-

type was put in long-term storage, while the first was earmarked to be cannibalized for spare parts. The second prototype, the plane that had been flown at Mach 2.22 five years earlier, logged 261 hours in 66 flights in the B-1B test program over the next 17 months. Then, at 10:30 am on 29 August 1984, disaster struck.

The second prototype had been airborne over the Edwards AFB test range for about an hour and was flying at an altitude of 3500 feet. The crew, which included Rockwell's chief test pilot, Tommie Douglas 'Doug' Benefield, a veteran B-1 pilot, along with Air Force Major Richard Reynolds and Captain Otto Waniczek, were in the process of setting up a stability and control test involving the reduction of power in an outboard engine. This would have involved swinging the plane's variable-geometry wing forward, shifting the center of gravity, but an apparent malfunction caused the plane to go out of control. The crew punched out of the crippled aircraft in the single crew-ejection capsule, a system that involved a 21-foot segment of the fuselage containing the entire cockpit area being blasted out of the plane and carried to the ground by three parachutes. The system had been part of only the first three B-1As and was replaced by four individual McDonnell Douglas

Top: In 1983, the second B-1A, still in gloss white was configured with B-1B systems for an extensive test program during which it logged 261 hours before it crashed in August 1964. The first of 100 B-1Bs *(above)* rolled out of the Palmdale factory one month later.

B-1A

Above and below: The first prototype B-1A (originally designated YB-1A) in gloss white with Strategic Air Command band around her nose. The wonderful Michael Badrocke cutaway *below* shows the aircraft's titanium inner structure and the impressive series of weapons with SRAM missiles on rotary launchers.

A major difference between the configuration of this original B-1A and the B-1Bs that eventually went into service *(opposite)* was that the newer aircraft have a movable weapons bay (see the drawing on page 176) that permit a wider variety.

The cutaway shows the aircraft with its variable geometry wings fully forward at 15 degrees, while the shaded areas aft of the wings show their positions relative to the aircraft when fully swept at 67 degrees. The B-1B shown *opposite* has its wings swept slightly to the midpoint between the two extremes.

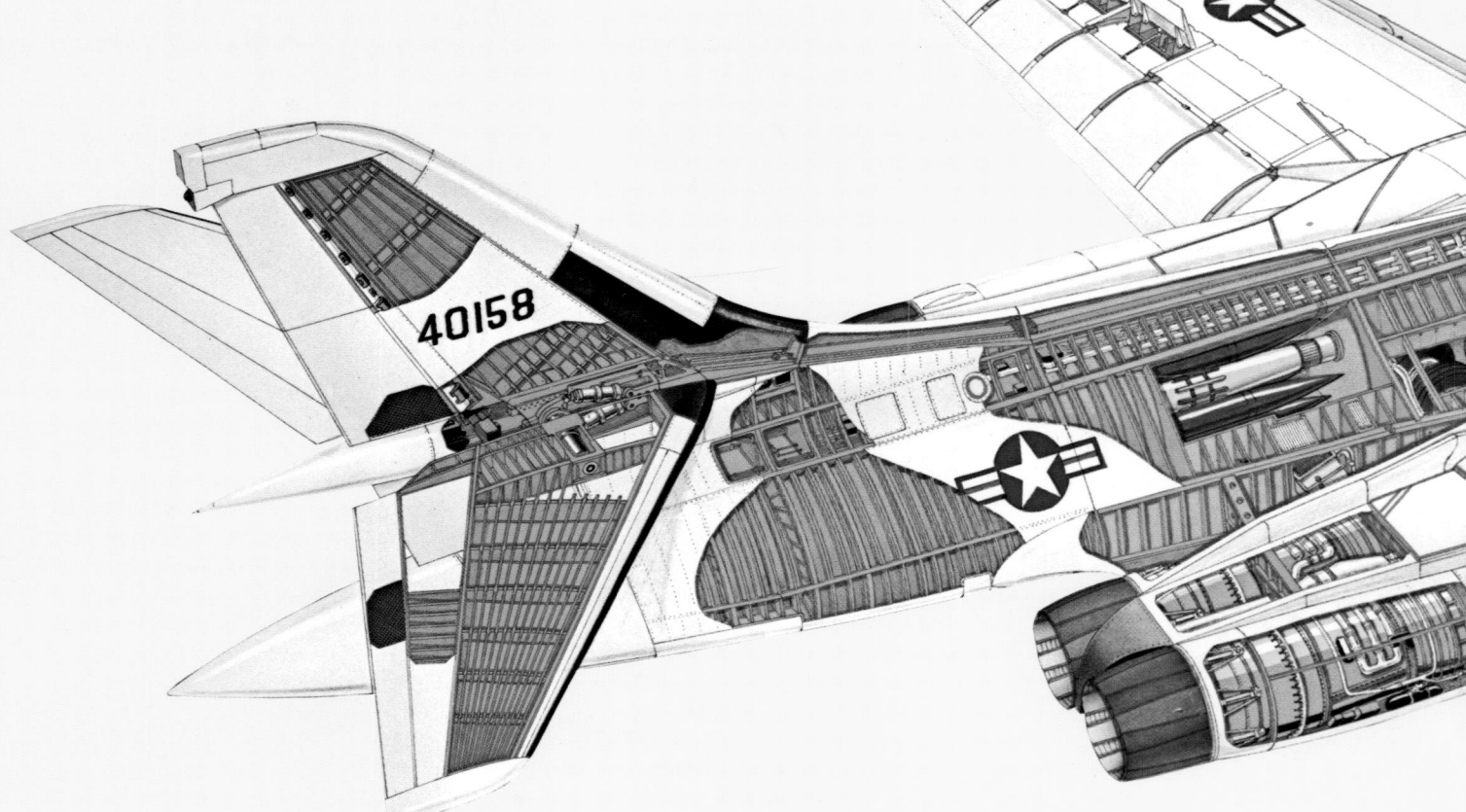

The pins that are inserted in the holes of the swivel joints (see the wing root area in the drawing *above*) are so perfectly matched to size that they had to be placed in liquid nitrogen to shrink them prior to installation at the factory!

Like the XB-70 before it, the B-1A was originally painted gloss white, a color intended to reflect the flash of a nuclear blast. The B-1Bs *(above right)*, however, are painted in dark European 1 camouflage which tends to absorb radar and make the aircraft hard to track visually when it is flying the type of low-level mission it would likely perform in wartime.

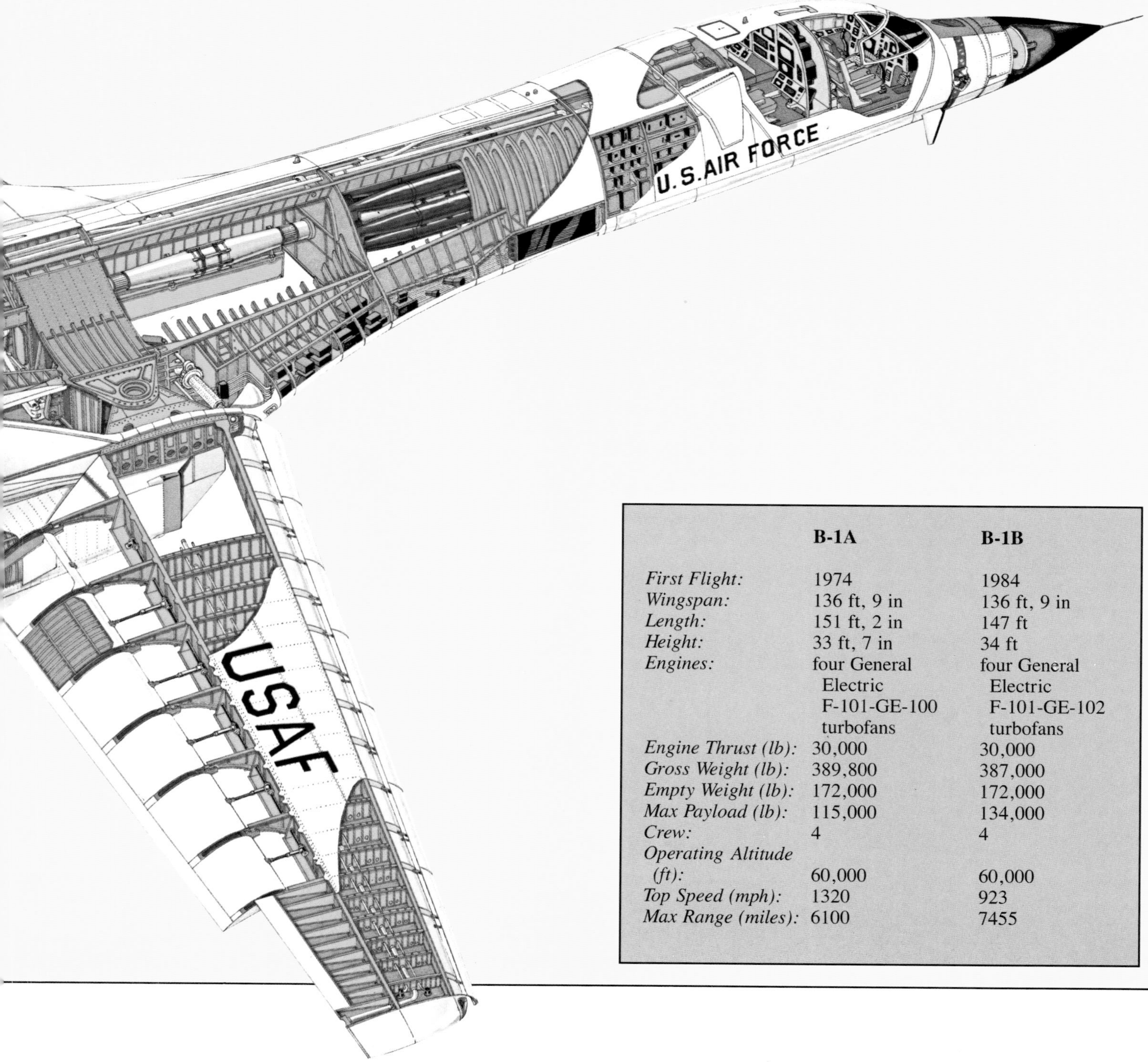

	B-1A	B-1B
First Flight:	1974	1984
Wingspan:	136 ft, 9 in	136 ft, 9 in
Length:	151 ft, 2 in	147 ft
Height:	33 ft, 7 in	34 ft
Engines:	four General Electric F-101-GE-100 turbofans	four General Electric F-101-GE-102 turbofans
Engine Thrust (lb):	30,000	30,000
Gross Weight (lb):	389,800	387,000
Empty Weight (lb):	172,000	172,000
Max Payload (lb):	115,000	134,000
Crew:	4	4
Operating Altitude (ft):	60,000	60,000
Top Speed (mph):	1320	923
Max Range (miles):	6100	7455

Aircraft Escape System (ACES) ejection seats aboard the fourth B-1A and all the production B-1Bs. The huge capsule slammed into the desert floor just 200 feet from the fiercely burning wreckage of the bomber. Doug Benefield was killed outright and the other two crewmen were injured.

It was against this somber backdrop that Air Force Secretary Verne Orr presided over the rollout of the first brand new B-1B just five days later, on 4 September 1984. 'We don't build bombers to go to war,' said the Secretary. 'We build them to keep from going to war. May it never fly in anger.'

INSIDE THE B-1B

The three years of B-1B development, both on the factory floor and in the two converted B-1A test beds, had yielded a much refined aircraft. The avionics were a decade newer, the bomb load greater, and the radar signature vastly smaller. Though the B-1B was the same size as the B-1A, its image on radar was one-tenth the size, thanks to redesigned engine nacelles and radar-absorbing composites.

The new aircraft looked much like its elder sister, except for the redesigned nacelles. In terms of appearance, the *most* obvious difference between the B-1A and the B-1B is *color*. Whereas the B-1A rolled out in gleaming gloss white with red, white and blue markings, the first B-1B appeared in the dark hues of the European I camouflage scheme. Though it appeared as a blackened bronze under the shimmering desert sun, the new color scheme consisted of two shades of dark olive green and one of dark gray. These colors, which were specifically developed for low visibility against wooded, rocky, Northern Hemisphere terrain, are also being used on many USAF tactical and airlift aircraft destined for operation in Europe in time of war.

Technically, the B-1B, like the B-1A, is listed as a multirole, four-engine heavy bomber designed to penetrate Soviet airspace carrying either conventional or nuclear weapons. In reality, it is designed to prevent nuclear war by demonstrating to the Soviet Union that if they attacked, the United States could penetrate their airspace with equally destructive weapons. More flexible than Intercontinental Ballistic Missiles, manned bombers could be launched if an attack seemed imminent and then be recalled if the threat did not materialize.

The four major components of the B-1Bs are the airframe, the engines, the offensive avionics systems and the defensive avionics systems. The contractors for these components are respectively, Rockwell International's North American Aircraft Operations (also responsible for overall integration), General Electric, Boeing Military

Above: Lt Col Leroy Schroeder *(right)*, B-1 program chief test pilot, explains the features of the B-1 bomber aircraft cockpit to astronaut Gordon Fullerton. Pilots love the fact that the B-1 has a control stick rather than a traditional 'big airplane' yoke. *Right:* The first B-1B on the factory floor at Palmdale in June 1984. It would make its first flight four months later. *Overleaf:* The production pace at Palmdale picked up rapidly in 1985.

Airplane Company, and the AIL Division of Eaton Corporation. These four major contractors were backed up by 5200 subcontractors throughout the United States.

The B-1 airframe was simply the largest combat aircraft produced in the West in over a quarter century. The original B-1 design was so important that it was copied in part by the Soviet Union's Tupolev design bureau when they were working up the drawings for their Tu-28 (NATO codename 'Blackjack') bomber, which will be deployed in the 1990s. The fuselage is nearly 150 feet long and built of aluminum, titanium and non-metallic composite components. The tail unit is made of titanium and aluminum alloy components, with movable surfaces driven hydraulically with fly-by-wire backup. The wings are of the variable-geometry or 'swing wing' type. They can be swept back to 67 degrees and forward to 15 degrees, using four hydraulic motors that can be operated by only two of the plane's four hydraulic systems. A torque shaft connects them and keeps the two wings symmetrical. The wings are constructed primarily of aluminum and contain fuel tanks. The B-1B airframe has been structurally strengthened to accommodate a 477,000 pound takeoff weight, an 82,000 pound improvement over the B-1A.

The cockpit, located in the front part of the fuselage, has an accommodation for four crew members—pilot, copilot and the operators of the Offensive and Defensive Avionics Systems. Rather than using the cumbersome escape-capsule system of the first three B-1As, each crew station is equipped with a McDonnell Douglas ACES II ejection seat. There is, however, sufficient room for the crewmen to stand up and move around to avoid stiffness on long flights.

The engines are housed in specially designed nacelles located under the aft part of the wing root. The four General Electric F101 turbofans each deliver 30,000 pounds of thrust, compared with 17,000 pounds of

Above and right: Ready for delivery! B-1Bs at Palmdale are prepared to be turned over to Air Force crews from operational SAC squadrons.

thrust from the Pratt & Whitney turbofans of the B-52H, or 10,000 from the Pratt & Whitney turbojets of the B-52D. Where the B-1A was designed for (and tested at) speeds in excess of Mach 2, the B-1B is designed for what the Air Force calls 'high subsonic' (Mach .9) speeds at lower altitudes, although it has a Mach 1.2 capability. The range of the B-1B is greater than that of either the B-52 or B-1A, making it less dependent on aerial refueling. With aerial refueling, however, the B-1B can fly to any place in the world and back without stopping.

Within the framework of the airframe and pushed by the power of the engines, the 'heart' and 'mind' of the B-1B are its avionics systems, both vastly improved over those of the B-1A. The Eaton AN/ALQ-161 defensive avionics (electronic countermeasures, ECM) system was developed to support and protect the aircraft while it operates deep in the heart of hostile airspace. The system is controlled by computer hardware that can be constantly upgraded through both software and hardware modifications. Because the B-1 has no defensive weapons, it must depend on its defensive avionics to keep enemy interceptors and anti-aircraft weapons away.

Despite its sophistication—or perhaps *because* of it—the AN/ALQ-161 proved to be the B-1B's Achilles heel. Even as late as August 1988, a House Armed Services Committee investigation revealed that the system was able to accomplish only half of its intended mission, leaving the B-1B potentially vulnerable and aircrews probably yearning for the days when bombers were protected by a tail-mounted cannon.

It was suggested that the B-1B might be retrofitted with the ITT Avionics AN/ALQ-172, which was then in use aboard SAC's B-52 fleet, and which had 180 degrees of coverage, versus 120 degrees for the troubled AN/ALQ-161. Although the AN/ALQ-172 system was perceived as being more reliable, the cost of rewiring and reconfiguring the system installation was seen as a reason to continue with efforts to improve the AN/ALQ-161 system.

The offensive avionics include a high energy inertial navigation system, a Doppler velocity sensor, a radar altimeter, countermeasures displays and an Offensive Radar System (ORS). The ORS includes a low-observable, phased-array antenna, and provides low-altitude, terrain-following and precise navigational functions.

The offensive weapons themselves are carried in three internal bays and can also be carried on external weapons pylons. The two forward weapons bays are actually a 31 foot, three inch double bay with a movable bulkhead, which permits accommodation of the 20 foot, nine inch Boeing AGM-86 Air Launched Cruise Missile (ALCM), a weapon which the B-1A could not carry. In addition to eight ALCMs, which can be mounted on a rotary launcher in the forward weapons bay, the B-1B can carry eight Short Range Attack Missiles (SRAM) in the aft bay. By removing the ALCMs and centering the partition in the forward double bay, a total of 24 SRAMs can be carried. The B-1B could also carry up to 12 B-28 or B-43 nuclear bombs, or 24 B-61 or B-83 nuclear bombs *(see photo on page 188)*. For missions requiring conventional ordnance, 84 Mk32 (550 pound) or 24 Mk84 (2000 pound) high explosive bombs can be carried internally. Fuel tanks can also be carried internally, and weapons (including 12 ALCMs or SRAMs) can be carried on eight external pylon attachments located below the fuselage, adjacent to the weapons bay doors.

Placed in perspective, the B-1B's conventional bomb capacity is four times that of the B-29 Superfortress, the largest bomber of World War II, and three times that of the B-52s now in service. The B-29 could carry a single nuclear weapon when specially modified, and the B-52 can accommodate eight such bombs. The B-1B can carry between 12 and 24 free-fall nuclear bombs.

Right: Warriors of the North and the Northern Lights. B-1Bs of the 319th SAC's Bomb Wing at Grand Fork AFB, North Dakota are silhouetted against the Aurora Borealis.

THE B-1B IN SERVICE

The first flight of a production B-1B took place on 18 October 1984, six weeks after its rollout, and five months ahead of schedule. On 31 October, after initial inflight tests of the new aircraft's systems, it was flown the short distance from Palmdale to Edwards AFB, completing 4.8 hours of flying time. A third flight of 5.5 hours on 14 November completed the initial test program.

By June 1985, the second production B-1B had been completed and had undergone six weeks of flight tests. It was intended that the first B-1B should stay at Edwards, while the second would be the first to join the SAC as an operational aircraft. The aircraft was scheduled to be flown to SAC Headquarters at Offutt AFB, Nebraska, for ceremonies on 27 June, and then on to Dyess AFB, Texas, two days later to join the 96th Bomb Wing, its assigned unit. As planned, the plane took off from Edwards on the 27th with the Secretary of the Air Force, Verne Orr, on board. Shortly before landing, bolts from two cooling duct doors on the aircraft's port side worked loose and were sucked into the number one and number two engines, but the plane landed safely and was officially turned over to SAC.

Crews replaced the two engines so that SAC Commander General Bennie Davis could fly the B-1B to the 29 June ceremonies at Dyess. When the replacement engines were damaged during a run-up on the ground at Offutt, it was decided that the plane would remain there and General Davis would go down to Edwards AFB and pick up the first B-1B. Thus, it came to pass that on 29 June 1985, the first B-1B to be mustered into an operational US Air Force unit was also the first B-1B to have rolled off the assembly line.

By June 1986, the first anniversary of the B-1B's arrival at SAC's Dyess AFB, 15 aircraft had been delivered to the Air Force. By 1 October, when the 96th Bombardment Wing reached its Initial Operating Capacity (IOC) with the new bomber, 23 had been produced, and by 21 January 1987, when the first B-1B was delivered to Ellsworth, AFB, South Dakota, the total produced had reached 36. After having

Above: Accompanied by an FB-111 Aardvark and an F-4 Phantom, a B-1B unleashes a bayload of unarmed B-83 bombs during a February 1987 training mission. *Right: The Star of Abilene* was a veteran B-1B assigned to the 96th Bomb Wing at Dyess AFB near Abilene, Texas when she came back to Palmdale for routine service in September 1987. The tan hanger in the distance contained the super secret final assembly area for the mysterious Northrop B-2 'Stealth' bomber. The B-2 was rolled out of this building 14 months later.

190

delivered only four aircraft during 1985, Rockwell reached a point in December 1986 after which it would produce no fewer than four a *month*. Meanwhile, the 4018th Combat Crew Training Squadron at Dyess was turning out the crews to man the big planes.

On 14 April 1987 a Dyess-based B-1B took off on a 21 hour, 40 minute nonstop demonstration of the bomber's endurance capability. Taking off at a gross weight of 413,000 pounds — 73,000 pounds above normal for operational training missions — the aircraft covered 9411 miles on a course that took it across Alaska to within 160 nautical miles of the Soviet Union.

By the time that a B-1B was ready to go on display at the Paris Air Show in June 1987, Rockwell's four-a-month delivery schedule had put more than half the original order of 100 bombers into the Air Force inventory. Dyess AFB had reached IOC (Initial Operating Capability) with 15 aircraft in September 1986 and had its full complement of B-1Bs by December. Having received its first bomber in January 1987, Ellsworth AFB received its 35th, and last, in September. Grand Forks AFB, North Dakota, received its 17th, and last, B-1B in December as deliveries began to McConnell AFB, Kansas.

The 100th, and last, B-1B aircraft rolled of the final assembly line ahead of schedule at Palmdale on 20 January 1988, six years to the day after the signing of the B-1B development and production contracts in 1982.

Ceremonies marking the event were held in the Final Assembly Building before an audience of several thousand, consisting of company executives, Air Force officers, executives from the associate

These pages: B-1B checkout routines over the rugged Mojave Desert country near Edwards AFB included both low level and high level flights.

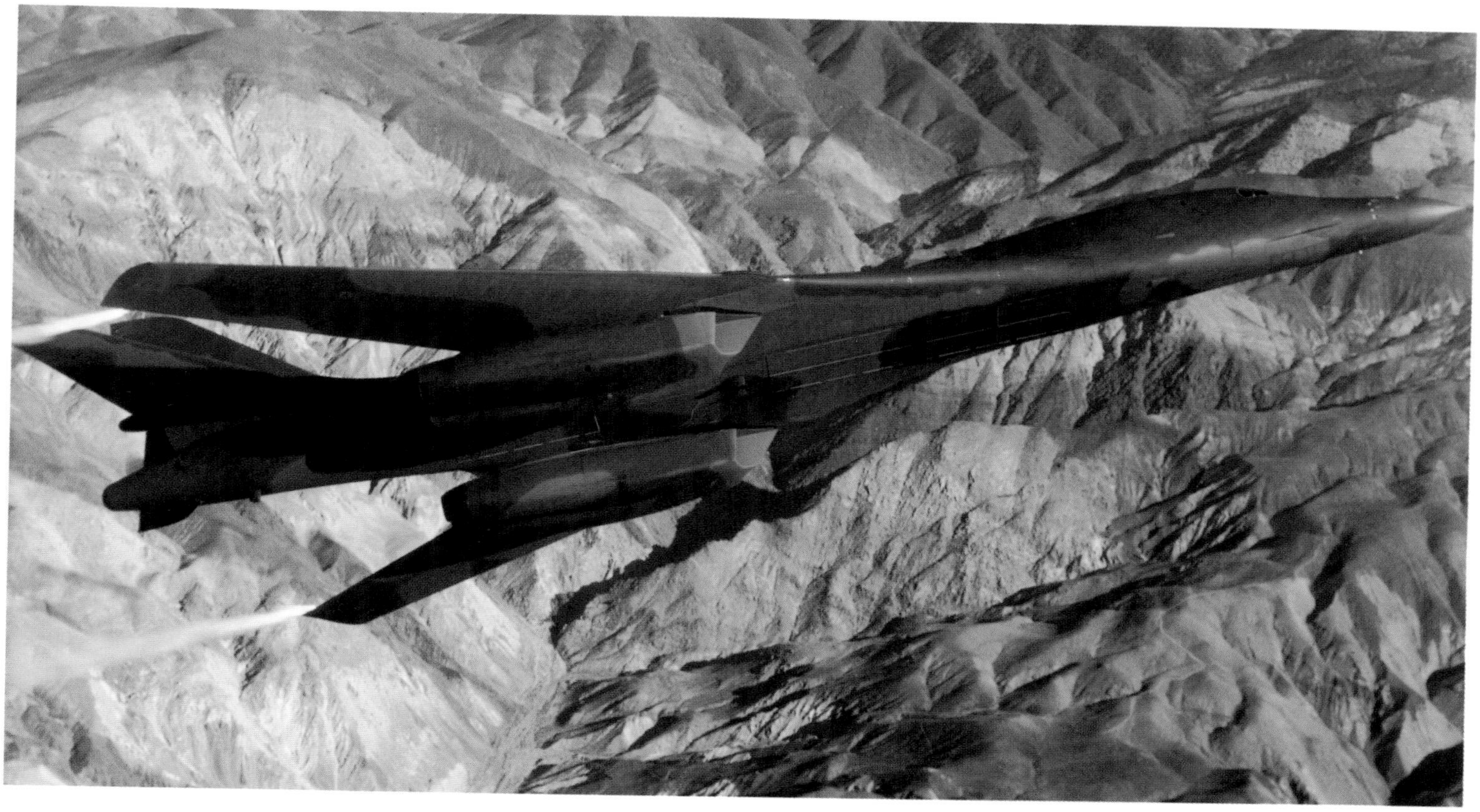

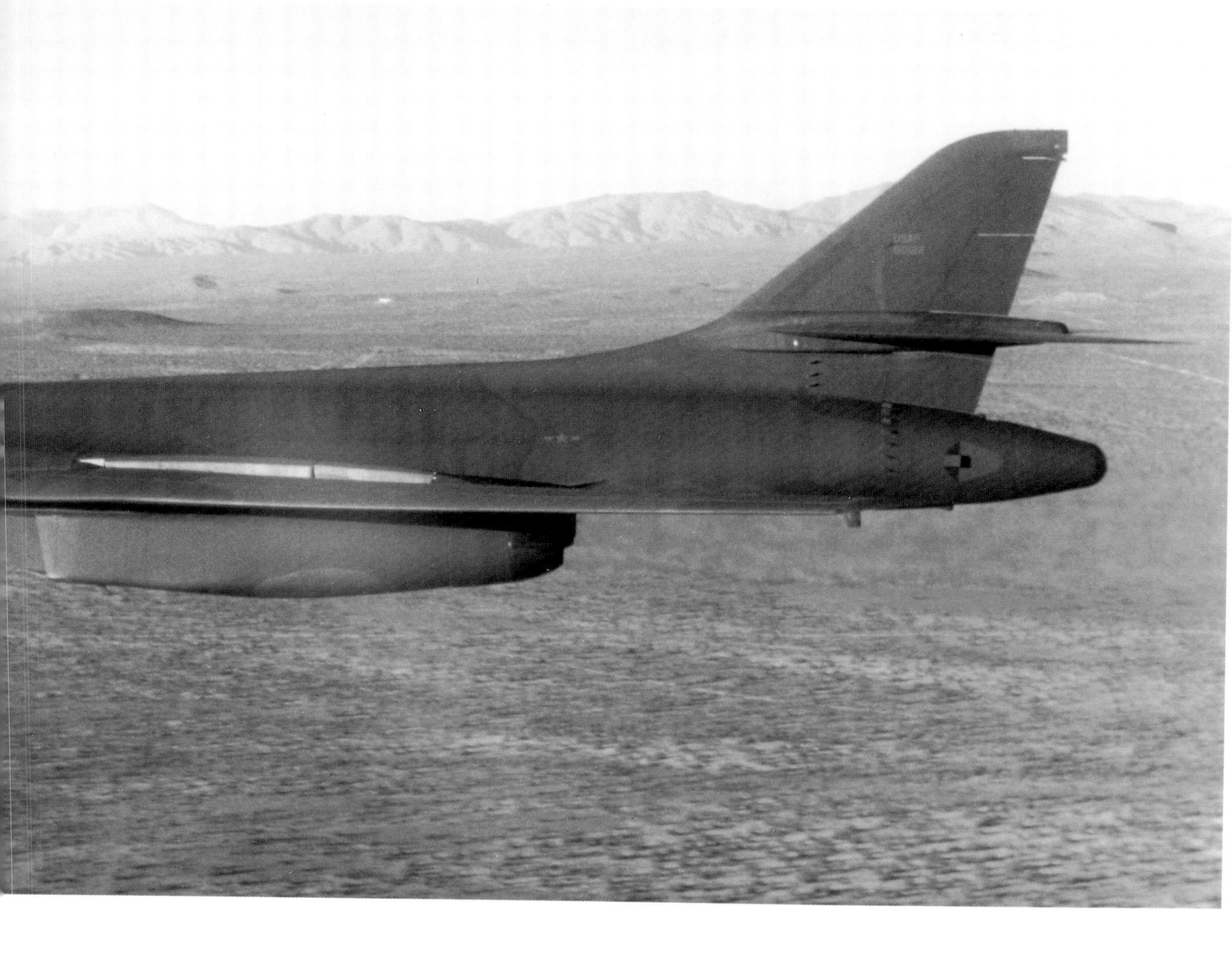

contractors, representatives from the B-1B industrial team of sub-contractors and suppliers, and civic leaders, as well as a large number of Rockwell employees.

Sam Iacobellis, president of Rockwell Aerospace Operations and master of ceremonies for the event, said, 'These firms, and the representatives who are here today, have been key players on the B-1B program. The way I feel today, each of them deserves an individual introduction.'

Robert Anderson, Rockwell chairman and chief executive officer, described the occasion as one of mixed feelings—sadness that it was ending, pride in what had been accomplished. 'Today marks an end, that is really a beginning. This B-1B rollout may be the end of the production run, but it marks the beginning of a new echelon of strength in our national defense. It's a day of sadness, a symbol of a job well done for so many fine people who now have new jobs and new challenges to seek. It is a day of vindication for the Air Force, for Rockwell, for our associates and subcontractors, who have proved to the nation that the old spirit of can-do is alive, and well, and living in thousands of companies scattered across this land.'

This 100th and final B-1B was officially delivered to SAC on 30 April 1988, two months ahead of schedule. This B-1B was also the 17th, and final, of the complement of aircraft assigned to the 384th Bomb Wing at McConnell AFB, Kansas.

With one B-1B having been lost in a crash on 28 September 1987 during a low-level training mission near La Junta, Colorado, the total fleet consisted of 99 aircraft at the time of the final delivery. Two more were lost in November 1988, bringing the total to 97. Three of this total (including the first B-1B) were assigned to Edwards AFB for test and evaluation and the remainder were assigned to SAC for operations and training at McConnell AFB (Kansas), Ellsworth AFB (South Dakota), Grand Forks AFB (North Dakota) and Dyess AFB (Texas).

As part of SAC's overall modernization program, the B-1B, along with the Northrop B-2 'Stealth' bomber (which first appeared in 1988), will give the Strategic Air Command its most effective force since the days of Curtis LeMay in the 1950s. If the B-52's record is any indication, much of the B-1B fleet will still be in service in 2015.

These pages: Beneath a thundering overflight by a B-1B and an F-106 chase plane, the 100th and last B-1B rolled out at Palmdale on 20 January 1988. *Overleaf:* Officially, pilots do not roll the B-1B.

An interview with Ed Ford, B-1B Test Pilot

A Rockwell International test pilot in the B-1B program, Ed Ford joined the company in 1985 after a career in the US Air Force. While with the Air Force, Mr Ford served two tours in Vietnam and spent time with the Strategic Air Command, the Military Airlift Command, the Pacific Air Forces, and finally with the Air Training Command. The interview was conducted in September 1987 at Rockwell's B-1B test facility at Palmdale, California, at a time when about two-thirds of the B-1Bs had been built and test flown.

Yenne: What I'm after here is really not so much an interview but to get some of your impressions, from a test pilot's point of view, of the B-1B. I'm also interested in your comments generally about how it handles.

Ford: It's a magnificent airplane at low level. It's one of the best. One of the things that surprises the fighter guys who were flying cover for the B-1B in training exercises is the quick acceleration, quick turn and very quick roll rate. If they weren't right there—ready to go with it—the B-1B would leave them behind on the climb. The F-106 that we fly as a chase plane can't stay with it initially.

Yenne: Have you flown the B-52, and how does it compare to the B-1B?

Ford: I enjoy flying a B-52, but it's a big, slow-responding airplane. There's just no comparison. It's a big airplane and it acts like a big airplane. It flies high, while the B-1B was made to fly low—although the B-1B can go higher than people say it can. Above 30,000 feet you have to sweep the wings, you have to go fast, so you're right in the critical Mach most of the time. They had to design the B-1B with the variable inlets. They changed those from the B-1A—and that reduced the 'warp factor' of the aircraft, so to speak. You can't get the same speed that you can with the variable inlet veins, of course. That's a fact of engineering.

The B-52 will get down low and it'll go, but goes about half the speed of the B-1B, and it puts out quite a bit of radar. You can't maneuver the B-52 around at the low level terrain like you can the B-1B. The B-1B can respond. It can really do some nice things that the B-52 can't. So there's no real comparison between a B-1 with the wings back and a B-52 in any condition.

The only time that the B-1 ever acts like a big airplane is at a very heavy gross weight with its wings forward. Now, you can have the same heavy gross weight, sweep the wings, start going fast and bam! It flies great from that point on. It's a configuration in which the airplane handles magnificently. When you get the wings *back*, the airplane can fly at Mach .85 all day under military thrust conditions without using the afterburners. The range between Mach .85 and Mach .90 is where just about all the work is done.

When you put the wings back, the airplane rolls and performs quite like a fighter. It's got great acceleration and great climbing capacity. It's just a really nice, comfortable airplane to fly. We hold it down to three Gs, but that still gives us plenty of room to turn.

We can't turn as tight as fighters do, but the roll rate of the aircraft is just as quick as a fighter's.

Yenne: Do you roll it?

Ford: No. We're not allowed to roll it, but I'm sure the airplane is quite capable of being rolled. Most of the time when you're pulling out of a low level run and you're pulling up really quick—you roll it to the 120 degree position to level it off.

Yenne: Is it designed so that you can land with the wings fully swept?

Ford: Yes. If you get your wings all the way back and they break and you can't get them forward, then you have to land at a little bit faster air speed. It's very unusual for the wings to malfunction on the aircraft. It's a good system.

One time an Air Force crew had a malfunction and brought the airplane back to Edwards AFB. The Air Force people at the test facility there thought that it would take more than 15,000 feet of runway, so they figured the B-1B would go onto the lake bed beyond the runway. This pilot stopped the airplane quite easily in the allotted time. He coasted to the end of the runway, but could have stopped it within 9000 feet. This airplane has some of the best brakes I've ever seen on an airplane. These are great brakes. No doubt about it.

Yenne: Does having a stick rather than a yoke help?

Ford: Oh, having a stick is wonderful! Yokes are for big airplanes. (*Laughs*) No, I think all airplanes deserve a stick, even if

they're big airplanes. I think it's much better for you. All the pilots in the military are trained with sticks anyway to begin with in. It's just a natural thing. I like an airplane that's got a stick in it.

All the SAC crews that are coming out of B-52s just love the B-1, mainly because it's great for refueling. When you first start refueling the B-52, it's very tedious, but the B-1B reacts to it right away. There's no delay like there is in a B-52. Once the pilots get used to it, the B-1B is a very easy airplane to refuel.

Yenne: Specifically, what sort of B-1B test work do you do here at Palmdale?

Ford: My main job here is B-1B production testing. I'm generally the only guy here. I fly just about every sortie out of here when a test flight involves a Rockwell test pilot. Every B-1B sortie out of Palmdale generally has one Rockwell pilot, an Air Force pilot and two Air Force guys in the back. I'm generally the Rockwell guy. There are other pilots, both Air Force and Rockwell, who fly the test birds (B-1Bs number 1, 9 and 28) at Edwards AFB. *Their* primary job is to do most of the data point testing. They test it over there, then they approve it here, and then we test the same points on the *production* airplanes to make sure that they work according to how they should work.

We keep in fairly close contact with them all the time. That's the important thing with an airplane that you're concurrently testing *and* producing. It saves time and money, but at the same time you're putting out airplanes, and you're going to have to call them back occasionally to update the equipment, as the new equipment gets tested and put in onboard.

Yenne: Is most of your test flying over Edwards AFB?

Ford: Yes. We do all of our test flying over at the Edwards AFB facility. It's perfect for what we need. We have our own individual radar control support at Edwards, and they talk to us on a discreet frequency. Of course, they're controlling a few other airplanes too.

Yenne: What's a typical flight routine for you in one of these check-out flights?

Ford: The typical flight normally lasts three to three and one-half hours, sometimes four, depending on whether we refuel. We generally take off at 321,000 pounds gross weight and climb into the air, do some doublets—which is just a stick shaking type of an affair—just to make sure the airplane isn't going to fall apart, and to see that it stabilizes after we jerk it around a little bit.

We do a wind-up turn or so, and then we sweep the wings and get

Below: In addition to his work in the cockpit of the B-1, Ed Ford occasionally would take a turn at the controls of an F-106 chase plane.

down to 5000 feet and check the trim on the airplane at Mach .85. Then we climb up to 10,000 feet, do some more wind up turns with the airplane with the wings swept to make sure that the air data computers are putting out the proper stall indications for the aircraft. We also check the trim at 10,000 feet, then climb on up to 15,000 feet and do some more checks of the computer at that altitude.

At the same time we're also checking the temperature controls on the aircraft, the air conditioning, and the pressurization. We dump everything and repressurize, then we climb on up to 25,000 feet, where I do the engine work. I do a lot of slam throttles—bringing the throttles out—especially on the first flight. I do them one at a time, to see how the engines are going to react. We do it slowly at first to make sure that they go into afterburner and come back, and that they're tracking normally with no stall indications. We also check the jog throttles—secondary controls—at the same time. We then drop down to 20,000 feet and we shut all the engines down—one at a time, not all at one time. Of course, we're shutting the generators off, too, so we're checking the electrical systems. We shut them all down, restart them in a different variety—it's either entering a cell or cross-bleed starts from the other side—checking the transfers for the air to make sure that we can start them both directions.

Finally, we'll go into a high-altitude bomb run where the Air Force radar bombardier is checking all of his bomb releases, his SRAMs and all the other weapons. The Air Force guys are the ones exercising the weapons bays.

After we go through the weapons bay exercises—that's a high altitude bomb run—we'll give the bombardier a low bomb run and let him check his radars and bomb releases. Then we'll chug back around and we'll do the ECM activity, which is the Eaton AN/ALQ-161 that's had so much publicity. It's coming along quite well, although there's still some work to be done on it. The equipment that we have on board—all the bands for jamming, for acquisitioning enemy radars that we simulate—work excellently.

The bomb runs generally take an hour's worth of work. From there, if we have a tanker, we'll go up and grab on, check the air refueling system, fly a little boom time. We break off from there and descend on down, sweep the wings again and check the terrain following radar. We do open loop runs first to make sure that the system is working properly. Then we'll couple up with the autopilot and we'll fly a group of low level runs. Right now, we're stepping down to 500 feet. We open-loop down to 200 feet just to see how the equipment is operating down there. It operates quite well.

Next, we'll climb back up and check all the flap configurations and the stall speeds with gear coming down. We just run the whole gamut there, exercising the gear a few times, making sure it's going to come up and down. We'll let the guys in the back set up their equipment to see how that's functioning, then we come back to the pattern and we shoot an airborne instrument landing approach. Then we'll come in and shoot a bunch of visual patterns and exercise the airplane, letting it hit the runway a few times, letting the gear roll, and checking to make sure that everything is operating properly.

Sometimes, when we have a problem with a specific airplane, we may be airborne a little longer while we're trying to troubleshoot it. Any time we get into a situation where we have problems, we take a break and talk directly to control. They have all the engineers sitting in the room while we're flying, and if we have a problem, we discuss what's going on and we try to figure out what's the best way to correct it.

Yenne: How many test flights do you generally run on an individual plane?

Ford: We're averaging about three sorties per aircraft right now (September 1987). On some of them we've gotten up to six or seven sorties on them. Those were basically clean airplanes, except for the just one or two items that needed more work, or when we've repeated a test. We've had a couple of airplanes that were close to 'selling' on the first flight. This is everybody's goal, to sell them on the first flight. With all the equipment being so closely monitored by your on-board computer system, you know everything that goes wrong, so it's pretty tough to sell them on one flight. You get an average of nine to ten hours on an airplane, and the Air Force buys it and takes it away.

It's just like anything else. The more an airplane flies, the better it gets. Airplanes are just that way. You sit them all on the ramp and they start pouting, they want to break on you. You fly them every day and they just hum beautifully. That's how most airplanes are. You give them their periodic maintenance and get them in the air!

Yenne: SAC certainly seems to like to fly their planes, to keep them in the air.

Ford: That's what it's all about. You've got to keep them in the air. The more you can get them in the air, the better they operate without major problems.

Yenne: I imagine that for test pilots you've got to be on your toes constantly, you can't take anything for granted.

Ford: You can't. You don't really know, especially when you fly an airplane for the first time. You assume that everything is going to work out properly on it, but there's no guarantee. So that means you have to be up on everything. That's why a lot of communication goes on between the guys at Edwards AFB and us over here at Palmdale. We're on a constant vigil while we're in the air. If something goes wrong, everyone just takes a deep breath, takes a look at exactly what it is and analyzes it really well before continuing on with the mission. We take care of a problem before we press on.

It also requires that we don't take unnecessary chances. When something goes wrong with an airplane on a first flight and we're not quite certain what it is, we'd rather get it back and get it on the ground in a hurry, and then let maintenance figure it out and find out what was *really* going wrong with the airplane. On a large airplane like this, you have so many complications that could build up from one seemingly minor incident that could lead to an inflight emergency down the line someplace.

A lot of people think of test flying as these guys that go jump in an airplane, kick the tires, light the fires and press on to the limits. Let me tell you, that may have been the way it was many a year ago, but now everything is very controlled and everybody's in on the picture. Before we go out to fly, we have briefings, and we know exactly how far we're going to try to take an airplane. Then we bring it back and they analyze all the data that we recorded in flight, and what they get in briefings from the pilots and the engineers.

Then we get together and they say that we can go another step. You take a step at a time. This has reduced the number of crashes in test flying significantly. Very seldom do you see us losing airplanes around here. It's very well controlled, and that's as it should be. It takes a little bit more time to do it like that, but then you have the data... *and* the airplane.

Below: A B-1B bomber with its F-106 chase plane close behind. These F-106s were on loan to the program from the Tactical Air Command in what would be one of their last official functions before being retired after a 30-year career as America's leading interceptor.

THE SPACE SHUTTLE

All of the manned spacecraft that were used by the United States and the Soviet Union in the first two decades of their respective space programs were designed to be used once, and once only. The Soviet Vostok, Vokshod and Soyuz, and the American Mercury, Gemini and Apollo craft were all ballistic re-entry capsules. They could be controlled in space and directed *prior to* re-entry, but upon return to the Earth's atmosphere, they were simply falling objects, which deployed their parachutes and floated down.

The idea of a winged, aerodynamic spacecraft that could make an airplanelike landing actually predates the idea for ballistic re-entry capsules. The latter were chosen because they were far simpler in design and thus could be designed and built much more quickly. In the late 1950s both the US and the USSR wanted to put a man in space as soon as possible. Ballistic re-entry technology accomplished the job by 1961 for both countries. A winged spacecraft, such as the American X-20 Dyna-Soar (Dynamic Soaring Vehicle), though being built at the same time as the Mercury capsules, would not have been ready for space flight until about 1965. If there hadn't been a space race, there might never have been ballistic re-entry capsules.

THE IDEA COMES TO LIFE

The Boeing X-20 Dyna-Soar, which had been an Air Force program, was canceled in 1963 just as its first spacecraft was nearing completion. However, it wasn't long before NASA picked up the thread. By then, Apollo was in its heyday and NASA was already looking ahead to future programs that would utilize a reusable 'space plane' and a versatile means of navigating in space.

It is certainly true that a complex space plane would be more expensive to develop and build than a ballistic re-entry capsule. However, it is equally obvious that, over time, a reusable spacecraft would prove to be cheaper to operate than a capsule that must be completely replaced for each mission. Since the idea of a reusable vehicle appealed to NASA, the Space Shuttle Transportation Systems (STS) was born. Even the *name* underscored NASA's conception of how this new vehicle would function.

All of the major aerospace companies submitted proposals for the new craft, but by February 1969 NASA had narrowed the field to four, issuing study contracts to Lockheed, General Dynamics, McDonnell Douglas and North American Rockwell. All four companies had exceptional backgrounds for the task, but North American Rockwell (soon to be Rockwell International) not only had experience in the

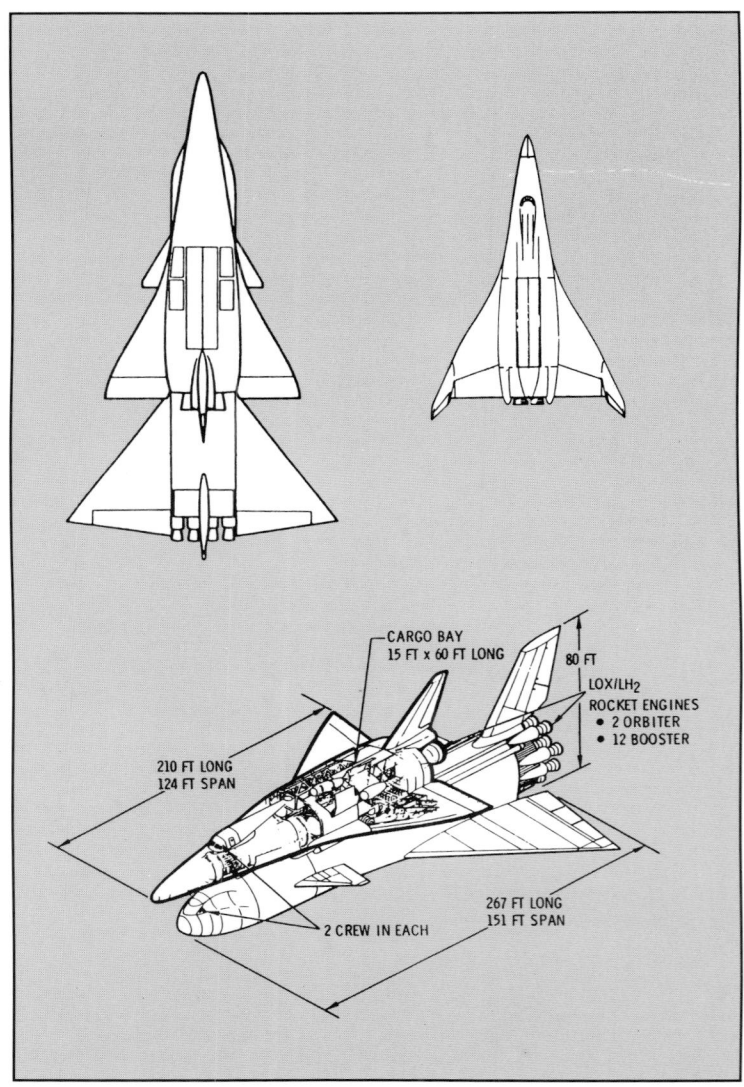

Above: This 1971 Rockwell STS proposal envisioned a scenario in which both the Orbiter and the launch vehicle would be winged, manned, reusable craft. (Two versions of the Orbiter are shown.) The configuration would change, but the payload bay size was already fixed by Defense Department requirements for their planned satellites.

Right: The Orbiter *Columbia* (OV-102) at Launch Pad 39 at Kennedy Space Center, just prior to the 12 April 1981 first ever Space Shuttle flight.

Apollo program, but also with the X-15, which was the closest thing to a space plane that had ever been built.

In March 1972 NASA decided upon a configuration for the Space Shuttle. On 26 July 1972 Rockwell was issued a contract to go ahead with the final design of the spacecraft portion of the system. Morton Thiokol would build the two Solid Rocket Boosters (SRB) and Martin-Marietta would handle the huge fuel tank that would supply liquid hydrogen and oxygen for the engines that would be built into the spacecraft itself. Together, these four elements—the spacecraft, two boosters, the external tank—constituted what would be called the Space (or Space Shuttle) Transportation System.

The overall system would stand 184 feet high on the launch pad and weigh 4.5 million pounds (fully fueled) at launch. The spacecraft portion, called the Orbiting Vehicle (Orbiter), was 122 feet long and had a wingspan of 78 feet. It was the size of a small airliner, weighing 75 tons. It had a 15-by-60 foot cargo bay capable of transporting up to five satellites to be launched in space. In fact, both NASA and the Defense Department had now decided to *phase out* the use of expendable boosters for the launch of nearly all unmanned satellites. Though it never could have been predicted at the time, it was a decision that would prove costly by the late 1980s.

The Orbiter was designed to be piloted by a flight crew of two but was capable of routinely carrying seven or more 'mission specialists' or 'payload specialists' who would help launch satellites or operate scientific experiments. It was the first US spacecraft to utilize an oxygen-nitrogen atmosphere (like the atmosphere on Earth or in Soviet spacecraft), rather than pure oxygen like Mercury, Gemini or Apollo. It was designed for an optimal mission of seven days.

The Orbiter had an aluminum framework, and its exterior was covered with thermal protective materials to shield the spacecraft from

Left: The Orbiter *Enterprise* (OV-101) is loaded atop the Boeing 747 carrier plane that was used not only for OV-101's earth atmosphere glide tests, but for transporting all the subsequent Orbiters between landing sites and launch sites. *Above left: Enterprise* returns to the Edwards AFB runway after a 1977 glide test.

Above: The Orbiter *Challenger* (OV-99) was the second of the STS series to be configured for the actual space flight. It is seen here under construction with its basic structure and crew compartment in place. *Below:* Rockwell crews put the finishing touches on *Challenger.*

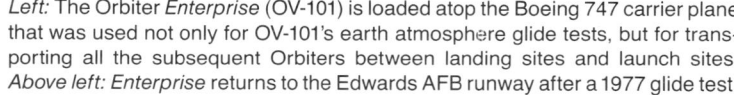

204

The STS Orbiter

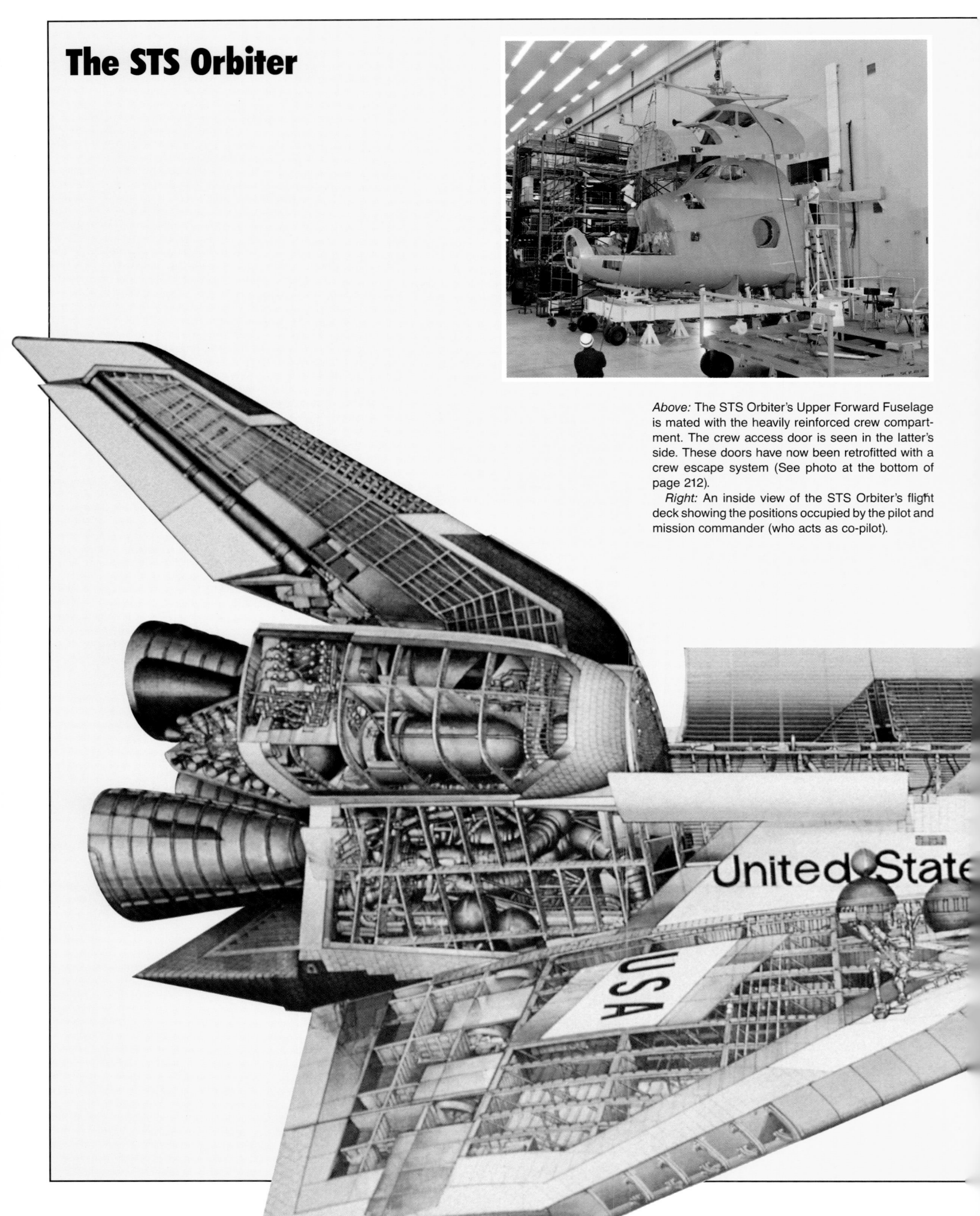

Above: The STS Orbiter's Upper Forward Fuselage is mated with the heavily reinforced crew compartment. The crew access door is seen in the latter's side. These doors have now been retrofitted with a crew escape system (See photo at the bottom of page 212).

Right: An inside view of the STS Orbiter's flight deck showing the positions occupied by the pilot and mission commander (who acts as co-pilot).

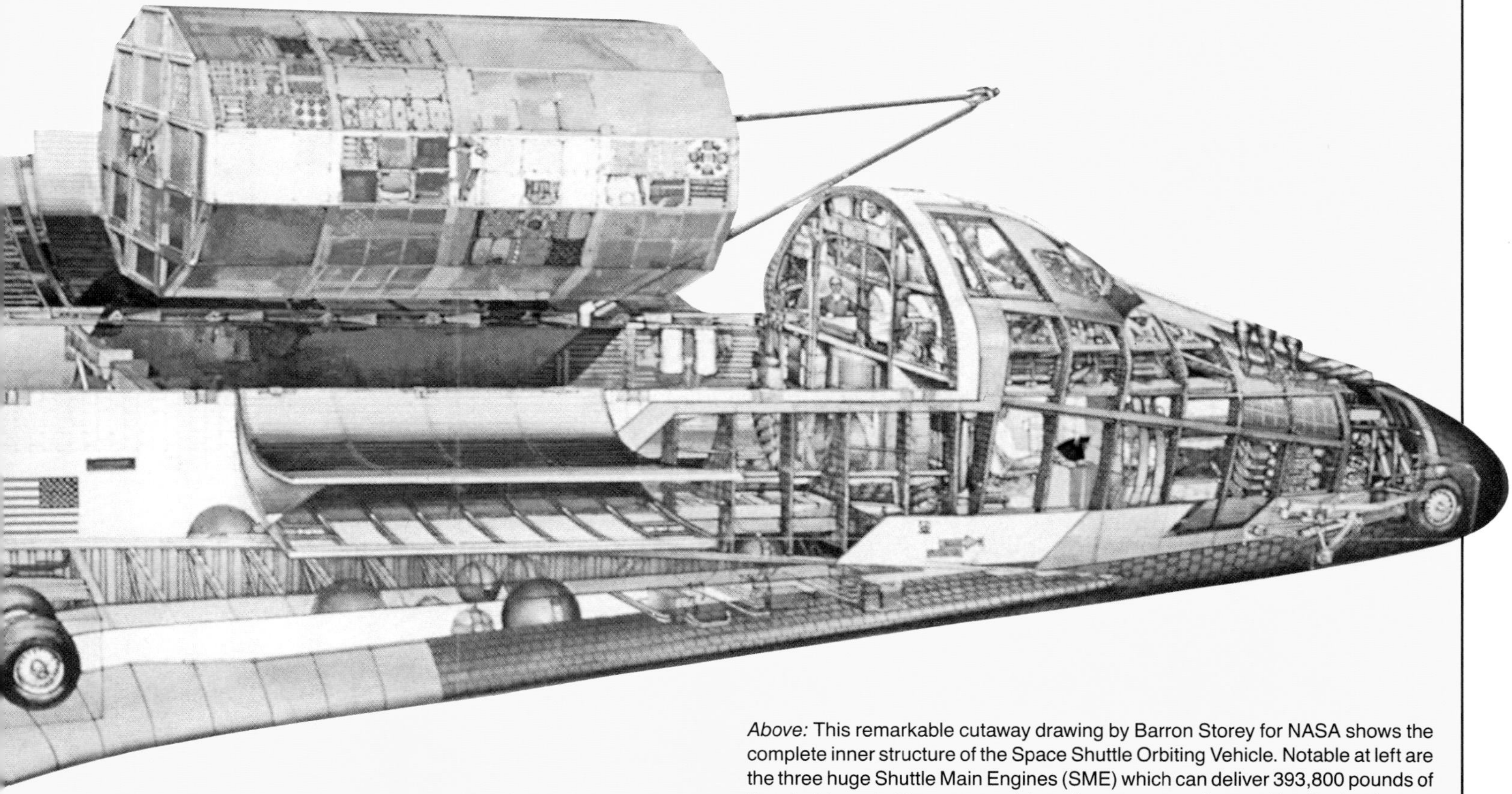

Above: This remarkable cutaway drawing by Barron Storey for NASA shows the complete inner structure of the Space Shuttle Orbiting Vehicle. Notable at left are the three huge Shuttle Main Engines (SME) which can deliver 393,800 pounds of thrust at launch. These powerful engines are manufactured by Rocketdyne, a Rockwell subsidiary.

This Orbiter is shown with landing gear stowed and its payload bay doors open. The Canadian-built Remote Manipulator System (RMS) arm is shown pulling the Long Duration Exposure Facility (LDEF) module from the bay. The 21,400-pound LDEF was launched by the Orbiter *Challenger* on 8 April 1984, for recovery by a future STS mission.

solar radiation and the extreme heat of atmospheric re-entry. The *top* of the craft was covered with coated silica tiles, and the *sides* with coated flexible sheets that could protect the ship at temperatures below 1200 and 700 degrees Fahrenheit, respectively. The bottom of the Orbiter and the leading edge of the tail were covered with glossy black silica tiles that protected them at temperatures below 2300 degrees Fahrenheit. A gray reinforced carbon material covered the nose and wing leading edges for protection above 2300 degrees Fahrenheit. Beginning with the third Orbiter, many of the white tiles were replaced with advanced, flexible, resuable surface insulation blankets (AFRSI), or silicon fiber blankets, which resulted in a half ton of weight savings.

The Orbiter's three main engines, located in the aft fuselage below the tail in a triangular pattern, were manufactured by the Rocketdyne Division of Rockwell International. Each could deliver between 375,000 (sea-level) and 470,000 (high-altitude) pounds of thrust. These liquid fuel engines are capable of seven and one-half hours of continuous use without maintenance or overhaul. Given that the engines are used on the average of only eight minutes per mission, the engines can be used for 55 separate missions, unless especially heavy payloads are being lifted into orbit.

As originally planned, the Space Shuttle was to make its maiden voyage in 1979, restoring a manned space flight capability to the United States just five years after Skylab and only four years after the Apollo-Soyuz flight. In early 1980 the Space Shuttle was scheduled to fly into space to rescue the Skylab Space Station which had been floating untouched for six years, and by the end of 1981, the Shuttle was to have made as many as 22 flights. However, this was to remain an unfulfilled dream, as 1979 came and went without a Shuttle flight, and Skylab plunged helplessly into the atmosphere and burned up, scattering a shower of fiery debris. The STS program had been the victim of delays, clipped corners and budget cuts that never had plagued the Apollo program. A proposed fleet of more than ten Orbiting Vehicles was reduced to six, and then to five.

The first Orbiter was completed by Rockwell's Palmdale, California facility and delivered to Edwards AFB, where testing began in February 1977. This first Orbiter was designated OV-101 (Orbiting Vehicle, first) and nicknamed *Enterprise* after the Hollywood starship in the television series and movie *Star Trek*. The *Enterprise* was never intended for actual space flight, but was to be used solely for tests that would be conducted in Earth atmosphere. A Boeing 747 transport was specially modified to carry the Orbiter on its back during the initial test because the Orbiter was not designed to take off in level flight. The 747 was also used later in the program to transport the Orbiters from place to place within the atmosphere.

The first free flight of the *Enterprise* came on 12 August 1977, with Gordon Fullerton and Fred Haise at the controls. *Enterprise* was released from the 747 at 22,800 feet, whereupon the crew glided the huge spacecraft prototype to a perfect landing. In May 1979, after successful flight tests and eight months of structural tests, *Enterprise* was mated to the shuttle launch vehicle system at Kennedy Space Center (KSC), with astronauts John Young and Robert Crippen at the controls, for further tests. Meanwhile, in March 1979, the Orbiter *Columbia* (OV-102)—the first space flight-rated Orbiter—arrived at KSC.

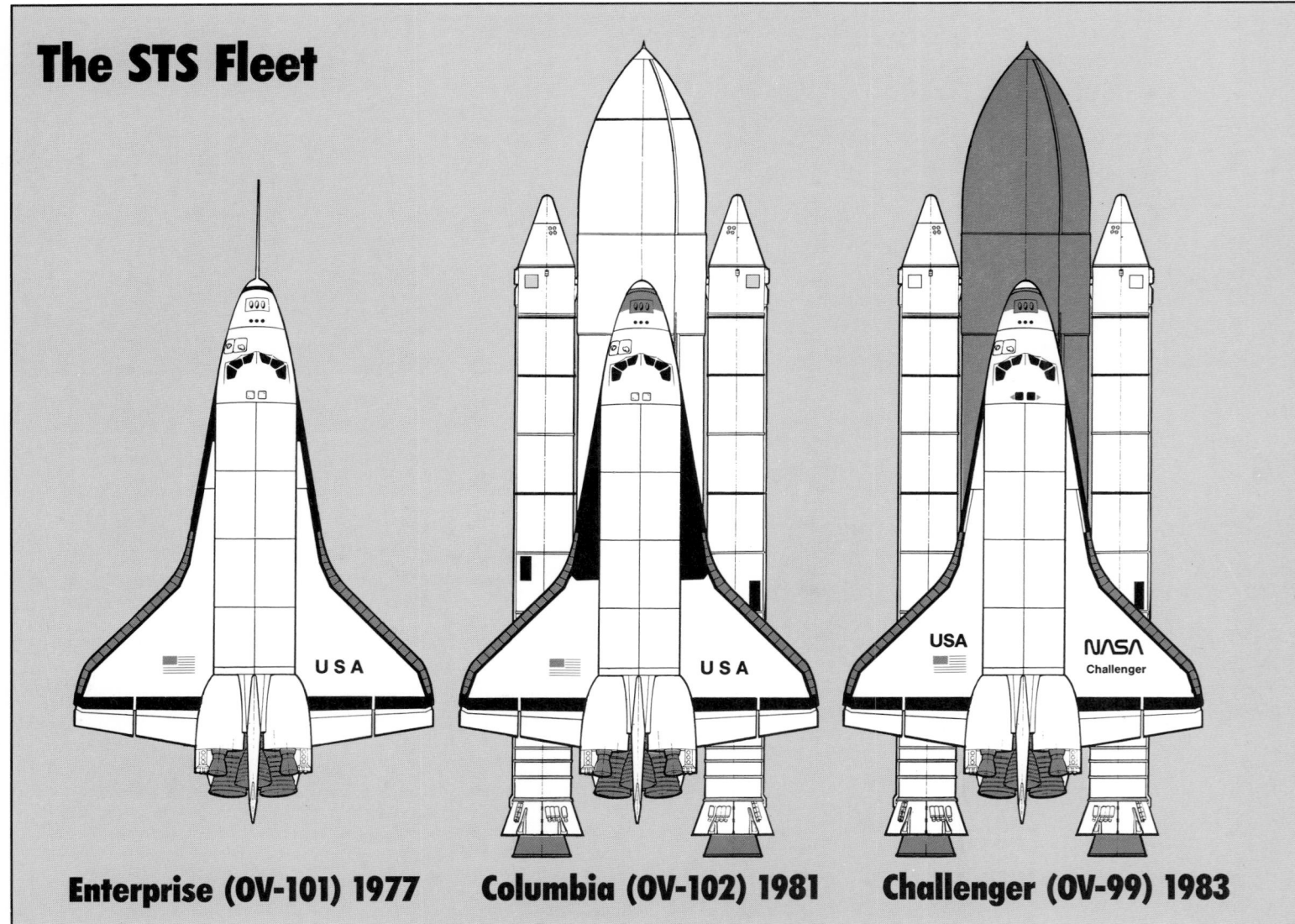

The STS Fleet

Enterprise (OV-101) 1977   **Columbia (OV-102) 1981**   **Challenger (OV-99) 1983**

STS Specifications

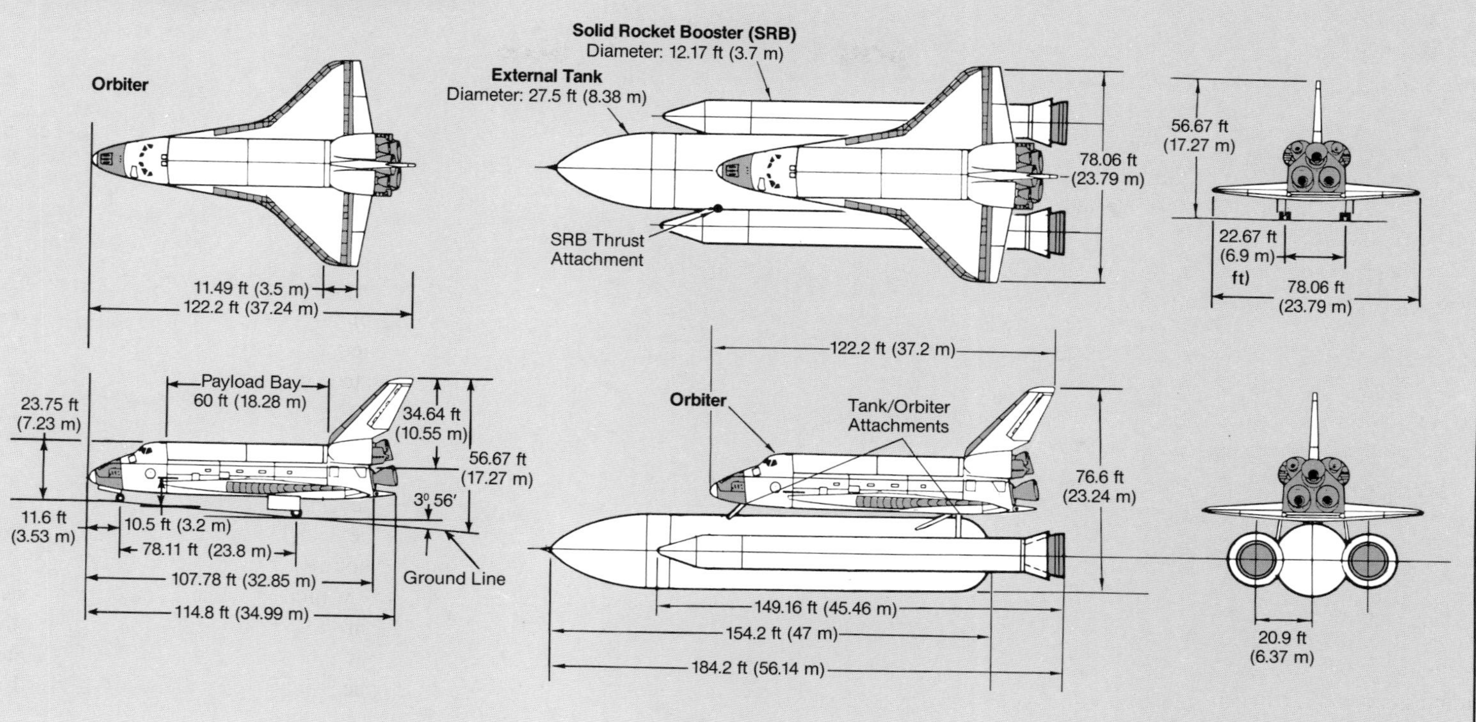

Orbiter

11.49 ft (3.5 m)
122.2 ft (37.24 m)

Solid Rocket Booster (SRB)
Diameter: 12.17 ft (3.7 m)

External Tank
Diameter: 27.5 ft (8.38 m)

SRB Thrust Attachment

78.06 ft (23.79 m)

56.67 ft (17.27 m)

22.67 ft (6.9 m) ft

78.06 ft (23.79 m)

Payload Bay
60 ft (18.28 m)

23.75 ft (7.23 m)

34.64 ft (10.55 m)

56.67 ft (17.27 m)

11.6 ft (3.53 m)

10.5 ft (3.2 m)

78.11 ft (23.8 m)

107.78 ft (32.85 m)

114.8 ft (34.99 m)

3° 56'

Ground Line

122.2 ft (37.2 m)

Orbiter

Tank/Orbiter Attachments

76.6 ft (23.24 m)

149.16 ft (45.46 m)

154.2 ft (47 m)

184.2 ft (56.14 m)

20.9 ft (6.37 m)

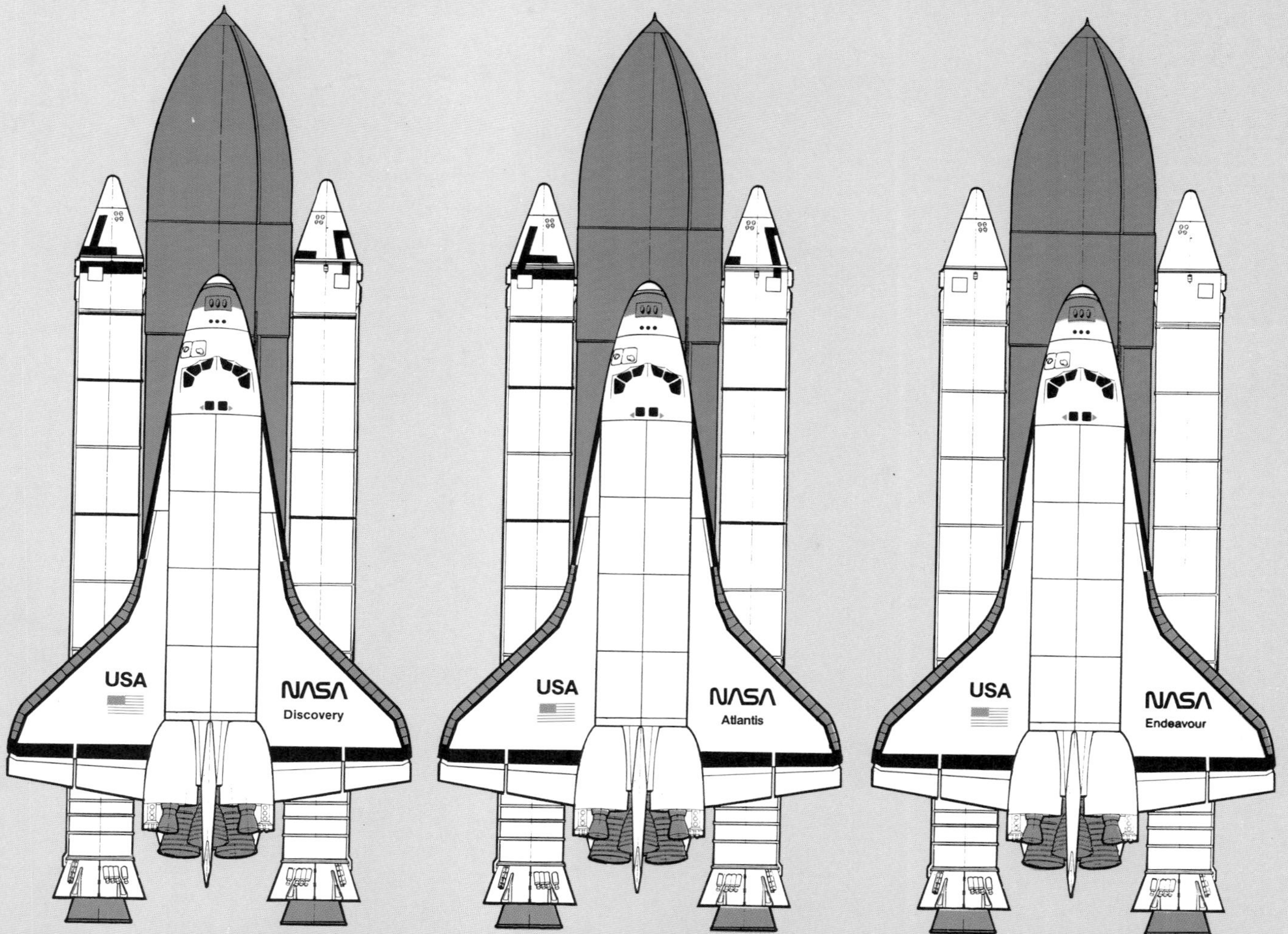

Discovery (OV-103) 1984

USA

NASA Discovery

Atlantis (OV-104) 1985

USA

NASA Atlantis

Endeavour (OV-105) 1992

USA

NASA Endeavour

THE STS IN SPACE

After two years of extensive tests and revisions to the engine and heat shield, *Columbia* made its first flight on 12 April 1981. This historic flight marked the twentieth anniversary of the first manned space flight, but it came three years and one month behind the schedule set in 1972 when the program had begun. In retrospect, for the enormous leap in technology that STS represented, the delays now seem to be of little consequence. Young and Crippen remained in orbit for 54 hours before returning to Earth for a picture-perfect landing at Edwards AFB.

Joe Engle and Richard Truly took *Columbia* up for another 54-hour flight in November 1981, marking the first time a spacecraft had flown in, and returned from, space *twice*. During 1982 two further flights were made with *Columbia*, extending the Orbiter's duration in space to seven, then eight days.

The first four *Columbia* flights were planned, and executed, as the STS test flights. Although some scientific experiments were carried out on board, they were missions during which the various facets of a very complex system were checked, rechecked and cross-checked. STS-5, flown by *Columbia* in November 1982, was the first *operational* mission. It was the first mission to carry more of a crew than just the two pilots, and the first during which satellites were launched.

STS-6, launched on 4 April 1983, was the second operational STS mission and the first flight to be made by the second orbiting vehicle, *Challenger* (OV-99). Originally built in 1975 as a structural test vehicle, *Challenger* was rebuilt and configured for space flight after *Columbia*'s maiden voyage. *Challenger* made three flights through August 1983, and in November, *Columbia* returned to space carrying the European Space Agency's sixteen ton Spacelab module in its cargo bay.

Below: Astronaut James van Hoften in the payload bay of the Orbiter *Challenger* during the April 1984 recovery of the Solar Maximum Mission ('Solar Max') Satellite, which is seen in the background. *Right: Challenger* during STS-7 in June 1983. The two cradles in her payload bay contained satellites that were launched during the mission.

210

THE HALCYON DAYS

The years 1984 and 1985 seemed to portend a new golden age for routine manned space travel. During these two years, *Challenger* made six space flights and NASA brought two more Orbiters on line. *Discovery* (OV-103) was launched on its first flight on 30 August 1984, and was in the midst of its fifth flight a year later. *Atlantis* (OV-104) made its debut on 3 October 1985 and flew again in November. Twice—in April and October 1985—the system saw two launches during the same month.

During this period, more than 70 American men and women flew in space, including a US Senator and several payload specialists representing private industry. Meanwhile, mission specialists from the European Space Agency (ESA) and other non-US space organizations flew with the Shuttle. Ulf Merbold of West Germany, who boarded the Shuttle in November 1983, was the first foreign payload specialist. During the succeeding years, this practice became common, as three Germans, a Canadian, a Frenchman, a Mexican and a Saudi prince joined NASA crews aboard the Shuttle flights.

For 1984 and 1985 the STS program logged 93 days in space and launched over one dozen satellites. Even more spectacular was the Shuttle's retrieval and return to Earth of defective spacecraft. By this time, it began to appear that the NASA/Defense Department decision to phase out expendable launch vehicles in favor of using STS to launch virtually all satellites *may* have been sound. Time would tell.

Well before the end of 1985 the Space Shuttle Transportation System had made space flight appear routine. Programs were underway for teachers, journalists and private citizens other than Senators and aerospace engineers to have an opportunity to participate in STS missions. In fact, the first teacher in space flight was scheduled for early 1986. Had *Columbia* been launched in December as planned, 1985 would have seen all four Orbiters in space during the same year. Unbeknownst at year's end, that possibility would soon be lost forever.

Above and right: The Orbiter *Challenger* (OV-99) was flown for the fourth time on Mission 41-B, which was launched on 3 February 1984. It was the STS program's tenth flight and featured the 'free-flying' SPAS module which took the photo above.

DISASTER AND RETRENCHMENT

The year 1986 promised to be the best yet for the STS program. There were 15 missions scheduled in addition to the one that had spilled over from December. Included were observations from space of Halley's Comet during its once-in-76-years turn past the sun, the launch of the Galileo spacecraft that would penetrate Jupiter's atmosphere, and the launch of the Hubble Space Telescope. When 1986 started, NASA, for the first time, had a full fleet of four Orbiters ready to meet the challenge of a 15-mission year. For two years, from November 1983 to October 1985, *Challenger* and *Discovery* had carried the entire load of the Shuttle program. *Atlantis* came on line in October, and two months later *Columbia* was back in service.

On 12 January *Columbia* was launched on its first flight in over two years, returning to Earth safely six days later. The next Shuttle flight was scheduled just a week after this return. This time, it would be *Challenger* making its tenth flight, the most ever flown by any Orbiter. The mission would include the launch of a communications satellite and involve observations of Halley's Comet. Most notable, however, would be the fact that this mission would inaugurate the 'Teacher In Space Program,' with Christa McAuliffe, a 37-year-old high school social studies teacher, slated to teach the first classroom lesson to be broadcast from outer space.

After several weather-related delays, *Challenger* lifted off the Cape Canaveral launch pad for the tenth and final time at 11:38 am on 28 January 1986. Christa McAuliffe's students in New Hampshire and students across the nation watched as the crisp, white bird rose into the blue sky. Just one minute after launch, a small tongue of flame licked out of one of the huge Solid Rocket Boosters as an O-ring seal failed. Two seconds later, the booster slammed the side of the external fuel tank, rupturing it and causing a leak of liquid hydrogen and liquid oxygen. Ten seconds later, the leak from the fuel tank was a torrent, and at the 73.2-second mark it ignited and began to consume *Challenger* and her crew. At the 73.6-second mark, a massive explosion occurred, ripping the Orbiter apart. The two Solid Rocket Boosters careened across the sky like blinded, panicked animals, only to be destroyed 37 seconds later by ground controllers when they began to arc back toward a populated area.

As had been the case with the Apollo 1 disaster 19 years and a day before, NASA suspended its manned space flight program while an investigation was conducted. Steps were taken to redesign the Solid Rocket Boosters when it was determined that a failed O-ring seal had precipitated the loss of *Challenger*. Unlike the Apollo 1 situation, however, Rockwell's portion of the system—specifically the Orbiting Vehicle—was cleared of having been at fault in the tragedy.

A presidential commission set up to investigate the accident did recommend some changes in Orbiter design, including the installation of a crew escape system. *Columbia* had been configured with ejection sets on its first four missions, but these were removed when crew size increased because it was not possible to position every member of the crew in a place where an ejection seat would function. Furthermore, ejection seats would work to save crew members only in certain specific instances during a very limited time during the mission. Other changes directed by the presidential commission included asking NASA to adopt a much less demanding schedule for the STS fleet.

NASA's response to this directive was that a less demanding schedule, combined with the two year delay that was now expected, as well as the earlier decision to use the STS for nearly all satellite work, would mean *fewer* satellites could be launched, and virtually none would be launched for at least two years. Against this backdrop, NASA and the Air Force quickly began issuing new contracts for expendable

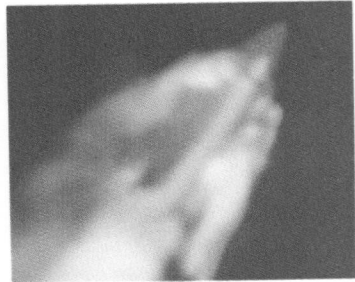

Above: The Orbiter *Challenger* was destroyed 73 seconds after launch on 28 January 1986. *Below:* After the tragedy, Rockwell retrofitted the Orbiter crew hatches with an emergency escape system. *Right:* The Orbiter *Atlantis* on Kennedy Space Center's Pad 39B in October 1986 for emergency contingency procedure tests.

launch vehicles of existing types and resumed their study of ways to develop new types.

For space operations that *required* STS, the less demanding schedule, along with the loss of one of the STS fleet, meant further serious delays. To address this situation, NASA requested funds to build an additional Orbiting Vehicle to replace *Challenger*. Under a previous contract, Rockwell had already been building and stockpiling structural spare parts such as wings, fuselage segments, etc. NASA suggested that these could be used to construct the framework of the new Orbiter and that the other program subcontractors could be asked to build one more of all the components they had recently produced for *Discovery* and *Atlantis*. Rockwell could, in turn, assemble the new Orbiter at Palmdale as it had all the others. The NASA proposal was accepted, and on 15 August 1986 President Reagan announced that a replacement Orbiting Vehicle would be ordered under the designation OV-105, although actual authority to proceed with assembly of OV-105 did not come until 1 August 1987.

In the meantime, on 8 June 1987, NASA administrator Dr James Fletcher announced a program for elementary and secondary school students to name OV-105. 'It is fitting that students and teachers, who shared in the loss of *Challenger*, share in the creation of its replacement,' he said.

On 10 May 1989, President George Bush announced that OV-105 would be named *Endeavour*, after one of Captain James Cook's exploration ships. Rockwell had already devoted two years to building OV-105, which was scheduled for completion in April 1991, with a first flight scheduled for early 1992, eight years after *Challenger* was destroyed. The new vehicle would feature the latest upgrades and modifications introduced on other Orbiters in the fleet, and would incorporate all new technology evolving from current flight activities.

THE RETURN OF THE SHUTTLE

After numerous delays, the STS program became operational once again at 11:37 am on 29 September 1988. Although the program stand-down had lasted 32 months, far longer than anyone had expected, the launch of *Discovery* with Richard Covey and Frederick Hauck at the controls represented no small triumph. No system as complex as the Space Shuttle will ever be completely foolproof, but *Discovery* and the entire STS mechanism and all procedures had been combed with the finest-toothed comb that NASA, Rockwell, Morton Thiokol, Martin-Marietta and the other contractors could find.

On 3 October, after 64 orbits, 1.7 million miles and the launch of a Tracking and Data Relay Satellite (TDRS), *Discovery* touched down at Edwards AFB. It was the kind of mission that would have been called 'routine' in 1984 or 1985, but no one was using such a word in 1988.

The next step in the re-establishment of STS as a viable operational system came on 2 December with the launch of *Atlantis* on the four-day STS-27 mission. Things were not 'routine' this day either, and as the program moved cautiously toward eight to 10 missions scheduled for 1989, there was a great deal of optimism where there once had been little or none.

Rockwell's STS Orbiter had more than two dozen successful missions to its credit before the Soviet *Buran* (*Snowstorm*) spaceplane made its first unmanned flight in November 1988, but didn't carry a crew into space for more than a year. If imitation really is the sincerest form of flattery, the Soviets paid Rockwell the ultimate tribute of copying the overall configuration for *Buran* and her sister ships exactly after the STS Orbiter!

At the time that the Shuttle Transportation System was put back into service in the fall of 1988, the Orbiter *Endeavour* (OV-105) was in its initial assembly stage. The mid fuselage, wings, elevons, body flap,

	United States Space Transportation System	Soviet Union Kosmolyet (Space Flyer) System
Number of operational Spacecraft (1 Jan 1989):	3	2
Number of successful Space flights (1 Jan 1989):	26	1
First space flight:	12 April 1981	15 Nov 1988
Launch vehicle:	(self-contained)	Energia
Launch weight (entire system):	4.5 million lb	5.37 million lb
Height (entire system):	184.2 ft	200 ft
Launch weight (Orbiting vehicle):	240,000 lb	235,000 lb
Landing weight (Orbiting vehicle):	212,000 lb*	184,000 lb
Length (orbiting vehicle):	122.2 ft	118 ft
Wingspan (orbiting vehicle):	78 ft	79 ft
Wing area:	2690 sq ft	2690 sq ft
Payload bay size:	15 × 60 ft	15 × 60 ft
Crew cabin volume:	2325 cu ft	2472 cu ft
Number of thermal tiles:	27,500**	38,000
Maximum duration in space:	c 30 days	c 30 days
Touchdown speed:	220 mph (±5%)	220 mph (±5%)

* 147,980 lb completely empty (dry) weight.
** *Atlantis* and *Discovery* only. *Columbia* had more tiles.

The milestone STS-26 mission began with the launch of *Discovery* on 29 September 1988 *(above)* and ended 96 hours later when *Discovery* touched down at Edwards AFB *(below)*. The Soviet Orbiter *Buran (below left* on its Energia booster) is an aerodynamic clone of the Rockwell Orbiter.

216

rudder-speedbrake, lower forward fuselage and the orbital maneuvering system/reaction control system pods were at Rockwell's assembly facility in Palmdale, California. The payload bay doors were scheduled to arrive at Palmdale in late 1989, and the wings and lower forward fuselage had already been mated to the mid fuselage.

The thermal protection system (TPS) was being installed on the mid fuselage, body flap, elevons and orbital maneuvering system/reaction control system pods. The TPS installed on *Endeavour* was identical to that installed on *Discovery* and *Atlantis*. The aft fuselage, forward reaction control system, upper forward fuselage and airlock were still at Rockwell's Downey, California facility, however, and were not scheduled to be transported to Palmdale until 1990.

There were several systems improvements or modifications to the Orbiter fleet that were in progress prior to the *Challenger* accident due to the down time, and all of these improvements, upgrades and modifications were incorporated into *Endeavour*. These modifications included improvements made to the primary reaction control system thruster, fuel cell powerplants, auxiliary power units, main landing gear axles and brakes, main landing gear brake electronic boxes and hydraulic systems, nose wheel steering, thermal protection system between the reinforced carbon-carbon nose cap and the forward edges of the nose landing gear doors, strengthening of certain areas of the wing and mid fuselage, and incorporation of the capability to jettison the crew ingress/egress side hatch, an emergency egress escape pole, and an emergency egress slide.

Endeavour would also incorporate a pyrotechnically-deployed drag chute under the vertical tail for use by the flight crew after main landing gear touchdown.

Symbols of the STS program during its recovery phase in the late 1980s were the flight of *Discovery* (OV-103) on STS-26 and the construction of the OV-105 Orbiter, which is pictured *above* underway at the Rockwell's Palmdale plant in 1988. The first mission after the 1986 *Challenger* disaster, STS-26 was launched *(right)* on 29 September 1988.

SPACE SHUTTLE TRANSPORTATION SYSTEM MISSIONS
(1981-1988)

Mission Designation and Orbiter	Crew	Launch Date and Duration	Satellites Launched
STS-1 *Columbia*	John W Young, C Robert L Crippen, P	12 April 1981 (54 hrs 21 min)	(Orbiter test flight)
STS-2 *Columbia*	Joseph H Engle, C Richard H Truly, P	12 November 1981 (54 hrs 13 min)	(Orbiter test flight)
STS-3 *Columbia*	Jack R Lousma, C Charles G Fullerton, P	22 March 1982 (192 hrs 5 min)	(Orbiter test flight)
STS-4 *Columbia*	Thomas K Mattingly, C	27 June 1982 (167 hrs 10 min)	(Orbiter test flight, with DOD payload)
STS-5 *Columbia*	Vance Brand, C Robert F Overmyer, P Dr Joseph P Allen, MS Dr William B Lenoir, MS	11 November 1982 (122 hrs 14 min)	Anik C-3 (Canada) SBS-C (US Commercial)
STS-6 *Challenger*	Paul J Weitz, C Karol J Bobko, P Donald H Peterson, MS Dr Story Musgrave, MS	4 April 1983 (120 hrs 24 min)	TDRS (US)
STS-7 *Challenger*	Robert L Crippen, C Frederick C Hauck, P Dr Sally K Ride, MS Dr Norman Thagard, MS	18 June 1983 (146 hrs 24 min)	SPAS-01 (W Germany) Anik C-2 (Canada) Palapa B (Indonesia)
STS-8 *Challenger*	Richard H Truly Daniel C Brandenstein, P Dale A Gardner, MS Guion S Bluford, Jr, MS Dr William Thornton, MS	30 August 1983 (145 hrs 9 min)	Insat 1B (India)
STS-9 (41A) *Columbia*	John W Young, C Brewster H Shaw, P Owen Garriott, MS Dr Robert A Parker, MS Dr Byron K Lichtenberg, PS Dr Ulf Merbold, PS (ESA)	23 November 1983 (247 hrs 47 min)	ESA Spacelab 1
41-B (10) *Challenger*	Vance D Brand, C Robert L Gibson, P Bruce McCandless II, MS Ronald E McNair, MS Robert L Stewart, MS	3 February 1984 (191 hrs 16 min)	SPAS-01 (W Germany) Westar 6 (US Commercial)
41-C (11) *Challenger*	Robert L Crippen, C Francis R Scobee, P Dr George D Nelson, MS Dr James D van Hoften, MS Terry J Hart, MS	6 April 1984 (167 hrs 40 min)	Long Duration Exposure Facility deployed (Solar Maximum Mission spacecraft recovered and repaired)
41-D (12) *Discovery*	Henry W Hartsfield Jr, C Michael L Coats, P Judith A Resnik, MS Richard M Mullane, MS	30 August 1984 (144 hrs 56 min)	Leasat 2 (US Navy) SBS-4 (US Commercial) Telstar 3-C (US Commercial)
41-G (13) *Challenger*	Robert L Crippen, C Jon A McBride, P David C Leestma, MS Dr Sally K Ride, MS Kathryn D Sullivan, MS Paul Scully-Power, PS Marc Garneau, PS	5 October 1984 (197 hrs 24 min)	Earth Radiation Budget Satellite (US)
51-A (14) *Discovery*	Frederick H Hauck, C David M Walker, P Anna L Fisher, MS Dale A Gardner, MS Joseph P Allen, MS	8 November 1984 (191 hrs 45 min)	Anik D-2 (Canada) Leasat 4-1 (US Navy) *Satellites recovered:* Palapa B-2 (Indonesia) Westar 6 (US Commercial)

Mission Designation and Orbiter	Crew	Launch Date and Duration	Satellites Launched
51-C (15) *Discovery*	Thomas K Mattingly, C Loren J Shriver, P James F Buchli, MS Ellison S Onizuka, MS Gary E Payton, PS	24 January 1985 (73 hrs 33 min)	Secret DOD satellite
51-D (16) *Discovery*	Karol J Bobko, C Donald E Williams, P M Rhea Seddon, MS S David Griggs, MS Jeffrey A Hoffman, MS Charles D Walker, MS Senator EJ 'Jake' Garn, PS	12 April 1985 (167 hrs 54 min)	Anik C-1 (Canada) Leasat 3
51-B (17) *Challenger*	Robert F Overmyer, C Frederick D Gregory, P Don L Lind, MS Norman E Thagard, MS William E Thornton, MS Lodewijk van den Berg, MS Taylor G Wang, PS	29 April 1985 (168 hrs 9 min)	ESA Spacelab 3
51-G (18) *Discovery*	Daniel Brandenstein, C John Creighton, P Shannon Lucid, MS Steven Nagel, MS John Fabian, MS Patrick Baudry, PS Sultan Al-Saud, PS	17 June 1985 (169 hrs 39 min)	Morelos 1 (Mexico) Arabsat 1B (Arab Satellite Comm Org) Telstar 3-D (US Commercial)
51-F (19) *Challenger*	Charles G Fullerton, C Roy D Bridges, P Dr Story Musgrave, MS Anthony W England, MS Karl G Henize, MS Loren W Acton, PS (Lockheed) John-David Bartoe, PS (USN civilian)	12 July 1985 (190 hrs 45 min)	ESA Spacelab 2
51-I (20) *Discovery*	Joe H Engle, C Richard O Covey, P James Van Hoften, MS John M Lounge, MS William F Fisher	24 August 1985 (170 hrs 28 min)	AUSSAT-A (Australia) ASC-1 (Australia) Leasat 4 (US Navy) *Satellite recovered and relaunched*: Leasat 3 (US Navy)
51-J (21) *Atlantis*	Karol Bobko, C Ronald J Grabe, P Robert Steward, MS David Hilmers, MS William A Pailes, PS	3 October 1985 (97 hrs 15 min)	Secret DOD satellite
61-A (22) *Challenger*	Henry W Hartsfield, C Steven R Nagel, P James F Buchli, MS Guion S Bluford, Jr, MS Bonnie J Dunbar, MS Reinhard Furrer, PS (W Germany) Ernst Messerschmid, PS (W Germany) Wubbo Ockels, PS (W Germany)	30 October 1985 (168 hrs 44 min)	ESA Spacelab D-1 (entirely devoted to W German programs)
61-B (23) *Atlantis*	Brewster H Shaw, Jr, C Bryan D O'Connor, P Mary L Cleave, MS Sherwood C Spring, MS Jerry L Ross, MS Rodolfo Neri Vela, PS (Mexico) Charles Walker, PS	26 November 1985 (165 hrs 5 min)	Morelos B (Mexico) AUSSAT-2 (Australia) Satcom Ku-2 (US Commericial)

Mission Designation and Orbiter	Crew	Launch Date and Duration	Satellites Launched
61-C (24) *Columbia*	Robert L Gibson, C Charles F Bolden, Jr, P Franklin Chang-Diaz, MS Steven A Hawley, MS George D Nelson, MS Robert Cenker, PS Congressman Bill Nelson, PS	12 January 1986 (146 hrs 4 min)	Satcom Ku-1 (US Commercial)
51-L (25) *Challenger*	Francis R Scobee, C Michael J Smith, P Judith A Resnik, MS Ellison Onizuka, MS Ronald E McNair, MS Christa McAullife, TISP Gregory Jarvis, PS	28 January 1986 (73 seconds)	*Satellites destroyed:* TDRS-B (US) Spartan (US)
STS-26 (26) *Discovery*	Frederick H Hauck, C Richard O Covey, P David Chilmers, MS George C Nelson, MS Michael Lounge, MS	29 September 1988 (96 hours)	TDRS-B (US)
STS-27 (27) *Atlantis*	Robert L Gibson, C Buy Gardner, P Mike Mullane, MS Jerry Ross, MS William Shepherd, MS	2 December 1988 (105 hrs, 6 min)	Lacrosse (US, DOD)
STS-29 (28) *Discovery*	Michael Coates, C John E Blaha, P James F Buchli, MS James P Bagan, MS Robert Springer, MS	13 March 1989 (119 hrs, 40 min)	TDRS-D (US)
STS-30 (29) *Atlantis*	David M Walker, C Ronald J Grabe, P Mary L Cleave, MS Mark C Lee, MS Norman E Thagard, MS	4 May 1989 (97 hours)	Magellan (Launched toward Venus)
STS-28 (30) *Columbia*	Brewster Shaw, C Richard N Richards, P David Leesma, MS Mark Brown, MS James Adamson, MS	July 1989	(DOD)

Key:

		PS:	Payload Specialist (usually not a NASA astronaut and associated only with one specific payload carried on the mission)
		TISP:	Teacher In Space Program participant
C:	Mission Commander (flies in copilot's seat)	DOD:	US Department of Defense
P:	Orbiter Pilot	ESA Spacelab:	This European Space Agency laboratory module filled the entire payload bay each time it was carried, so that no satellites were launched on these missions.
MS:	Mission Specialist (usually a NASA astronaut associated with several, or all, of the projects on the mission)		

SPACE SHUTTLE TRANSPORTATION SYSTEM (STS) MISSION DESIGNATIONS

The first nine space flights of the system, between 1981 and 1983, were divided between *Columbia* and *Challenger* and were designated STS-1 through 9 consecutively. Mission 9 also carried the second designation, 41-A, which was the first application of a new nomenclature system under which all subsequent Shuttle missions were designated.

In this system, the first digit is for the NASA *fiscal* year in which the mission was *originally scheduled* (NASA fiscal years begin in October). The second digit referred to the mission launch site, with 1 assigned to Kennedy Space Center and 2 assigned to Vandenberg AFB. The third digit is a letter indicating the order in which the mission was *originally* scheduled within the fiscal year. Thus, 41-A is read as the first mission scheduled to be launched in fiscal year 1984 from Kennedy Space Center.

Under this system a mission would be designated before its launch and would have retained the same designation throughout its planning stages, even if it fell behind schedule. For example, mission 51-B was planned to follow 51-A, but actually took place after 51-C and 51-D. Missions would also be canceled without affecting the designations of other missions. For example, mission 41-G followed mission 41C when missions 41-E and 41-F were deleted from the roster. With the 32-month cancellation of flights in 1986 and Vandenberg AFB mothballed as a launch site, the old system was reinstated, although some 'STS numbers' would not be in order. The September 1988 flight was called STS-26, or simply 'Mission 26,' while STS-28 and STS-29 were not launched in numeric sequence.

NAA MODEL NUMBERS

GENERAL INDEX

PHOTO CREDITS

All photos and artwork are courtesy
of Rockwell International Corporation
with the following exceptions:
American Aviation Historical Society 49
(bottom)
Michael Badrocke 58-59, 90-91, 178-179
(bottom)
Boeing Airplane Company 35 (top)
McDonnell Douglas Corporation 35
(middle), 156 (both)
NASA 120-121, 125 (top), 157, 159
(both), 161 (both), 163, 164 (right), 166,
167, 170, 171, 204-205 (bottom), 208,
209, 210-211, 212-213 (all), 215 (both),
216-217, 221
Sabreliner Corporation 146-147
TASS 214
US Air Force 54-55 (both), 62, 84-85
(all), 112 (bottom), 124-125 (bottom),
128 (all), 129 (bottom), 132-133
(bottom), 177 (top), 180 (bottom)
© Bill Yenne 21 (top), 25 (top), 45, 53,
65 (bottom), 77, 89, 109 (top right),
206-207 (bottom)